WITHDRAWN

PRO FOOTBALL

*The History of the Game
and the Great Players*

Other Books by Robert Smith

Nonfiction

Baseball in America (1961)

Modern Writing (1955)

Heroes of Baseball (1952)

Writing Fiction (1952)

Baseball:
A Historical Narrative (1947)

Fiction

The Ordeal of Mr. Blair (1959)

One Winter in Boston (1950)

The Human Image (1945)

Hotel on the Lake (1943)

PRO FOOTBALL

*The History of the Game
and the Great Players*

Robert Smith

DOUBLEDAY & COMPANY, INC.

GARDEN CITY, NEW YORK

1963

for two good friends

JACK PETERS

and

HANK STOREY

with whom I have played, watched, or talked football

on countless happy afternoons

Contents

Author's Note

Rather than attempt the task of listing all the men and women, in football and around it, who gave me a hand in gathering the material for this book, I will limit myself to saying that professional football players, active or ex, and those men I happened to meet who coach or direct the clubs or help publicize their doings or who work in the league offices are the finest people in sports. It may simply be that they haven't got used to being successful yet. But I suspect that, besides being the greatest sports spectacle ever devised, professional football is also the breeding grounds for a type of gracious, unpretentious individual that will one day do our country proud.

Let me disclaim at the very beginning any pretension to omniscience in football, or in any sport. Whenever an ordinary man like myself writes a book of this sort he is bound to omit the names of many practitioners who own perhaps stronger claims to public honor than any of those included. This was not meant to be a list of names, or an honor roll, or even a day-to-day history. It is part history and part recollection, and above all an appreciation of a sport I once tried to play and have always been enraptured to watch.

Chapter I

The Dark Backward and Abysm

Football, I suppose, must be one of the most elemental of games, for it has been played for centuries, in various forms, under many different names and since long before there were any sports writers to celebrate it. English-speaking people have always played it. It is first remembered in England as a sort of mass shoving contest and what few could bear to watch it could only be horrified at it, or be tempted instead to hurl themselves into the press. The football, in the earliest days, was a bladder or a stuffed leathern bag, or any other yielding object, usually lost in the swarm of struggling bodies, as many as fifty or a hundred on either side, and sometimes without any effort at all to keep the sides even. The goal might be an imaginary line between two bushes or trees, or the corner of a street, the boundary of a town or neighborhood, or merely the end of a fence or field.

It was played in city streets, as a form of shindy, except that no sticks were used and the ball was large and bouncy. Or it was played in the country, over pastures and dells, with a playing field that might reach for a mile. Everyone who chanced upon the struggle might get into it and some might suddenly find themselves in it who wanted to get out.

Football sometimes would involve all the young males of the town. Often windows would be smashed, fists would fly, ladies would faint, angry shopkeepers would curse wildly but in vain as the struggling "sides" surged up one street and around a corner, screaming, rallying each other, yelling for mercy as they tumbled beneath the feet of the mob.

In Boston, at the time of the massacre, football was sometimes thought more of a menace than the Redcoats. And in England, more than a century before that, the town fathers of Manchester had adopted the following resolution against it:

". . . There hath bene heretofore a great disorder in our toune . . . and the inhabitants thereof greatly wronged and charged with the mending of their glasse windowes broken yearlye . . . by a company of lewd and disordered persons using that unlawful exercise of playing with the football in ye streets . . . breaking many men's windowes and glasse at their pleasure and other great inormyties. . . ."

Football was indeed a yearly rite then, with its own season, as kite-flying and cricket and boating all had their particular times of year. It was the season when there was still no snow to freeze a fellow's feet and not warmth enough to lure a boy to the seashore or the bank of a brook, when it was chilly enough to encourage a lad to run and jump and wrestle and shove, and yet pleasant enough to be outdoors when school was over.

Although it was played by grown men, by farmers, and soldiers, and even by courtiers in the earliest days, called sometimes camp ball, or hurling, it became among the English and among the colonial Americans a schoolboy game eventually. It usually developed as a sort of class rush, a test of masculinity and an initiation into the ritualistic brutalities of the adult world, and at the same time an ecstatic taking part in a common struggle in which self could often be so submerged that the flesh grew almost impervious to pain. It was always bloody, full of private dirty work, and everlastingly reviled by authorities who saw in it no real sportsmanship or inspiration, only an appeal to the lowest instincts and a release for the vilest impulses.

Kings and councils forbade it, and insisted that God did too. Men warned their sons against it, schools abolished it, policemen put a stop to it, and laws punished its exercise. Yet football thrived, kept raising its head in newer and wider fields, and made room for itself sometimes where neither man nor nature had allowed space for it to be played.

In 1314, the laws of Edward II set forth sanctions against the "hustling over large footballs, from which many evils arise, which God forbid," And Great Britain's first King James debarred it from his court, as he did all violent exercise, but with a special word for football, which he deemed "meeter for lameing than makeing able the users thereof."

One Philip Stickles, writing of English football before Shakespeare was born, protested that it "may rather be called a friendlie kind of fyghte than a play or recreation, a bloody and murthering practice than a fellowly sport. . . . For dooth not everyone lie in waight for his adversary, seeking to overthrowe and picke him on the nose . . . ?"

All the same the bloody and murthering practice thrived through the centuries. In colonial New England, it became a traditional delight for boys to kick the pig's bladder about after the Thanksgiving feast, or on butchering day. And eventually every English public school had its own version of the game, depending on what sort of room they had to play it in and how much regulation they had been able to develop.

At Rugby, football was "Bigside" for it was played on Old Bigside field (the other side, naturally, from Littleside). Here it was frequently the Sixth form against the rest of the school, or School against Schoolhouse, and there were only a very few rules to inhibit the inormyties the lads might practice as they tried to work the ball up the field against the massed opposition, except that it was traditional that the ball should be kicked, not propelled with the hands. There was a rule to forbid "offside" play—that is, attempting to clear a path by going ahead of the ball. But the boys used to spar and struggle and shove to get kicking room and naturally many a kick went astray in the struggle. It was bruising, wild, frantic, and bitter as a battle.

When William Webb Ellis of Rugby, in the early 1800's, grew impatient with the aimless struggle and, having caught the ball, set out to run with it, while some of his own teammates as well as all the opponents tried to hurl him to the ground for his unsporting act, he made the move that started the development of modern football. But it was a long time before his dastardly deed won approval, even at Rugby, and for a time its practice was limited to players who had made a "fair catch."

At Eton, where there was no big field on which to play, football became the Wall Game, for it was played along a high brick wall, the ball being put in play through a "scrummage"—a gathering of players right against the wall. The outer edge of the field was marked by a furrow plowed in the grass and the goals by marks on the wall. Offside play, known as "sneaking," was frowned on here too. And when the acquisition of a field gave rise to the Field Game, the Wall Game was still played steadily. And the limitation of players to eleven on a side, a necessity in the cramped play space, extended to the Field Game and finally after many years to American football.

This addiction to the forced limitations of the game, like the urge that keeps American kids playing stickball when there is space enough for baseball, brought two other forms of the game into being. At Westminster Abbey, where there was no play space at all, the boys played a form of football known as the Game in Cloister, with one can only imagine what forms of bloody devastation upon each other's persons as they struggled over the stones. Then, when some buildings were cleared to make an open space nearby, the Game in Green developed. But the boys kept right on playing the Game in Cloister too.

In all these games, the essential aim was the same—to kick the ball into or across a goal. And in all of them, offside play was forbidden, to build a long tradition that cramped the American game for years.

Football was not played in English colleges, for it was considered a small boys' game, often having no rules to limit the score, the number of players, or the time consumed. Indeed, most football games ended only when the school bell sounded, the dark grew too deep, or the police descended. And it remained a secondary school game even after the sides were limited to twenty-five and then to fifteen, and strict rules had been developed—and after the Americans had worked out a dozen devices for getting around the rules.

In America, the game grew as it had in England, except that the colleges rather than the secondary schools used the class-rush form of the game. Throughout the early nineteenth century, football at the big eastern colleges almost always meant the freshman against the sophs, early in the college year. The football was a large round ball, sometimes leather-covered, sometimes rubber. But the "game" was just an excuse for a free-for-all, with the football a sort of chip on the collective shoulder of the sophomore team. The ball usually was "put in play" when a daring freshman moved up and laid a toe or a finger to it. And then the various class members would set upon one another, until finally the ball broke through one class or another to the "goal"—or the authorities put a stop to the riot.

At Harvard, football day was known as Bloody Monday. The sophs met the freshmen on the Delta, the site of the latter-day Memorial Hall, and they severally and collectively did each other down until there was hardly a whole pair of pants, an unshredded shirt, or an unbloodied nose in the crowd. Teeth were knocked loose, ribs cracked, legs and arms broken, exactly as Philip Stickles had set forth almost three centuries before when he wrote of football players who had "the sleights to become one betwixt two, to dash him against the hart with their elbows, to butt him under the short ribs and peck him on his neck, with a hundred other such murthering devices."

In 1860 both the college and the town authorities had had their fill of these murthering devices and by their order Bloody Monday was abolished. The college thereupon went into mourning. They conducted funeral rites for "Football Fightum" and erected a tombstone in his honor. They also predicted, with the shrewdness of their ilk, that he would some day be reborn in those very environs. About fifteen years later he was, in the guise of a sport.

Yale too used football in the early nineteenth century as a

freshman-sophomore contest. While Princeton is supposed to have originated the flying wedge, as it applied to intercollegiate football, the Yale freshman class used that formation in 1840, in greatly enlarged form, to smash through the bewhiskered sophs who lined up several deep against them. In 1860, the New Haven authorities, as well as the Yale faculty, ruled an end to this form of football-gone-mad.

Still another form of football, sometimes called "association," was played intramurally at several of the eastern colleges, notably Nassau Hall, the college in Princeton, New Jersey, and Rutgers, in New Brunswick, twenty-five miles away.

Nassau, which was not yet called Princeton, had been a long-time rival of Rutgers, particularly over the possession of a Revolutionary cannon that was supposed to grace the Nassau campus. The Rutgers boys took regular delight in stealing this cannon from the Princeton campus and setting it up on their own. And the Princeton bloods of course would steal in by night, using carriages and wagons, and carry the little cannon home.

The big college sports of that day were rowing and cricket. But there was a new game called base ball, or the New York Game, that was growing in favor then and both colleges began to develop teams. In 1865, the contest over George Washington's brass cannon was brought to a final and frustrating event, when the Nassau boys sunk the thing up to the trunions in cement and nothing less than dynamite would ever budge it more. Then, to rub the victory in, the Princeton team trimmed Rutgers in 1866 by a score of 40-2, at base ball.

There was nothing left for Rutgers then but to sit and stew. The cannon could not be recovered and base ball, it was evident, was simply not their game. The rivalry bubbled along in the form of taunts and written exchanges until 1869, when a bunch of the Rutgers boys who felt they had grown pretty clever at association football challenged Nassau Hall to have a go at them in *that*.

Young men had been playing almost the same form of football at Princeton as they had been playing at Rutgers: twenty-five to a side, with a black rubber ball, which could be kicked or "butted" with the shoulder. There were two essential differences: The Nassau game permitted batting with the fist and allowed a free kick—that is, a kick in which the opponents had to stay ten yards away from the kicker until he booted the ball—after a ball had been caught on the fly or on the bounce. The Rutgers game did not permit either.

The Princeton boys were delighted at the opportunity to find another game they could beat Rutgers in. They quickly agreed to a series—one game at New Brunswick, on November 6, 1869, using Rutgers rules; one game at Princeton, on November 13, using Princeton rules; and a rubber game at New Brunswick on the twentieth.

Rutgers, using their own rules, won the game at New Brunswick, and Nassau Hall, using *their* rules, won the game at Princeton. The rubber game was never played, because the faculty at Princeton became alarmed when their young men began to devote more thought and study to this silly game with a round rubber ball than to the binomial theorem and the declension of Latin nouns.

At both Princeton and Rutgers the game (which came to be called "soccer," a corruption of the abbreviation "assoc.") was practiced steadily on campus. Within a few years, both teams were playing once more against other colleges in the East.

Yale's version of the game was affected by the enrollment of a boy from Eton, who brought along his version of the Field Game. David Schley Schaff arranged interclass contests in the English game at Yale and finally was able, despite police and faculty interference, to field a team to represent the college.

At Harvard, the corpse of Football Fightum had stirred in its shallow grave until finally there was an organized team to carry the college colors. One day the team from McGill University, of Montreal, came to Cambridge to exhibit their form of rugby football. A very interesting game, the Harvard young men allowed, but hardly suited to college play. McGill, however, trimmed Harvard at rugby and soon thereafter the Harvards took over this game, with its big oval ball, as its own. Harvard therefore became the school that really introduced rugby football to the United States.

This game, played under "accommodation rules," sometimes using fifteen players and sometimes eleven, grew in popularity in the big eastern universities until by the 1870's Columbia, Pennsylvania, and Rutgers, as well as Harvard and Yale, had all abandoned association football for the Canadian style, which was still recognizable as rugby, with plenty of offside play (constantly deplored in the press by Henry Chadwick, British-born New York sportswriter and acknowledged Father of Baseball).

Each of the Big Three colleges contributed its own special influence to the new game: Princeton, apparently the roughest type of play and organized "offside" interference; Yale, the crafty formations and the devious rule evasions that gave the game its variety; and Harvard, the essentially softening influence that the game needed to keep it from developing into a periodic gang-fight. (Harvard suspended its football schedule for a season until the other colleges agreed that slugging with the closed fist, even once, should be cause for ejection from the game.)

Rugby football, as played in America, was rough enough, without any fist-fighting. A bloody bandage around the head was a common sight at an intercollegiate match. The rule against slugging did not bar striking an opponent in the face or on the head and neck with the side or the heel of the open hand. Indeed, it took nearly half a century more to get this exercise out of the game.

Eventually, in 1876, a convention of the eastern universities was called to set up uniform rules of play in football. The rules of rugby were generally adopted, except at Yale. Fifteen players were to make a team and touchdowns were to be included in the scoring. Yale subscribed to the convention rules three years later, when the other schools all agreed to the eleven-man team, as in the Eton Field Game.

The convention met annually thereafter and continued to experiment with the rules, not so much to "improve" the game as to find a code some new members would agree to. The old "demoralized association" game was gone from the colleges for good (to come back as soccer). But what the American colleges were playing was not really rugby either. American boys simply could not refrain from offside play. Rutgers in its game with Nassau had thrown guards out ahead of the "dribbler"—the man who nursed the ball along with his feet—and rules or no rules American rugby players just could not resist clearing a path for the runner by sparring with would-be tacklers, shouldering them aside, or grabbing and holding. When the unwritten rugby rule was invoked against Americans they got around it by letting their interference seem accidental. Finally this type of guarding was officially countenanced by a rule that prohibited only blocking "with extended arms." From that time forward, blocking became a part of the game and turned rugby into American football, a game as different from its parent as baseball is from rounders.

Chapter II

Football for Love or Money

I saw my first professional football game around the time of the First World War, when I was too young to understand it completely. But from what I recall of it, only the players really knew what was happening and sometimes, in the crush of encroaching fans, they themselves lost temporary track of the game.

The game was played on a rocky, unshorn field near Boston, between a team named the Shamrocks and another team whose name I never hope to recall. I remember only the wild shouts of players and fans as the ranks of men in bright green jerseys would surge forward, while their opponents groaned, cursed, and flailed their arms. The spectators were close behind the backfield on every play and could barely restrain themselves from getting into the scrimmage. It was a disorganized and disorderly spectacle—not too different perhaps from the favorite lithograph on my boyhood bedroom wall of a crush of football players surmounted by one triumphant warrior with a bloody bandage on his head—but not at all like the richly caparisoned, disciplined, or at least ritualized spectacle of college or high school football. This could not, all agreed, ever replace the college game. It was simply a group of young men, too old for high school and too poor for college, trying to pretend they were in the same league as the real heroes of the great autumn sport—the Brickleys, the Mahans, the Hardwicks, the Oliphants, the Coys, and the Pollards.

Yet, long before that day, men had started to play football for money; and men who were supposed to be playing it for fun, or

for glory, were taking pay for the job. Oddly enough, many of the
very first professionals played the game for fun, while great
numbers of the college amateurs were playing for board, room,
books, tuition, and salary. Even the prep schools of my era recruited high school football players, often outbidding colleges,
and keeping some young men on their campuses so long that
when they left at last they were nearly too old to play. One star
football player of my youth stayed in prep school until he was
twenty-eight, earning a better living at athletics than he might
have scratched up at day wages in industry.

The first football pros were really semipros: that is, they made
only a small share of their living at football and needed a full-
time occupation to keep the bill collector out of the front parlor.
They were paid per game and the stipend varied widely, depending on their fame. A big-name star, who would have several
teams bidding for him every weekend, might get half a hundred
dollars, while a squint-eyed tackle from the local granite quarry
would take home a five-dollar bill.

It is generally accepted that this form of "professional football" first took root in Pennsylvania, within a fifty-mile radius of
Pittsburgh, where young businessmen who had built their muscles in the mines used to play rugby football on free afternoons.
In the 1890's, outside the colleges, association football was still
played as widely as rugby. Although the rugby "scrum" had been
abolished by 1890, the rush-line scrimmage of the American
game still, to a spectator, looked a good deal like the original
head-to-head huddle of the opposing teams. In the middle nineties, more than three men had to charge before the ball was
snapped if a violation was to be called and men in the rush-line
could still lock ankles, even though they could no longer legally
use their hands and fists on the opposing blockers or tacklers.

The scrum had disappeared because the Americans had invented a way of squirting the ball back (by stepping on one end
of it) to a specified player instead of letting it be heeled out haphazardly to anyone who could reach it first. The new scrimmage
line formalized the snapping back of the ball and so divorced the

American game forever from its parent. Practically every rule ever developed to keep the game within bounds had been stretched far out of shape by the Americans anyway. For instance, in the early versions of the game, the rule for putting the ball in play by kicking it had been so diluted that the "kicker" could just touch the ball to his toe without ever letting it out of his hands, and would then wheel in behind the charging agglomeration of interference that formed the flying wedge.

The early pros, or rather semipros, of the 1890's followed the college rules, and most of them had played or were still playing in one of the eastern colleges. It is vain to try to decide just when and where a man first took pay for playing football. Certainly many of the college teams of the nineties subsidized athletics just as generously as any independent team ever had; and intertown rivalry in football in some areas had grown as violent as a baseball rivalry. Baseball teams throughout the land had been hiring ringers for decades.

It is fact that as early as 1893 a strapping Princeton graduate —one of a trio of husky athletic brothers—agreed to play for the Greensburg (Pennsylvania) Athletic Association football team for twenty dollars and expenses. He was Lawson Fiscus, who had first played college football in a Pennsylvania town called Indiana and who then went to Princeton to win renown as the strongest man in school—and the fleetest halfback. Fiscus, a rangy, broad-shouldered man of twenty-eight, with a mustache that might have adorned a German general, served as coach of the club as well as ball-carrier and eventually brought his two brothers along to play on his side against such teams as Latrobe, the Jeannette Athletic Club, and the East Side Athletic Club of Pittsburgh.

All these clubs were manned by young businessmen, most of them former college players, who were playing the game more for excitement and glory than for money. But as the members yearned more and more for victory, they began to reach out to the college rosters for rugged ringers to match the ones their rivals presented. Many of early football's greatest names appeared on the rosters of these Pennsylvania clubs. The Latrobe team in 1897 listed Walter Okeson, an All-American from Lehigh who became a famous college football official, and Doggie Trenchard, an All-American from Princeton.

Protective equipment was scanty indeed in the 1890's. Most players were satisfied to wear a pair of ribbed shin guards, such as hockey players favored, plus the standard laced canvas "smock" (invented by Ledou P. Smock, Princeton '79) which included padded moleskin knee pants. Helmets were almost unknown. If a football player wore any headgear at all, it would most likely be a small knit cap such as merchant seamen wear in the winter, and it would carry the club colors. In this era, Yale football players began to grow their hair long on top, chrysanthemum style, so that no hat would fit over it. This was not for protection, but merely as a badge of their profession. The bushy hairdo, for some time, became the accepted insignia of the boy who played on the varsity.

The tough lads from the mill and mining towns of western Pennsylvania, however, had little regard for such affectation, although they might breed a mustache, if they were able. (Latrobe's first paid player was a sixteen-year-old lad from the town of Indiana named John K. Brallier. He could not grow whiskers but he quarterbacked his high school team and the local normal school team as well—and then allowed himself to be talked into playing quarterback for Latrobe for a ten-dollar fee, plus expenses. He went on to Washington and Jefferson College, played football there, and played later for West Virginia University. But he continued to steer the Latrobe eleven from time to time, and when West Virginia found itself unable to pay its football players as agreed, he signed with Latrobe for $150 for the season.)

Blocking in the nineties was still elemental. A specific rule had been passed in the eighties to prevent the use of hands and arms to bar would-be tacklers from the runner. (The rules *still* said it was illegal to interfere at all, ahead of the ball.) The body blocking was done usually face to face, or even back to face, or with an occasional dig of the shoulder into the chest. The rugby rule that forbade tackling below the waist was repealed and players were urged to tackle low, so as to capture the runner's legs. The only low blocking, however, was done by the Indians. (The Carlisle Indian School was close by.) They had a special way of hurling themselves against an opponent's legs and rolling over like a moving barrel to sweep his feet from under him. This method, which eventually became the recommended style, was long known as Indian blocking, or the Indian roll, and even to-day some old-timer may observe that an end who is dumped on his face has been "Indianized."

A Carlisle Indian named Isaac Seneca, who was also the first Indian ever named on an "All-American" eleven, played with Greensburg at the turn of the century while Latrobe carried on its roster a big aborigine called Shelafo. Seneca, according to old-timers who recall his deeds, was as fast and as rugged as Jim Thorpe and might have outdone the more famous Indian had he found more area to play in. As it was, his name lived on past its normal expectancy because he participated in one of the not infrequent free-for-alls of the professional gridiron, when the invaders from Latrobe traded kicks and punches with the doughty men of Greensburg, one November Saturday in 1900.

Partisans of both teams piled into each other after quarterback Kennedy of Latrobe dumped the rugged Seneca on his duff with more energy than finesse and the big Indian rose up and belted Kennedy in the mouth for his trouble. Coach Russell Knight of Latrobe, hastening out to separate the embattled braves, was tomahawked en route by a doubled fist and immediately both benches, the sidelines, and the distant waiting buggies boiled over. Eventually the riot simmered down; but before Greensburg would go to Latrobe to play the return match on Thanksgiving, the team sought assurances that they could invite their sheriff along to help restrain the crowd. Sheriff Seanor brought twenty deputies with him and not an angry blow was struck—except for what few might have been dealt out anonymously in the scrimmages.

The rivalry between Latrobe and Greensburg had always been bitter. (After one Latrobe victory, in Greensburg, the victors seemed ready to demolish the town, and fears were expressed over the town hall steeple.) Betting was heavy and pre-game promotion was ardent. Latrobe had the best marching band in America, the locals insisted, and they called it out to lead the parade when their imported pros marched down to the playing field. The ladies all carried long silken ribbons with the team's colors and used little horns to toot their pleasure when our side made a gain.

In one of the early Greensburg games (against the Jeannette A.C.), the great Lawson Fiscus, the "Samson of Princeton," nearly precipitated a riot when he took deliberate aim with a shod foot at the jaw of a prostrate ball carrier and let him have it, fracturing the jawbone. But when Latrobe and Greensburg met, there was no need for an outrage like this to set the blood to boiling. The towns openly despised each other and gloated over victory, or mourned a defeat, as madly as if every maiden's sacred honor had been at stake. When Latrobe beat Greensburg one year, the Greensburg boys refused to deliver up the ball—the winner's traditional trophy. Latrobe had to come get it. They did, because they were bigger and stronger that year, but they took home a few fat lips and left some drifting teeth behind.

Footballs, in those days, were sometimes made of rubber, inflated with a hand pump. But the expensive ones were built of panels of leather enclosing a rubber bladder that was blown up hard and laced in tight. It was nearly round, hard to throw, and not the sort of thing to be toted about in one hand in the manner of some of today's quarterbacks.

The game, while it had no forward passes, had plenty of lateral pitchouts, for the quarterback was continually tossing the ball to one of the backs. In punt formation he even passed it back to the kicker, who stood only eight yards behind the line of scrimmage. It was no longer the grinding "block game" of the very earliest days, nor was it, after 1894, nearly so dangerous a game to play as it was during the flying wedge era.

The reforms of 1894 put an end to the phoney kickoff and the mass momentum play. With only three players allowed to start before the ball, and with the rule that required every kick to travel at least ten yards, the thundering herds behind which the ball carrier would hide at kick-off time (the kickoff being a touch of the ball to the boot) could no longer be organized. But, because linemen could line up in the backfield, momentum plays from scrimmage were still possible and could still smash into a stationary defensive line with something of the force of a bull charging through a broken fence. Runners would pop through the line again and again—often being shoved free by the strong-arm backfield men who followed them—and would then dodge and scamper through the scattered opposition, to the wild delight of the crowd. Deception was not complicated, but it was often practiced—on "crisscrosses" or on "tackle around" plays.

The basic formation was the old-fashioned T, with the full-back a stride further back than the two halfbacks, and the quarterback squatting low behind the center, deeply bent at both knees and waist so that he was actually closer to the ground than the center was, and could peer right into that player's upside-down face. The play was given by a number or a letter signal, and the starting signal, when the ball was passed back, would be a mere opening of the fingers or extension of the hands to receive the ball.

The nearest thing to a forward pass was the quarterback kick, or onside kick as it was eventually called. The quarterback on this play would endeavor to plop the ball gently into the air, so that one of the other backs, on the dead run, and knowing about where the ball would drop, could gather it in and travel on with it. The ball was a free ball, however, and the opposition too could pick it up and take off with it, so this play often backfired.

Kicking in the early game was of prime importance, a goal from the field, for a time, counting more than a touchdown. (Originally a touchdown counted nothing at all but merely gave the attacking team the right to attempt to "convert" the touchdown into a goal by drop-kicking or place-kicking it over the goal posts. This feature is retained in today's point-after-touchdown conversion.) The great players were nearly all great kickers. The punt was vital too, for there were but three downs in a series, instead of four, and the punt was counted on to move the opposition back.

One of the greatest of the early-day kickers, among the pros, was Ed Abbatticchio, who later won fame as an infielder with the Pittsburgh Pirates. Ed played for the Latrobe pros at the turn of the century, and sportswriters who had to record his great deeds (he was acknowledged the greatest fullback of his day) at first refused to commit his full surname to print. He was just "Awful Name" to them. To the fans around Pittsburgh he was "Mr. Punt," or "Abby."

As in all professional play, be it baseball, football, or merely weight-lifting, there was, in those distant days, occasional talk of sell-outs. And there was wild bidding too for the services of the college stars.

The Latrobe team fired their coach, a former Pennsylvania star named A. E. Bull, because he was (wrongly) suspected of "selling out signals" to the enemy. (Coaches in that day played with the team. Even college coaches, when the varsity played a semipro or independent eleven, were permitted to take part in the game.) And one of Latrobe's mightiest linemen, a tackle named Charles Lloyd Barney, who was supposed to be the strongest man alive (he once lifted a whole football team on his shoulders), and who wore his golden locks nearly as long as Samson did before he got his free haircut, had to hide his glowing head in shame one day when it was learned that, in a weight-lifting contest at the Showalter Opera House, on which many wagers were riding, he "lay down" for a few hundred pieces of silver.

Latrobe and Greensburg often schemed against each other to capture the top stars of the area. When Doggie Trenchard, Princeton's All-American end and then coach at West Virginia, signed to play with Latrobe, the Greensburg backers outbid their rivals and set out to kidnap Doggie (his hair was shaggy as a dog's) at the railroad station. But the lads from Latrobe got wind of the plot, met the train one station west of Greensburg, piled Doggie into a hack, and drove over deeply rutted roads to Latrobe, where Doggie played thereafter for seventy-five dollars a game.

The play itself in this era, although it was always rough, was usually clean. There were bruises and bloody noses aplenty but seldom any serious injuries and few complaints. The old pros, most of them veterans of the bloody intercollegiate wars of earlier days, gloried in their toughness. Physical strength, stamina, and sound wind were everything. A football game was a fearsome and stirring experience, in which almost any man—even guards and tackles—might be called on to run with the ball. It was as bloody sometimes as a bare-fisted fight (although slugging had been outlawed) and made equal demands on the heart and body. The game, until the reform of 1894, had lasted ninety minutes, divided into two periods. In 1894 the periods were shortened to thirty-five minutes each. The men on the rush-line, as the scrimmage line was still called, crouched head to head with their opponents and bulled it out from the instant the ball was passed back. No substitutes were allowed except by permission of the referee and he never granted permission except for obvious serious injury on the field of play.

Backfield men crashed head-on, without helmets, into the line, and sometimes into the spine of a slow-moving "interferer." Strong ends and fullbacks would often set their backs against the ball carrier and shove him through the massed opposition by main strength. And once he broke into the open he could fend off tacklers with his hand and arm.

This was a hard-boiled era anyway, when many newspapers still carried sports news on the same page as news of the raids on "sporting houses" or the arrests of disorderly persons. Gentleman Jim Corbett, at about this time, proved himself no gentleman when he spit into the eye of Jim Jeffries, whom he chanced to meet in a Philadelphia saloon. (Jeffries, who one suspects may have been alive to the uses of a publicity buildup, was restrained by Corbett's brother from mixing it, without charge, right there.

They were to fight later for a large purse.) The college football team of the University of Pennsylvania retreated each summer to a camp in Ontario where they grew hairy and tough as they concentrated on improving the wind and building the biceps.

Professional football, despite crowds of five thousand or more, was still not expected to be as thrilling a spectacle as college football. The early professional promoters, even though they recruited their stars from near and far, could not range as widely as the big colleges to draw in the top-notch players. Nor could many of the professionals devote themselves to the game as single-mindedly as a college athlete could. Most of the pros had to work at a full-time trade during the week. The top-rated college stars let nothing fret them but football during the season, and a few of them were earning a stipend more handsome than they might have picked up with the pros. Yet the pro game grew quickly and spread before long into Ohio, and east to New York and to Philadelphia were Connie Mack organized a football team to match his baseball club and to wear the same honored name: Athletics. He even used one or two of his baseball stars, including big Rube Waddell, in the lineup. But some who tried the game (and Waddell was one of these) quickly decided that baseball was more their style. For one thing it was almost impossible to play seventy minutes of football while waiting for a hangover to heal, or even while wearing an extra ring of lard around the middle. The Athletics of the baseball diamond were not all of them quite athletic enough to mix it in the scrimmage line for minutes on end.

Christy Mathewson of Bucknell, however, was one athlete who could earn a paycheck at either football or baseball. Even before he had become a star pitcher with the New York Giants, he was playing football for money. (Football made money for him on the baseball diamond too, because one of his early baseball managers gave him a raise after seeing him boot a field goal for Bucknell.) Christy decorated the bench in two games for the Pittsburgh pros against Connie Mack's Football Athletics, in 1902. The games were played in the same week in Pittsburgh and, after a scoreless tie on a muddy field, Pittsburgh beat the Athletics for the "National Championship."

These games marked both the beginning and the end of the original National Football League which, except for the teams in Pittsburgh and Philadelphia, never really got off the drawing board. It had been organized on paper with two teams in Philadelphia, one in Pittsburgh, one in New York, and three others in Pennsylvania, including the steel-mill monsters from Homestead, who had been cleaning up every team in the county for two seasons. Promoters of the teams, in most of the towns, simply backed out at the prospect of dumping still more money down the dark hole that always seemed to swallow as much cash as a sports promoter in those days could ever collect. In a few of the Pennsylvania towns—Homestead, Latrobe, Jeannette, and Greensburg—money to keep the stars contented, to buy team sweaters (at twenty-five dollars apiece) and to provide the pants and shin guards and belts had been solicited from local merchants, collected in a high-crowned derby at the games, or had been promoted through diverse "socials" or public entertainments.

The Latrobe team one year raised seventy dollars toward the cost of uniforms by holding a football festival in Doherty's Hall featuring "exquisite melody" by the Latrobe Cornet Band and a "watermelon walk" for the small boys. Regularly at the close of each season in Latrobe, the team held a minstrel show in Showalter's Opera House, where Doggie Trenchard and Walter Okeson won roaring applause for their vocalizing.

Stratagems of this sort, however, did not seem likely to provide capital enough to keep afloat a whole league whose teams would have hundreds of miles of travel to log each fall. Enthusiasts who joined the project and pledged their fortunes to it dwindled at last to Connie Mack and W. C. Temple of Philadelphia and the president of the league, David J. Berry, a man who should be enshrined somewhere someday as the true father of professional football in this country. Berry, like most other sports promoters of the early days, was a newspaperman to begin with and actually put on a uniform to play with the first team he organized, in Latrobe. A sturdy and enterprising young man, bearded like a French count, he was always on the go, finding new teams to lick, organizing all-star contests, recruiting college players from all over the state. In practice one day, his jaw was broken by Captain Harry Ryan of the Latrobe team, which Berry was coaching, and Berry then retired from active play.

Berry headed the Pittsburgh team in 1902, when the league was formed. He was a church deacon now and a successful printer. He put out a beautiful thirty-two-page souvenir program for the championship game with Philadelphia and his kid brother peddled 2500 in less than an hour. But the enthusiasm Berry managed to stir up in and around Pittsburgh did not spread to the other towns, although Youngstown, Ohio, and Homestead (where the team was financed by Carnegie Steel) had had professional teams for two or three years. Even with the backing of local merchants it was all a promoter could do to hold his team together through a schedule, without sending it to Chicago and back. A player in Greensburg one night pulled down a building that overlooked the new park because he just could not bear to see three dozen non-paying spectators up there devouring the game for free.

While there were some three hundred professional football players in the country at the turn of the century, and more developing in the colleges, the bidding for the stars made it seem sometimes as if there were hardly players enough to go around; and some of the better players would appear in two or three different lineups in a season. Albert Kennedy, Latrobe's star quarterback, also played for the New York Athletic Club. Bemus and Hawey Pierce, the rugged Indian brothers from Carlisle, played for several teams in Pennsylvania and also graced the lineup of the Syracuse All-Stars. Dr. Roller, the two-hundred-pound guard from DePauw who played for the New York A.C., also wore the colors of the great Duquesne Country and Athletic Club of Pittsburgh, the D.C.A.C., which was operated by W. C. Temple, former president of the Pittsburgh baseball team. (The letters D.C.A.C., according to a triumphant Latrobe rooter whose team outscored this "unbeatable" outfit one day, really stood for "Defeated Champions and All-Around Crokers.")

The few games that were actually played in the "National Football League"—all involving Pittsburgh and one or the other of the Philadelphia teams (which were named Phillies and Athletics, after the baseball teams)—drew moderately well, despite bad weather. The first game, played to a scoreless tie on Thanksgiving Day, 1902, had drawn an enthusiastic crowd; and Connie Mack was persuaded to stay over two days to play again.

Before the second game began, however, it was obvious that instead of the ten thousand fans that were expected, there would be hardly half that number on hand. Connie, fretting over his heavy payroll, refused to field his team until the guarantee was in his pocket. So, while the crowd shuffled and stamped impatiently, Dave Berry sent his minions scurrying about to scare up what cash lay loose. It began to look as if there would be no game until one of the spectators, learning the cause of the delay, offered Connie his personal check for the entire sum. Connie boggled a moment, not recognizing the name (he never could keep names straight anyway). Then someone whispered to him that he was dealing with the number one man at Carnegie Steel. That was good enough for Connie, who took the check away and gave the sign to start the game.

It was a bruising game, like the first one, and looked like another scoreless tie. It grew dark, and the crowd began to dwindle. Then the Philadelphia quarterback was hurt and had to be helped off the field. His replacement, a little fellow named Weir, soon brought disaster down upon his team. Settling under a high punt, with hands and arms ready to clutch the ball, Weir grew nervous at the presence of several husky Pittsburghers, including the mighty Arthur Poe of Princeton, who stood hard by ready to demolish him. (There were no fair catches in that day.) He let the ball slip and the Pittsburghers pounced upon it, smothering little Weir and taking the ball away from him on the Philadelphia nine-yard line. After two short plunges, the Pittsburgh fullback, Ellis of Harvard, smashed his bare head into the Philadelphia line while his quarterback, the left halfback, and a monstrous guard named Kirkhoff all piled up behind him and shoved him through the massed defenders and right across the goal line.

There were but ten seconds left to play in the final twenty-five-minute half when a Pittsburgh kick went out of bounds. The referee blew his whistle and half the people present, including manager Dave Berry, thought the game was over. Berry snatched up the muddied football, wrapped it snugly in a newspaper, and started home, while several of his players plunged for the dressing room. But the referee had merely called the play back because of an offside and after he had assessed the penalty he looked in vain for the ball. Berry then was recaptured, the ball was returned to the field, and Pittsburgh kicked again. This time poor little Weir dropped the ball again and Poe, who was right upon him, deftly booted it over the goal line (kicking a free ball in that day was part of the game). An undersized Indian named Miller, playing left half for Pittsburgh, scurried after the ball like a terrier and fell upon it in the end zone, to make the Philadelphia humiliation complete.

Dave Berry took the ball home finally then, while the joyous Pittsburghers pranced and shouted all around him. He could not have known, in that moment, that this game marked the end of his National Football League—as it marked the last time to this writing that the Pittsburgh team has won any sort of professional football championship.

But Berry had many other troubles in football besides quick whistles, stingy gate receipts, and a broken jaw. (Collisions of the bare head and unprotected jaw were common in early football, although the game did not produce the number of torn ligaments and serious fractures that marked the more heavily armored game of a later day.) Berry, like every part-time sports promoter, had to be a combination diplomat, coach, organizer, salesman, cheerleader, peace officer, bill collector, and clubhouse lawyer. He once had to come bustling home from a promotion tour to deal with a guard named MacKenzie, who had staged a one-man strike in midseason to get more wages. And one Saturday afternoon, when a crowd awaited reopening of the bloody feud between Latrobe and Greensburg, the Greensburg team, having driven onto the field in their horse-drawn omnibus, refused to disembark until they had seen the color of the guarantee. They whipped up the horses and made off again too, until Berry, having gathered up cash enough, ran after them and proved it was truly in hand. Another day, in Greensburg, when the famous Cornet Band, the pride of Latrobe, had accompanied the team to a game and had marched all through the streets of Greensburg, the Greensburg management halted them at the gate and made them all cough up the price of admission.

Football of this sort could not, by today's standards, be described as "professional." The promoter often enough found himself at the season's end shelling out more than he had taken in. Dave Berry, however, what with one stratagem or another, managed to keep the ghost walking regularly on the appointed day.

Berry's enterprise, despite the league's failure, infected others in the county until, by the time the new century was well started, there were a half dozen well-equipped and well-established professional (or semiprofessional) teams in the Pittsburgh area—as well as several more in nearby Ohio. Industrial teams from the steel mills and railroad plants sometimes played on the Colosseum field in Pittsburgh before fair-sized crowds who paid to get in. And in many cities throughout the East football teams were formed of college stars and other young men who hungered after the game and called themselves professionals.

Another "Championship" in 1902 was won by the Syracuse All-Stars who played in the Indoor Tournament in New York City staged at Madison Square Garden by an enterprising Irishman named Tom O'Rourke. Even though the field he could mark out was only seventy yards long and thirty-five yards wide, O'Rourke managed to draw in over three thousand customers at a time. He staged two games each night of the Tournament—a preliminary between two local clubs, and a big game between two of the four teams in competition for the championship. Reporters for the polite press found it ineffably funny that

O'Rourke should lure in "ribbon clerks, bartenders, and cab drivers" to cheer the play just as if they were college boys. The spectators were given slips of paper with cheers printed on them, and were actually encouraged to desecrate the names of some of the big universities by lending their unlettered throats to the singing of the university songs. They even undertook to wear colored streamers in their lapels—getting the colors all mixed up, of course, as anyone might expect who tried to teach college manners to lowly persons.

Lettered or not, however, the spectators at Madison Square found the football games well within their understanding, and they never failed to set the big arena to roaring. Spectators in that day, even in colleges, came to football games expecting to see blood flow, and the crowd that attended the first (and best) game of this indoor tournament was not disappointed.

The championship was actually settled in that first game, played on December 29, 1902. The Syracuse All-Stars, who won the tournament, featured the Warner brothers (not a motion picture) from Cornell; the two big Indian brothers from Carlisle, Bemus and Hawey Pierce (who had recently played for Pittsburgh); and a dashing young man from Williams College named Phil Draper, who had made four touchdowns against Yale. Opposing them this December night, on the soft loam of the Garden floor, was the New York A.C., which listed seven big men from Penn on their roster, as well as Kingdon, a 220-pound lineman from Columbia, known up there as "the giant guard," who had played for Connie Mack's Athletics in the Pittsburgh series.

The game would seem helter-skelter to a modern audience, and probably not worth spending a half hour to watch. The first kick-off bounced off behind the boxes, was retrieved against the wall, and run back some fifteen yards. The ball carriers (who often included the guards) would quickly lose their footing in the soft earth and go sprawling when they tried to change direction sharply. Yard lines, all carefully drawn before the game began, were erased in a few minutes, until all measurements were guesswork.

But there were three stand-up fist fights, just as everybody hoped, besides uncounted blows struck in the scrimmages. Carver, the Syracuse end, took random pokes at half a dozen opponents, until Teas, the 212-pound center from Pennsylvania (and the only substitute who entered the game) banked his fires for him with a solid uppercut. The Carlisle Indians, always deemed fair game, and both of them men who were not the least bit slow to wrath, took a few potshots from the New Yorkers, until eventually Bemus Pierce (who was still playing professional football twenty years later) rose up and smote his tormentors hip and thigh. At this signal both lines abandoned football for a more direct assault upon each other with foot and fist. The two umpires and the more peaceable members of the squads managed to effect a truce, however, and no more open blows were exchanged until Stehle, the New York right end, around whom Phil Draper had made the longest run of the evening, expressed his disgust by dealing young Draper a punch in the nose. This uprising was quickly quelled and the game proceeded—with the stands in a continuing uproar.

When the game moved toward its close, someone in the stands, or elsewhere, announced in too loud a voice that time was up. Time was not really up. There were five minutes of the second twenty-minute half remaining. But the spectators, who had been straining at the railing right along, rushed out of the stands and engulfed the players, making further play impossible.

Syracuse, having earned five points when Boettger of Princeton had plunged over the goal line from two yards out, was declared the victor. Glenn Warner, Syracuse left tackle, missed the conversion, as he had missed two previous attempts at goals from the field. The New Yorkers had lost a desperate bid to defer, or even elude, their doom, when their own umpire—a Mr. Wench of the New York Athletic Club—refused to let loyalty to the club influence his sense of right and wrong. As the teams were lining up for the touchdown play, several New Yorkers deliberately put themselves offside, perhaps believing that the final whistle was near and a little stalling would mean a tie. Umpire Wench called out "New York offside," whereupon the ball was snapped back, tossed by quarterback Moore to Boettger, and carried quickly over the line. Captain Kennedy of New York immediately insisted that the violation be called and the penalty exacted, but Umpire Wench wisely canceled the call and it was several minutes before the clamor died down enough so that Referee Smith could be heard announcing his decision that the score stood.

Haphazard play of this sort was common in football for many seasons. For one thing, the rules carried loose ends aplenty. It was permissible, for instance, to recover a fumble out of bounds, so that opposing players could go scrambling right among the sideline spectators and fight for the ball on the cinders. A kickoff might be returned from anywhere and often was. Latrobe players once had to plunge waist-deep into a creek for the first kickoff and run it back through the end zone. Officials at the professional games eventually gave up trying to keep the peace and would let the players slug it out until a truce was struck. If they had started to call all the personal fouls there might not have been time left to play the game. As a result, in many of the early professional contests, the police would have to enforce the final whistle.

But boys in the early part of our century were raised on roughhouse play. Football skills—a willingness to take and give a bump, or to escape a tackler—were frequently developed in games like "Hill-Dill," "Hoist the Green Sail," or "Red Rover," which consisted chiefly of headlong tackling in an attempt to capture opponents, and wild dodging, squirming, or bucking to elude entangling arms. Boys who returned from "play" often sported, all unknowing, clotted blood, dangling blouse buttons, and ripped sleeves and could not understand the growing horror on their mothers' faces when sonny walked in the door. As these boys grew older, they found opportunities to play football, and if they could not attend college, they would form football clubs of their own. Occasionally they might earn backing enough to afford the hire of an enclosed field or at least a wooden stand so that they could pay an occasional college star to help do in some precious enemy. And a few persisted, through lean times and good, until a league was formed to enfold them.

In the first five or six years of the new century, football remained the favorite fall pastime of so many young men that there were football games both outdoors and indoors from late summer until nearly spring. It took a famous team like the All-Stars from Syracuse, or the Philadelphia Athletics, or the Watertown (N.Y.) Red and Blacks, to draw a well-paying crowd. But even when the Knickerbocker A.C. of New York played the Warlow A.C. of Whitestone, there were ravening fans enough to rattle the roof of Madison Square Garden. The two teams had played themselves into a battle royal (which the police put a stop to) when they met outdoors. And when, in December 1902, they played on the skimpy gridiron Tom O'Rourke laid out in the Garden, the spectators were screaming for blood. They got it, too. Nearly a dozen players were knocked senseless during the fray and there was almost as much time out as there was time in. When Leahy, the New York star, bucked over for the tie-breaking touchdown, his fans fell upon him before he could convert the goal, and he had to make his kick with paid customers all round about him and half-blocking his view of the posts.

A short time later when the Syracuse All-Stars came back to the Garden to meet the Orange A.C., some roughneck on the Jersey team kicked Bemus Pierce in the face and broke his nose. He was led to the locker room streaming blood and barely able to see.

These were lusty days in the city. At Grand Central Palace, two teams of "ballet girls" put on an exhibition of rugby. And at Manhattan Casino two "artists' models" gave a fencing exhibition, in tights of course, with a "female police force" on hand to "prevent undue excitement." Down on the Bowery, Big Jack Martin agreed to meet Joe Levy, the Duke of Essex Street, in a goose-eating contest, in which the first man to pack away six pounds of selected goose meat would take the prize. In Helena, Montana, Bob Fitzsimmons fired his manager by knocking him unconscious at the ladies' entrance of the Finton Hotel.

And back in New York, Tom O'Rourke, when it grew too cold to play outdoors, revived football again in Madison Square Garden, with teams like the new club from Franklin, Pennsylvania, which starred most of the former Philadelphia and Pittsburgh players, and the Red and Blacks from Watertown, where Phil Draper of Williams College had played professional football. O'Rourke dressed the games up this season by decking his officials out in top hats, patent leather shoes, and white gloves, as if they were attending an opera rather than an organized bloodletting. And this tempted the Franklin crowd one day to cook up a play aimed straight at the referee (the great Hinkey of Yale). Down he went into the loose loam of the Garden and over him rolled the entire Franklin eleven. When he arose his gloves were no longer white and his high silk hat had become eligible for a comic strip. Hinkey laughed it off, however, and the game went on.

Chapter III

Bulldogs, Tigers, and Boilermakers

Throughout the early 1900's football remained a brawling game, dominated by kickers, with relatively little protective equipment. A few helmets (the fullback sometimes was the only man to wear one) appeared before the start of the century; they would seem comic measured against the military-type headgear required today. They were made of hard leather, padded inside, but fitting like a skullcap, with leather earflaps.

Deception of a sort was used more frequently, with the quarterback pretending to pitch the ball to one man, then flicking it over that man's head to the runner beyond. Or halfbacks would crisscross, as in a modern reverse, and one would hand the ball to the other before he hit the scrimmage line. Every play into the line meant an enormous pileup, with ends, quarterback, and halfbacks on the offense all straining to shove the ballcarrier ahead and the entire defensive line, plus most of the backfield, rushing up to stem the tide. Often the defensive quarterback alone would remain between the runner and the goal if the runner could be forced through the opposition. And the runner was not counted "down" until he surrendered.

Bloody noses were actually of very little account in such play. Gashes on the scalp or forehead, though superficial, could bleed heavily and blind a player. But such injuries were not deemed serious by the players—except that they might require removal from the field for patching. President Theodore Roosevelt, however, thanks to the improvement in photographic reproduction, chanced to see a picture of a battered Swarthmore star, his face black with blood, being led to the sideline. And that caused the doughty exponent of the strenuous life to cry "Enough!" In 1905, he called in representatives from the big eastern colleges and insisted that they get the bloodshed out of the game or abolish it altogether.

After a White House conference that involved representatives only of the Big Three—Harvard, Princeton, and Yale—the major colleges in the East joined together to create a football rules committee that would open up the game. They legalized the forward pass (it had been used without sanction from time to time in an impromptu way), outlawed hurdling, and ruled that linemen could not line up in the backfield on the offense unless they were five yards or more behind the line. (Through the nineties, many college teams and the pros as well employed a "guards back" or a "tackles back" formation to add weight to their plunges, and it was standard practice for some teams to line up with the ends, in military parlance, "slightly refused"—i.e., a stride behind the line of battle.)

It was not the forward pass that opened up the game, however, for there were only a few players in the East who were practiced at this maneuver. Whereas some of the western and midwestern colleges immediately set out to develop this new play and use it to disrupt the defenses, the old line colleges resorted to it mostly as a desperation device. What really began to cut down on the carnage on the football field was the establishment of a "neutral zone" to restrain players of the opposing rush-lines from getting any closer together, before play began, than the length of the ball. Heretofore, the opposing linemen had lined up head to head, or chest to chest, and there was always some man-to-man scuffling before the ball was snapped. It was this that led to the merry slugging matches that had made the game so attractive to spectators and that sometimes would hold play up for several minutes, while the officials tried to pry the combatants apart.

The pass, when it first came in, was severely restricted. The ball could be thrown forward only when the passer was at least five yards, laterally, from the center of the scrimmage line. (The field had to be marked off with longitudinal lines to help the officials enforce this rule.) A forward pass, like a kick, could be recovered by either side, once it had been touched by a receiver. If it went out of bounds it was awarded to the opponents at the point where it crossed the boundary. If it was caught behind the goal line, it became a touchback and entitled the defending team to a free kick-out from the goal.

Most players of this era who resorted to the forward pass would heave the ball end over end, like a place-kick, cradling the ball against the forearm with the whole hand closed over the ball's blunt nose. A pass receiver would need a group of interferers to surround and protect him while he awaited the ball, for it would soar like a punt and give everyone on the field a chance to gather near the spot where it might fall. And many a player, right up to the century's teens, always thought the forward pass a freakish device, of somewhat doubtful virility.

Another 1906 rules change lengthened the "yards-to-go" in three downs to ten, rather than five, and this actually inhibited the pass, which might completely "waste" a down. The quarterback kick was still relied on by many teams, some of whom had quarterbacks who could boot the ball as accurately as they could pass. Still the forward pass gradually gained favor and by 1907 most of the colleges were working on pass plays of their own.

Among the pros at least the accepted passing formation became the "short punt" or even the regular punt formation, and the quarterback sometimes had an option either to pass or kick. On the short punt as on the regular punt formation the ends were split so they could hasten unimpeded downfield to nail the punt receiver or catch a thrown ball. The early rules, however, permitted a pass to travel no more than twenty yards from the line of scrimmage.

Backfield men, on a pass as on a kick, would usually devote themselves to protecting the passer—although they might take a short toss if the passer could not see an end in the clear. Linemen did not immediately learn to yield a yard or two of ground in order to give the passer more time. It was still deemed traitorous to allow an enemy tackler across the line without a do-or-die effort to drive him back.

The resemblance between the forward pass and the punt was further emphasized by the frequent use of the out-of-bounds pass on last down. Like the coffin-corner kick, this could immobilize a team near its own goal line, for the ball went over to the opposition on the spot where it crossed the sideline.

In 1910, the rules committee finally repealed many of the restrictions on the pass and put a final end to mass play by insisting that linemen could not line up in the backfield on offense at any time. It also made illegal the pushing and pulling of the ball carrier, which had often turned him into a human football and had made for an enormous crush of bone and muscle at the point of impact on a line play. (When the Franklin, Pennsylvania, team played the Watertown Red and Blacks at Madison Square Garden one night in December 1903, Kirkhoff, the giant Franklin guard, picked the ball carrier up and actually threw him across the goal line. Happily he clung to the ball while in orbit.) The rules committee also granted an extra down in which to make ten yards, and this provided the quarterback with a fine chance to pass before he was forced to kick.

For a long time, thereafter, the third down became the standard passing down, even among the pros, who were often inclined to indulge in more razzle-dazzle than the colleges were. This opening of the offense prompted some opening of the defense too. The center now began to play "soft"—that is, to hesitate or even withdraw a step or two when the ball was snapped, to guard against deception. Soon he became a "roving center" who was ready to shift his force to whatever spot the enemy attack was aimed.

There were still not too many professional football players available in the land and, among those, the few who were experienced with the forward pass, or a defense against it, were fewer still and much sought after. The center of gravity of professional football had started to shift now from Pennsylvania to

Ohio, as the players yielded to offers of better and better pay, and as recruiters roamed the land to hire away football players before a rival town could snatch them. Most of the Pittsburgh stars, and many of those who had played with Connie Mack, moved first to Franklin, Pennsylvania, where a rivalry (backed by a fat wager) was brewing between Franklin and Oil City. The Franklin backers scuttled about the East to buy up football beef before Oil City could smell it out and soon they had all the really famous players with them: Blondy Wallace, who had been Connie Mack's captain; Pop Sweet, the lightweight and fleet-footed center, who had already played for more teams than he could recall; big Doc Roller, who had come from Seattle to study surgery and always played football in kid gloves to keep his fingers in shape for his eventual profession, and who sometimes wore a Van Dyke beard on the football field; "Bull" Smith, the University of Pennsylvania strongman; and just about everyone else a football fan could name who was fit to play in the fastest company. The result was that when Oil City undertook to recruit its own team, there was no one left to hire except a few creaking old stars and some untried youngsters.

So Oil City surrendered, refused to field a team, and insisted the bet be called off. (The cash—amounting to some twenty thousand dollars—was already in escrow.) The bet was canceled finally and the Franklin team was eventually disbanded. But a brand new rivalry was already abubble, and many of the Franklin players found themselves being courted once more—this time by promoters from Canton and Massillon, Ohio, out where William McKinley and "General" Jacob Coxey had been born and raised.

The Massillon team was invented first. Eddie Stewart, a writer for the Massillon *Independent*, had seen a chance to buy up a flock of football jerseys at a close-out price and he grabbed them. They were all striped around the arm, so the team became the Tigers before he had any team to put into the jerseys. The Canton Bulldogs came into being as an answer to the Tigers—or as an answer to the challenge Eddie Stewart sent to his friend Bill Day of Canton. Day accepted, and then the two men scrambled to sign up football players. The leftovers from Pennsylvania were divided between the teams, with Blondy Wallace coming on as coach for the Bulldogs. Day thought he scored his greatest triumph, however, when he signed up (for six hundred dollars) Willie Heston, Michigan's most famous ball carrier, who had just finished his university career. But when Willie came to Canton, he spent most of his fee on fancy food and liquor and reached the training grounds in a semiliquid state. He was many pounds overweight and not too bright of eye. But he was willing—and he was Willie Heston.

Stewart, meanwhile, like so many sportsmen of that day (and of this) was more concerned with a victory than he was with the quality of the play or even the excitement of the spectacle. So he bought himself one of the lightweight footballs little boys played with and blew up by mouth, built of split leather, or an imitation, with a bladder inside like a toy balloon. The whole thing weighed hardly half a pound and to throw or kick it was like trying to play baseball with a sphere of celluloid.

The newly recruited Bulldogs, of course, had no notion of what they were in for and they practiced doggedly with the big regulation football, inflated hard as a pneumatic tire and heavy enough to sprain a stockinged toe.

On the day of the game, the Bulldogs entrained in a special car, hired a-purpose to carry the squad the eight miles to Massillon on the interurban choo-choo. They ran through their paces on the frozen grounds of the local insane asylum, where the game was to be held. When the game began and the Canton boys first took hold of the featherweight football they began to wonder if the inmates were not staging the affair. But their howls of protest were bootless. The agreement said in black and white that the ball was to be supplied by the home team, who was to have sole discretion as to its qualities. Anything written down and signed was deemed, in that distant era, binding and unalterable, so the Canton boys bent wryly to the task of playing football with a toy.

The first time they scrimmaged, Canton thought to run off

with the game by turning the great Willie Heston loose. Willie's weakness (he could run only to his right) was no secret in Massillon and the defense was stacked up to meet him as he dashed around end with the squishy football snuggled in his arm. No doughty tackler was needed, however, to lay Willie low. There was a patch of glare ice in his path, spread with rice straw, and Willie's feet, with their unyielding cleats, flew out from under him as soon as he struck the spot. Down went Willie with a thump that frightened little boys on the sidelines. Immediately the entire Massillon team, in the fashion of the day, leapt atop his carcass, smothering his cries, crunching his ribs, and nearly popping the football. When Willie was helped to his feet he had the strength only to stagger to the bench.

Although Heston got back into the game in a later period, and offered some rugged defensive work, he never gained an inch. (He played one more game as a pro, broke his leg in that, and withdrew from football forever.)

Massillon carried the day by a score of 14–4. Reynolds of Canton, in defiance of the laws of dynamics, had actually propelled that ridiculous ball over the goal posts for a four-point field goal. The Bulldogs trailed off despondently and rode their luxurious car home in silence except when one substitute, who had not even gotten into the game, burst into song.

"Shut up!" bellowed Bull Smith, a pro since Connie Mack hired him in 1902, and now nursing a fractured wrist. "Nobody sings when they've been licked!"

As far as Massillon was concerned the promotion had been a wild success. Heavy money had been bet, and collected, and there was plenty of legitimate money in the till too, for the field had overflowed with paying customers—a few of whom, in all likelihood, had come there as much to watch Christy Mathewson play umpire, or the great Arthur Poe of Princeton act the referee, as to see the famous professionals pretend they were home-grown heroes.

The Massillon-Canton feud was continued in 1906, nurtured some by the press as well as by the urge of bettors to even things up. This year there were two games scheduled, one in Massillon and one in Canton. The first game, featuring the new-fangled pass, was won by Canton 12–6. Massillon had brought an acknowledged expert on the forward pass, Peggy Parrott, down from Cleveland to startle their rivals with his dexterity. But Canton was ready, with the nimble Pop Sweet, who had heard all about the forward pass and knew how to defend against it. So Canton took home the football. They did not, however, take home the loot, for their coach, Blondy Wallace, who had been entrusted by the team with several hundred dollars to bet on themselves, was unable, he said, to get the money off. But he assured them he would have it all down, and more besides, on the second game.

The second game went to Massillon 12–6 and immediately thereafter the Massillon paper accused Wallace of bribing one of his own players to throw the game. Blondy, who had never been popular with his charges, took off for friendlier environs, not even waiting to pack, and threatened at long distance to sue the paper for libel. The paper immediately girded up its legal loins and made ready for the litigation, but Blondy dropped the suit at once and faded out of football, to turn up years later as "King of the Bootleggers" in Atlantic City, New Jersey.

The Wallace affair, which was followed by a dismal game with Latrobe, for which both the Bulldogs and the Latrobe team went unpaid, put an end to big-time professional football in Canton for about ten years. But the appetite for it remained and fans still talked about the wild scenes the Massillon-Canton games had prompted: the vision of Big Bill Edwards, the mountainous referee, lifting the water boy by the slack of his pants and tossing him bodily into the arms of the Massillon coaches who had tried to use him to sneak a play in to the quarterback, in defiance of the rules; the valiant Turner of Dartmouth playing two whole periods with a broken collarbone; the great Willie Heston taking his unscheduled header on the ice.

When professional football came back to Canton, in 1915, it brought Jim Thorpe with it. Thorpe, most famous athlete of his

day, was surely at that time the greatest football player alive. He
was not merely good for his era, or the best of a mixed lot, but a
remarkable performer for any day, that or this. He consistently
booted that big fat football eighty yards, without a wind. And if
the ball was brand new, and he felt like trying it, he would kick
it a hundred yards. He was the swiftest and hardest runner ever
seen in the field and could race from one goal line to the other,
in all his football regalia, in just a shade over ten seconds. Attempting to tackle this man was like trying to knock over a telephone pole with one shoulder; being tackled by him, not unlike
being struck by the blunt end of a telephone pole in the small of
the back.

Thorpe had a frightening habit of catching up with a runner
from behind and wiping him right off the field with a smashing
application of his mighty shoulder ("padded," some said, with a
sheet of metal to give it added authority). Like most big men
who play the game, Jim Thorpe found a special delight in violent bodily contact. Sometimes, it is true, he eluded tacklers by
"showing them a leg then taking it away," but often he just
hurtled into them like a truck rolling down a hill. And one of his
teammates even vowed that Jim more than once permitted an
opponent to catch a pass in front of him, just so Jim would have
the joy of blind-siding the poor man halfway to oblivion. When
the victim of one of these smashing tackles looked up from the
turf, still not sure if he lay in one piece or in two, Jim would
usually smile down at him and remark: "A fellow could get hurt
playing this game. If he don't take care."

Canton had other great men wearing its colors during this
renaissance, men like Greasy Neale, who scored six touchdowns
in one game; two more Carlisle Indians, Peter Calac and Joe
Guyon, fast and rough and durable (they played big-league football for a dozen years); big Howard "Cub" Buck of Wisconsin,
who eventually became a stalwart in the line for the Green Bay
Packers; and Charlie Brickley of Harvard, the country's greatest
drop-kicker, who accepted $3000 to play a few games for the

Bulldogs (most players received $75 to $150 a game, depending on how many periods they "worked").

The rivalry with Massillon was immediately revived and burned hotter than ever. As many as eight thousand people would turn out to see a Massillon-Canton game (three thousand was a fair-sized pro football crowd) and the heavy betters in each town plunged up to their necks—and then stood on the sidelines to rail at the hired hands if they failed to come up to snuff. Spectators sometimes wearied of waiting a decision on the gridiron and took to belting each other along the sidelines. Often there were wild scenes at the rail terminals as rival rooters piled out of the cars or took off in triumph for home.

The Canton-Massillon game was always for the "championship," because it was generally acknowledged that Canton could trim any other pro team in the nation. As for Massillon, they would hire up all the stars from the other teams and create a special squad just for the Canton game, so the Bulldogs would see a line-up of familiar and not always welcome faces crouched across the neutral zone. (Knute Rockne and Gus Dorais, the Notre Dame passing wizards, once wore six different uniforms in a single pro season.)

Jim Thorpe, like all the great players of his day, was a triple-threat: that is, he might pass, run, or kick, whenever he took hold of the ball. Before his days at Canton were over, he had begun to slow up a little although he still could be relied upon, when he really felt the urge, to get yardage if the need was desperate.

But Thorpe, according to those who knew him best, was given to dogging it a little on occasion, especially if victory seemed assured or further effort seemed useless. After his first few years with the Bulldogs, of which he became manager, Jim did not always appear in the lineup. In 1920, for instance, he missed the first three games completely. (The Bulldogs hardly missed him, for they did not even have so much as a first down completed against them until the third game.) When Thorpe did show up, in the fourth game, he entered late in the third quarter

and could not prevent a loss to Akron, who twice held the Bulldogs for downs inside the Akron fifteen-yard line. In a game at
Buffalo late that season, Jim left because the hopelessly muddy
going had made the ball thoroughly soggy and a scoreless tie
seemed inevitable. But after Jim left, Al Feeney of Notre Dame,
who had never missed a field goal in his life, tried a placement
kick for Buffalo and made the goal, for the game's only points.

Still Thorpe, right after the war, remained the commanding
figure in professional football. He was fleshier now than he had
been when he carried off almost all the prizes in the 1912 Olym-
pics. His rugged features were battered and slightly bulging, so
that he looked less like the noble savage than like some Irish
family's drinking uncle. And some of the fire had gone out of
him, perhaps as an indirect result of the dirty deal that robbed
him of all his precious Olympic trophies (one of them a miniature golden boat, given him by the Shah of Persia, and inlaid
with pearls). Jim had been contrite at the time, had acknowledged his "guilt" of having played a few baseball games for pay
before joining the Olympic team, and had sent back every medal
and trophy. But since then he must have learned as everyone
close to sports had long known that almost every college athlete
of note had taken pay at one time or another and still remained
an amateur. Even Ivy League colleges, through divers devices,
had kept their varsity players on a steady payroll all through the
training and playing period. (The entire Georgetown team at
one time played football on Sundays, under a list of phoney
names, as the "Washington Vigilantes.") But it seemed the
Paleface destiny to cheat and humiliate the Indian—even those
who, like Thorpe, were part Irish. When a group of sportswriters,
in Jim's later years, cabled the head of the Amateur Athletic
Union (then in London) that it would be a pleasant gesture to
recover for Jim, as the greatest athlete in the world, the trophies
he had honestly won, that dignitary, with characteristic grace, replied, "If Jim Thorpe is the greatest athlete in the world, he
doesn't need any trophies." (Jim by this time had grown philo-
sophical enough merely to note that the head of the A.A.U. had

been one of the competitors who lost out to him in his heyday.)

But Thorpe, to get back to the immediate postwar days, could still do nearly everything on a football field—although not so often and perhaps not quite so fast as when he had played under Pop Warner at Carlisle. He could even coach his team and recruit ballplayers from far away, or set up a killing by taking care to keep the betting odds from getting out of balance. Once he was injured on the field and made as if he were sure to miss the upcoming game with Massillon. The odds then began to drop until it was possible to find some real money ready to say that Massillon would win. Then Jim, the story goes, bet $2500. When game time arrived, and the throngs gathered ready to see the Thorpeless Bulldogs take their thumping, there was Jim all bright-eyed and bushy-tailed, ready to scamper out on the field, where he scored every point in the 23–0 victory for the Bulldogs.

It seemed altogether natural that Jim Thorpe should be made president of the league—when the pro teams got around to making one. This happened in 1919, in the most casual way imaginable, on a hot summer day in the showroom of Ralph Hay's automobile agency in Canton, Ohio. Jim was there that day, loafing on the running board of a new touring car. Also present, besides Ralph Hay, who was General Manager of the Bulldogs, were Leo Lyons of the Rochester Jeffersons, Joe Carr of Columbus (where there were a dozen independent football teams already), Frank Neid of Akron (which harbored, in addition to the Indians, Neid's team, an eleven sponsored by the Goodyear Tire & Rubber Company and known as the "Silents"), and Carl Storck of the Dayton Triangles.

The league first called itself the American Football Association but within two years changed its name to the National Football League. Each of the five cities represented that day was assessed twenty-five dollars for a franchise and each agreed to the simple code of ethics—consisting chiefly of an agreement not to dicker with college athletes until they had completed their courses (an agreement which was honored mostly by the violation of it, in later years). The league paid Thorpe no salary for his services but did permit him to decorate the Canton Bulldogs' letterhead with his new title of president. In 1920 (which for some obscure reason the league likes to pretend is its *real* year of birth) a number of cities applied for franchises and the price this time was one hundred dollars. Jim soon quit as president, because he wanted to devote his full time to playing the game and coaching his team (for which he did get paid), and Joe Carr succeeded him. Joe held the job until his death in 1949.

Thorpe moved on to Cleveland in 1921 and soon after that undertook to show the world that he could build a whole team of Indians that would never know defeat. This was the Oorang Indians, first named after a dog kennel in Indiana, Pennsylvania, but entered in the league as representing Marion, Ohio. They were not really invincible at all. Indeed, without Thorpe they sometimes seemed like very tame Indians indeed and once dropped a game to Akron by a score of 66–0. Their roster, however, was an awesome thing to read, what with all the tribal names mingled with a few Paleface monickers. There were Arrowhead and Deadeye and Gray Horse and Eagle Feather; Lone Wolf and Tomahawk; Running Deer and Wrinkle Meat; Big Bear, Black Bear, Red Fang, Red Fox, Little Twig, and Buffalo. Occasionally they would play ball with feathers on or with an Indian costume worn outside their football pads, and no one who ever saw them and heard their wild cries felt that he had been cheated, even if a few of the "Indians" traced their lineage to a thatched tepee in County Sligo.

By 1922, the National Football League included eighteen teams. The Canton Bulldogs won the championship that season, although they did not meet all the teams in the league, or even nearly all. Patronage was haphazard in some cities. There were frequent arguments over eligibility, for some teams still insisted on grabbing for college players who were still playing college ball, and sponsorship was sometimes uncertain. Franchises kept skipping around and teams occasionally handed back their franchises in an argument with league authorities. The schedule was unwieldy and the championship always in question, because any football team was likely to beat almost any other on a given Saturday and some of the teams never faced each other. In 1926, for instance, there were twenty-two teams in the league, some of which played only four league games. (The winner that year was the Philadelphia team, which listed its home port as the suburb of Frankford and called itself the Yellowjackets.)

One of the most successful franchises was the one issued in 1921 to the Staley Starch Company of Decatur, Illinois (there was a Staley baseball team, too). George Halas, a husky young man who had missed making the grade as a baseball player with the New York Yankees and who had tried the previous fall to get himself a job with the Rochester Jeffersons as an end, was the player-coach of the Staleys, who eventually became the Chicago Bears. The Bears made George rich and helped place professional football on a par with baseball as the national game.

It was Joe Carr, however, who made the league successful, by clinging to his faith in the organization when franchise holders all around him were cutting their losses and hastening back to the rubber factory or the brokerage office. Joe came from Columbus, however, and in Columbus sandlot and professional football had long drawn as much patronage, sometimes, as the Ohio State University football team. In Joe's home town there were the Jungle Imps, the Wagner Pirates, the Linden Whistles, the Ohio State Stoves, and the Ralston Indians. Some of these were lightweight or middleweight teams, featuring grown-up high school stars, and some were heavyweight teams where fading professionals could still find a small payday. The Wagner Pirates were strong enough one year to hold the National League's Columbus Tigers even for half a game. All of them were used to the vicissitudes of weather and patrons. They knew adversity in every form and made out with rock-strewn playing fields, disappearing halfbacks, spectators that crowded on the plays, even wagon tongues and auto trucks that encroached on the playing area. Yet out of the Municipal League in Columbus came some top-notch football players. And many of the games were so cleanly played that hardly a penalty would be assessed all day.

(The officials, however, were not always so quick to call infractions as they might have been in school or college play.)

Most famous of the Columbus teams was the Panhandles, who eventually turned into the Tigers, and most famous of the Panhandles were the Nesser brothers, who made up most of the team when it began. One of the minor oddities of football has been the persistent appearance of pairs and even groups of brothers, sometimes to play side by side. Princeton of course had the Poes, kin to the great poet, and one of them bearing his name. There were six Poes who wore the Princeton togs between 1880 and 1901, the most famous being Arthur, who once carried the ball a hundred yards to score against Yale and who played for many of the early pro teams.

Mightiest and most miraculous of all, however, were the Nesser brothers, who included a father and a son, and the father's five brothers—and who had grandpa to help out with the water bucket and grandma Nesser to wash all the football jerseys by hand each week, and to cheer her lads on. The older Nesser boys had started to play football soon after their arrival from Germany at the close of the Franco-Prussian War (in which Nessers had fought on both sides). Brother Al Nesser saw his big brothers playing professional football while he was in grade school, and he immediately decided that this was the game for him. At the tail end of the nineteenth century Al played the disorganized game of the public schoolyards but as soon as he got his growth he answered the "call" for players to try out for the Rexall Drug team. (He arrived three or four hours early, to make sure he did not miss.) From that time forth, until age finally slowed him down, he played professional (or semiprofessional) football wherever he could, without regard for the size, the fame, or the reputed toughness of the opposition. But he, like all his brothers, put in his best years with the Panhandle A.C. of Columbus, named for the Panhandle division of the Pennsylvania Railroad, where Theodore Nesser, Sr., worked in the boiler factory— and where all the brothers had received their advanced education too.

The Panhandle A.C. was far more than a neighborhood team, or a group of boys who put a football team together with the help of their shopmates. All the Nessers were spectacular athletes and most of them played professional football for years. Most noted, perhaps, was Frank, who was one of football's greatest passers and kickers. He, like Jim Thorpe, whom he often faced on the gridiron, could stand behind one goal line and boot the ball over the other. Forty- and fifty-yard passes were commonplace with him and he could throw twice that far if need be. He could drop-kick the ball, too, better than any of his contemporaries, except Thorpe himself and Paddy Driscoll of the Chicago Cardinals. Brother Al was a mighty end, who played like a tiger, yet had only admiration for an opponent willing to mix it with him. Al played for half a dozen professional teams, in the National League and out, beginning in 1910 and winding up with the Cleveland Indians in 1931.

The oldest Nesser brothers, John, Pete, and Phil, were greenhorns in America at the turn of the century, having come over with mama on the slow steamship—six weeks on the Atlantic. But they took to the new game as zestfully as college boys. "Football," Mama Nesser told them, "was born for everybody to enjoy." John, in the early 1900's, was as good a quarterback as the game had seen. And Phil could have starred in any sport, for he matched the best performers of his time.

The Panhandle A.C. wore the colors of the Pennsylvania Railroad—maroon and gold. And they were able to challenge teams from far and near, for the whole crew, as railroad employees, could ride anywhere within reach on passes, and thus save considerably on travel costs. None of the Nessers got rich at the game, however, although Al and Frank stayed with it for many years. But riches were not all they had sought in America. If papa had been paid for the flexible stay-bolt idea he had brought with him from Germany, they might all have been millionaires —might even have owned the Pennsylvania Railroad today. But who the hell, they used to ask each other in their later years, wants to own a railroad?

Chapter IV

One Game—One Football

Slugging, in college circles, had become distinctly unfashionable when World War I was over but it cropped up now and then in the pro game which, despite heavy recruitment from the colleges, now listed many a Hard Knock graduate who might not even have finished high school—and where the will to win was more elemental and seldom diluted by gentlemanly traditions. The man in the pro ranks who was not ready to hand back as good as he got, be it fair blow or foul, was committed to a short career.

The game itself now bore only a faint resemblance to the game the old-timers had known. With the linemen rigidly separated by the neutral zone, both sides crouched low, with the attackers ready to drive their shoulders into the thighs, abdomens, or chests of their opponents, and the defenders preparing to belt the attackers about the head with their open hands, or submarine under their knees to clutch the ball carrier.

It was still legal to wallop an opposing lineman almost anywhere about his body with the open hand. Sometimes it was difficult to distinguish between the effects of such blows and the results of a few old-fashioned punches on the head, especially if the hands were given added conviction by the application of heavy friction tape.

The quarterback now no longer squatted with his belly nearly on the ground. The starting signal was given by a voice—a shouted number in the second "set" of numbers. (The first set would indicate, by code, the ball carrier, the play, or the "hole" the play would be aimed at, and would also give the number, in the second set, on which the ball would be passed.) Sometimes, as on a time out, the play would be decided on in a huddled conference and when the teams lined up the quarterback would call out: "First set called" and then go right into the second set. Between the first and second set there was usually a "hike"—at which call the team would shift into its running formation, or just tighten up in starting position.

Now that the rule required seven men in the line of scrimmage, it was a problem to gather the momentum needed to hit the opposition at full speed, or with concentrated power. As a result, ends and tackles occasionally turned into ball carriers and, on the starting signals, would wheel out of line and run through the backfield, where the ball would be slipped into their arms. This was the first reaching after the wingback formation that would soon alter the old-fashioned and standard T.

With the forward pass now thoroughly respectable, the ball was far more frequently in the air, where spectators might see it. A man was allowed to throw it as far as he liked—and some, like Frank Nesser or like John Levi of the Haskell Indians (who threw underhand) could hurl it a hundred yards. It was no longer a free ball if it fell to the ground and the attacking team did not lose possession of it if it dropped out of bounds or was caught behind the goal line. Nor could a potential receiver any longer be clobbered, without penalty, before he could lay hands on the thrown ball.

Every coach now added trick plays to his repertoire, sometimes involving a fake pass or a "delayed" pass, in which an end would come back to grab the ball and heave it diagonally downfield—the most valuable pass in the book, according to one contemporary authority. There was other razzle-dazzle too: end-around plays and tackle-around plays, fake handoffs of every sort, and sometimes a quick kick exploding out of a running formation.

But still the pass had not even begun to take over the game, as it seemed it might a couple of decades later. Some coaches averred that a pass "could not be thrown on the run" but should always be caught that way. It was not often that a halfback was sent out for any pass except a very short one and a pass earlier than the third down was daring strategy indeed, as was a pass inside the attacking team's own forty-yard line. The ball was still too big for most men to clutch it easily, and a number of quarterbacks still slung the ball flat-handed, with a sidearm sweep. But it was always passed in a spiral now and could be sent swiftly and accurately down to meet a receiver who was on the dead run.

Field goals were kicked chiefly by drop-kick, although there were fine place-kickers in this era too. The drop-kick, which had been a trick of slightly doubtful legality in the round-ball days, when the ball was tossed into the air to put it into play, was now accomplished by dropping the ball on its nose, then kicking it the instant after it had touched the ground. Great kickers like Frank Nesser, Paddy Driscoll, Jim Thorpe, and Charlie Brickley could score by drop-kick from the fifty-yard line. (Red Reeder of Army once enlightened the spectators at a game by booting practice drop-kick field goals first over one goal, then over the other, from midfield.)

Up until 1920 (at which point the rulesmakers decided that the game could not be improved further, except in trivial matters) there were a number of special oddities that would have bemused a modern spectator. The try for goal, which had gradually developed into a mere "point-after-touchdown," remained as a link with football's unpadded past, when only kicks could score. The scoring team, after a touchdown, could take the ball out to the five-yard line at the point opposite where the score had been made, and could then attempt to boot the ball over the crossbar—with the kicker all alone, or with a man to hold the ball in placement, while the defenders could rush toward him from the goal line with hands extended to block or deflect the kick. If the angle seemed too acute for the kicker, the scoring team might elect a punt-out, with their kicker punting the ball from the point where the score was made, out to a teammate, somewhere before the goalposts, with the goal attempt permitted from the point where the catch was made.

Substitutions in that day were limited, so that no man could return to the game in the same half, after once being removed. Every player played the game "both ways," and defensive strength and agility were as necessary as skill at running, passing, kicking, or blocking. Football seemed more fun then, to many who remember it, for, while weariness might overtake a man before the final whistle blew, there was a build-up of excitement from play to play. A fumble did not mean a sudden return to the bench, but rather a fierce effort to get the ball back immediately. There was no kicking specialist to come dashing in all spotless and fresh when a field goal seemed possible. Instead the bruised and muddied gladiator who had carried the ball into position and had perhaps vainly smashed twice at the line to make a score would now have to drop back and endeavor to dropkick the soiled ball straight and true and far across the standards.

There was one odd tradition that spoiled many a ball game for the spectators. Until 1925, it was unheard of that any game should require more than one football. The ball was expensive. More than that it was a trophy to be fought for and carried home by the victors. If it went into the stands, or into the creek, it had to be recovered and dried off and put in play again. As a result a rainy day meant a sodden, slippery, and heavy ball—almost impossible to kick, suicide to throw, and difficult to hold on to. Game after game, during an especially rainy fall (as 1925 was) would degenerate into a dull shoving and hauling contest, with every now and then a short and sorry kick to give the ball over to the other side, or an unseen fumble in the mud, with the holder of the ball not to be determined for a full minute, as men fought and slithered and grabbed at the ball in the mire.

Rain and a wet football may have contributed more than anyone knows to the strangulation of many a professional team. College boys, who would yearn for no matter how painful and narrow a victory over an ancient rival, could sit through a downpour with no loss of spirit and pray aloud for victory even when their heroes could hardly hold their footing. But spectators at professional games were often only mildly committed and came to see the play. Three muddy afternoons in a row might put a team in bankruptcy.

It was not until Iowa played Ohio State in October 1925, in one of the fiercest downpours of that cold and rainy autumn, that anyone thought of substituting a new football for the wet one. When the teams started the second half and the officials brought a shiny yellow ball out to replace the black and slimy object that had served the whole first half, sportswriters were moved to marvel. Never before, they told their readers, had such an oddity been seen on a football field. And would the victor, Iowa, take both balls home? Or what would be done, goodness knows?

(Baseball had been through a similar period, when players had been urged by the management to go into the stands after a ball that had landed there, and to force unwilling spectators to disgorge—yes, even to keep a sharp eye on the umpire, who might take the extra ball home in his pocket. A game would be held up in the early days while a ball was searched for in the grass, or to await its return, pounded and soiled as it might be, from over the fence.)

The pros, however, who were generally harder put for money than the colleges, were not quick to adopt this extravagance and they continued to wear out the patience of their spectators while they tried to pretend it was possible to play football with a leather object that was mostly mud.

Professional football, in the decade following War One, was still played largely for fun—or in the vain hope of staging a contest that would draw larger crowds from every quarter. In a few cities the game showed steady profit but in many places it was kept alive through the devotion of a promoter who would scramble to recruit players, book games, argue over guarantees, wangle publicity, peddle tickets, beg subsidies, patch equipment, dodge creditors, appease disgruntled players, then go coach the team, or even play in the game. Unhappily, most of the men who devoted themselves to keeping the breath of life in the professional game in this trying era had succumbed to hard times before the game had struck it rich. Not that any of them were in the game for riches. But some of them would have been made easier by a small show of gratitude on the part of the millionaires who moved into the game when it began to show the color of gold at the gate.

One of these forgotten heroes was Leo V. Lyons, who managed and coached and played end on the Rochester Jeffersons (who hopefully called themselves the Rochester Kodaks one season before the Kodak people decided that it was cameras and not football they wanted to sell). The Jeffersons had begun on Jefferson Avenue in Rochester—just a group of youngsters who wanted to keep on playing football, and who no longer had any school to play for. Leo joined the team in 1910 and took over the leadership two years later. He kept the team afloat for a dozen more seasons, losing in the process several large pots full of money, a hundred opportunities to better himself in business, and very nearly losing his poor patient wife as well.

His wife, after Leo had lasted past the age of indiscretion, had no objection to his devotion to football—as long as he did not try to play any more. But Leo—a lanky Irishman, with that half-smiling countenance that always seems to suggest its wearer is as ready for a fight as for a frolic—could not outgrow his love for football and sneaked himself into the lineup whenever he could manage. He was fast and tough and sure-handed, so he could hold his own with the best of them for many seasons.

Lyons, like all successful promoters, always thought in major league terms. If a team dared call itself champion of anything, Leo would challenge it to a game. If he needed a backfield man to draw a decent gate, he would wire the current All-Americans, wherever they might be, and coax them to come play for the Jeffersons.

If they would not respond to a letter or a wire, he might pick up and go after them by train and talk them into accompanying him to Chicago, or Cleveland, or wherever the next game was scheduled. More than once his recruits ran into storms or slow-downs that kept them from meeting the team at the appointed place and hour and then Leo would have to hustle indeed to fill his lineup. Once, lacking a backfield star, he recruited a mounted policeman in Chicago to play for him against the Cardinals—and the fans howled at the new recruit: "Hey, Jack! Where's your horse?"

But Leo had some of the best on his roster—and nearly had the best of all, Red Grange, whose college-boy "manager" accepted Leo's offer of five thousand dollars a game for the star, only to have Grange himself reveal that no one but C. C. Pyle could bargain for him. And Pyle had signed him with the Bears.

But before that dark day dawned, Lyons had signed many a college divinity and seen them star with the Jeffs. He hired as quarterback, in 1921, Williams College's most famous player, Ben Lee Boynton, the cocky, fleet-footed, and fast-thinking young Texan who could run a football team with the coolness and the craft of a man dealing faro. Benny, sleeves rolled up, helmet pushed back, eyes alert, would be sizing up the opposition even as he barked his signals and he seemed to own the devil's own instinct for spotting the sector where the enemy could least bear to have the next play strike. Benny himself was swift as the wind, elusive as a runaway razorback, a strong-armed passer, and an instinctive athlete. One day at the Bay Street Park in Rochester he sent his fans into hysterics when he sailed head-first clean over a would-be tackler's head, to land neatly as an acrobat on his neck and shoulders and flip quickly to his feet to run seventy yards to the goal line.

Also on the Jeffs' roster for a time was the mighty Elmer Oliphant of West Point, who earned letters in so many different sports at the Academy that he required a special order from the War Department to create a new marking for his sweater. (Elmer ripped his fine gray Army overcoat clear to the neck one day when he was forced to climb a wire fence after someone had forgotten to bring the key to the Jeffs' practice field.)

Hunk Anderson of Notre Dame played for the Jeffs and so did Nig Berry of Pennsylvania, who scored all the points in a 16–13 loss to the Chicago Bears one day by kicking two drop-kick field goals, from the thirty-seven and thirty-nine-yard lines, running ninety-five yards to a touchdown, and then kicking the point after.

By this time Leo was no longer getting into a football suit himself, although it was his job to tape the legs of his mighty hirelings, and even to supply four copies of *The Saturday Evening Post* each week—not for his charges to read between the halves, but for two of his rugged linemen to fold under their stockings as shin guards.

Leo's playing career was over in 1916—or should have been, had he heeded his wife. But Leo could not resist getting into one more game against a gang of iron moulders from Lancaster, New York, who met the Jeffs indoors in a night game at the New York State Armory, with both teams wearing rubber-soled sneakers. Leo begged the local newsman not to betray his presence in the lineup.

"All right," said the writer. "I'll give you an Indian name."

Leo led his team to victory that night but in the course of doing it was set upon by two mighty iron moulders who hauled Leo to the floor after he had caught a forward pass. Leo slid along on the bridge of his nose, with one iron moulder on his head and another on his back. When he was picked up, they had to take eleven stitches over his right eye. It was long past midnight when he appeared on his own doorstep, with an enormous gauze turban on his head. His wife screamed and benched her husband for good.

In the morning, Leo found that the newsman had been true to his word, for the Jeffs' right end listed in the morning paper wore an Indian name. He was "Man-Afraid-Of-His-Wife."

What usually made the "success" of a promoter like Leo Lyons, besides his willingness to think in major league terms, was energy and resourcefulness at recruiting. (Success is used in its Pickwickian sense, because Leo, like many other professional football managers of his day, never really found a surplus in his treasury and often had to toss his whole bankroll into the pot the players were collecting just to buy the tickets back to Rochester.)

Leo was always first off the mark when there was a player to be signed and frequently snatched recruits away from better-bankrolled teams because of his readiness to go right out in the pasture, if need be, to throw a bridle on a prospect. There was no draft in those early days, even after the league was formed, and every player was fair game. Leo signed Ben Lee Boynton, his greatest star, right out of the open-hearth steel mill in Pittsburgh, where Benny was learning the trade—and took him right away from Eugene Grace, who merely owned most of the steel company, and who had been assigned by the Akron team to fetch this prize package home for their own club.

Still, there was a special flavor to those more haphazard times, despite lean gate receipts and wearying day coach rides, so that men who shared them still relish their memories. Even the suspense of awaiting the arrival of the backfield star, whose failure to arrive might mean forfeit of the guarantee; the breakdown of the lumbering Pierce-Arrow that was carrying half the team on the thirty-mile trip to the game; the disappearance of the man with the gate receipts; the "guarantee" check that the bank would not honor; the baggage-car dressing room; the greasy lunch wagon; the ripped jerseys and the lost pants; the bootleg gin that floored the quarterback; the almost comically skimpy crowds—all these became tenderly mixed and intermingled with the memories of the pretty and admiring girls on the station platform; the lovely locker-room smell, compounded of steam and leather and new towels and sweat and wintergreen oil; the roughhousing; the tearful rejoicing at unforeseen victories; the one-hand snaring of a touchdown pass; the clean, fierce block that took an end right off his feet; the reckless taxi ride in muddied uniforms to catch the impatient overnight train to the next game; the all-night card games; the wild celebrations, and above all the delight youth takes in the reckless expenditure of its hours, as if they never need be counted.

Payment to football players as the twenties wore on seldom rose higher than $250 a game and occasionally even this stipend, usually given to the triple-threat backfield man, proved out of reach. "Exhibition" games, outside the league schedule, sometimes brought only $25 each to the players and nothing at all to the management. And sometimes all of them had to scratch for carfare home. Yet the game still lured men who might have done better by themselves in the auto plant, or the insurance office. Many of them liked to pretend that they were just "in it for the cash." But few of them were. They had to risk broken bones and torn ligaments—even six-week hospital bills and untended injuries of every sort. But only in football could they recover the special joy that team play provides—that feeling of intimate kinship, more even (for the roaring minutes of the game) than a family knows, that helps submerge private fears and erases pain.

Of course, as the league grew larger and more secure, and players were bound by contract to a single team and could not dicker with another, they occasionally found their lot not altogether joyous. The coach now, under no constraint to coddle or coax them, might barely acknowledge them on the street—in contrast to the way a college coach might have had to woo them to hold them on the squad. Their injuries sometimes brought them serious woe, even a release from the team, plus a heavy hospital bill. If one team let them go, they were seldom claimed on "waivers" by another team, which would have had to assume their contracts, but were usually released outright then hired by the team that wanted them at a lower wage. Often they felt neglected and unwanted—as did a man Paul Governali of the New York Giants told about, who, after an exhibition game in Dallas, wearing a deep gash under one eye that needed stitches, hauled himself into the locker room to find that everyone but the trainer—doctor, teammates, coaches—had taken off. The trainer had to take the stitches while the poor man lay—"just me and the trainer in an empty locker room two thousand miles from home, I on my back nude, with a towel between my legs, staring up at the ceiling while the trainer stitched me up."

Chapter V

Three Football Players and a Horse

The appearance of Red Grange of Illinois on the professional football field in 1925 marks, in most minds, the beginnings of respectability for the pro game. The auspices, however, were not always happy, nor even completely respectable, and there were, even in that joyous day, some dismal moments. Red was the first really national hero football had ever produced. Much of his fame he surely owed to the perfection of newsreel photography, that gave to the football fancy everywhere an opportunity to watch the easy-striding young giant making his incredible runs.

Red was no hired athlete, nor alumni pet, when he enrolled at Illinois to play football under Bob Zuppke. (His first year his fraternity brothers, with the help of a large paddle, had to "persuade" him to go out for the team.) What help he got was never enough to relieve him of the job of earning his keep all summer through delivering ice to the homes of his neighbors in Wheaton, Illinois. When Red's fame increased, there were publicity pictures aplenty showing him with a huge cake of ice slung over his shoulder on a pair of tongs, but the job itself was no publicity stunt. Famous or not, Red Grange toted ice all summer long and dutifully studied economics at the university, so that he might eventually go into business and repay his father for some of the sacrifices required to keep Red in school. (His father, a deputy sheriff in Wheaton, did not want him to play professional football.)

Red's unbelievable, and even inexplicable, skill at loping or slithering past all manner of would-be tacklers excited people so, even making them yell aloud in the motion picture theaters, that there was no curbing his fame, nor the appetites of the promoters who measured his worth at the box office. In 1925, as he approached his final game as a collegian, the clamor of the many who wanted to exploit his name, and of the many more who deemed such exploitation a form of sacrilege, grew to a howl. Red continued to score touchdown after touchdown on the gridiron, sometimes scoring all the points his team would make. Even when mud would slow him down, the very possibility that he might run free, with tacklers falling from him for all the world as if his britches had a spell on them, was enough to keep the spectators screaming.

As the final game (with Ohio State) grew nearer and nearer, the story gained currency that Red had already signed a pro contract, that he would play with the Chicago Bears on Thanksgiving, that he had made an agreement with theatrical promoter C. C. Pyle (immediately named Cash and Carry Pyle by a Chicago *Tribune* sportswriter) for Pyle to act as Red's business agent, and that he had also made an agreement to play a part in a Sydney Chaplin picture called *The College Widow*. Red denied these allegations in toto and in detail. "I have never signed even a *scrap* of paper," he insisted.

The name "Pyle" became a dirty word on the campus at the university and the students, who were talking of enshrining Red's number 77 jersey in a glass case forever, freely offered to lynch the mustachioed dandy who had sullied the name of their idol. At one point Red came very close to calling C. C. Pyle a liar, insisting that a statement attributed to Pyle about Grange's agreement to a professional offer had not a word of truth in it. Coach Zuppke and Athletics Director Huff held a conference with Grange, on the Tuesday before his final game, and the campus know-it-alls whispered that Grange had been directed to turn in his suit if he had indeed signed a pro contract. Said Grange: "I'm all mixed up. And I'm worried. But I don't intend to sign anything until I play my last game for Illinois." Thereupon he hastened home to confer, it was said, with his father, who was still telling newspapermen that it would be all right for Red to write for newspapers, or act in the movies, or make public appearances, but that "commercialized football" was a sinful business.

At home Red may still have been worried but he was agreeable and affable as ever to those who got a chance to talk to him. Was he going to sign with the Chicago Bears? He wouldn't say yes, nor would he say no. Meanwhile, the Bears and the Chicago Cardinals were winning football games from the likes of the Duluth Eskimos and the Rock Island Rockets, who had signed Jim Thorpe after he had been fired by the New York Giants for "failing to keep in condition" (Jim had started on his honeymoon when he was fired). And the crowds that came to see professional football games seldom exceeded six thousand, even though in one game you might see the Cardinals' great Paddy Driscoll attempt drop-kick field goals from as far out as fifty-five yards, and actually make them sometimes, too.

Red-hot rumors continued to erupt in Wheaton: Someone had come up with an affidavit from a real estate man in Kokomo, who deposed and said (to what end, who knows?) that he had seen with his own beady little eyes, a letter of agreement between Pyle and Grange, with Red's honest-to-God signature thereon. Red had missed football practice one day, and the president of the university allowed that if Red dared stay away from classes, he was going to find himself suspended. In good time, these grown-ups all cooled off to a moderate simmer and followed young Grange's good example of saying less and thinking more. Red's father allowed that "It was all up to Red" and Red himself, apprised of the wild protests on the campus against commercialization of the holy name of Grange, tipped off his decision when he said: "Most of those guys will forget me next year. Would they lend me a dollar then?" To suggestions that he might become a salesman, he shook his head. He might go into manufacturing or something like that, but as for selling, "I wouldn't have the nerve."

Zuppke denied that there had been any threat of stripping Red of his uniform but did urge publicly that Red stay on and get his degree. Major Griffiths, Lord High Executioner of the Western Conference, declared that if all these stories about signing with the Bears and signing with the movies were true, as they seemed to be, then Grange was ineligible to compete with athletes who had never accepted any checks or played professional ball under their right names. Oh no, said Bob Zuppke, not unless Red took money. And Red, with a good deal of heat, asserted once more that he had not accepted a penny.

Despite the fact that the Illinois team was supposed to have been "demoralized" by Red's missing practice, and guilty of being "carefree" (according to Zuppke) before the game, when they talked more about the fat contract Red was supposed to have signed than they did about the Ohio State team they were supposed to lick, Illinois beat Ohio State 14–9. Red's performance was sturdy if not spectacular. He made one brilliant thirty-seven-yard run with an intercepted pass and took off once more from scrimmage on a run of twenty-five yards. In twenty-one carries he averaged better than five yards a try.

After the game, the worst-kept secret of the season was released to the few who had not heard it: Red would sign with the Chicago Bears for a guarantee of three thousand dollars a game against a percentage of the gate.

"I'll be on the Bears' bench tomorrow but I haven't signed a contract," Red affirmed. But hadn't he even *talked* to the Bears? Well, he did have one talk with Sternaman (the Bears' manager), Red admitted. "He just telephoned to wish me luck and hung up without saying goodbye." There had been eighty-five thousand spectators at the Ohio State game and the Chicago promoters did not see why they could not draw in at least a quarter that many to see the Redhead break loose as a pro.

The following Sunday, in bitter cold, seventy-five hundred people watched the Bears beat the Green Bay Packers and

watched the great Red Grange, all huddled up in the current
status symbol—a new raccoon coat—watching the Bears from the
bench. He had signed, it was revealed, to play six games, beginning on Thanksgiving against the Cardinals and then, with
only two days' rest, against the Tigers of Columbus. What with
the intense publicity buildup he had been receiving (newsreel
men actually lived in his dormitory, leaving him no time for
study and hardly any for thinking), football fans were slavering
to see what mincemeat he would make of the play-for-pay boys.
It was generally accepted in college circles then that pro football
was no more than a feeble imitation of the real thing and that no
professional player would ever hurl himself into the fray for mere
money as a college man did for glory and The Game.

When the tickets for the first Red Grange game went on sale
in Chicago, at Spalding's store on State Street, the ticket line
stretched out the door, up to the corner, around the corner, down
an alley, and back again. The police were called out to prevent a
stampede, and ticket sales were quickly limited to two to a customer. All the seats that were available at the time were grandstand reserved seats at $1.75 each (speculators ate them up and
were quickly offering them to the people in line at $5 to $10 a
copy). If the printer hadn't been so pessimistic—or so relaxed—
twice as many would have been sold. As it was, half the crowd
had to come back on Tuesday, and they finished off the tickets in
an hour. At that point an alderman named Jacob Arvey let out a
roar of rage. Speculators, said Arvey, had blocks of five hundred
to fifteen hundred tickets. Besides, the Bears have no license to
perform and I'll put a stop to the whole thing! The Bears, however, needed no license, because the Chicago Cubs had a year-
round license on Wrigley Field. So despite the alderman, scalp-
ers, and cold weather, the game between the Bears and the Cards
went on as scheduled, in a snowstorm, on Thanksgiving Day,
1925. There were thirty-six thousand people in the stands, far
more than Red's guarantee called for and enough to assure Pyle
and Grange the juiciest payday they had ever seen. (The scalp-
ers found themselves stuck with a mess of grandstand tickets

when two thousand standing-room admissions were offered on the day of the game.)

The game itself, no matter what sportswriters or fans may have tried to tell each other afterwards, was a disappointment. Crafty Paddy Driscoll, the Cards' captain and famous kicker, took pains to angle his punts away from Grange, so the great redhead found only three opportunities to run back a kick. His longest return was twenty yards. His total gain from scrimmage, in the mud and snow, was thirty-six yards—his longest run being a seven-yard gain through right tackle. On punt returns he totaled fifty-six yards and he failed to complete a pass, although he tried six. The fans, some of whom had been telling each other beforehand that the whole game would be fixed to give Red a chance to run, booed wildly each time Paddy Driscoll aimed a punt where Red could not get it. Paddy's punts kept the Bears on their heels all afternoon. (And "Paddy's pig," the Cardinal mascot, delighted all the small boys in the stands.)

At the end, neither team had a point to its name. Red Grange took home twelve thousand dollars and a black eye. But before he could get off the field he had to shake the hand of every Cardinal player and of every fan who could reach him.

At Wrigley Field, the following Sunday, twenty-eight thousand spectators gathered to watch the Columbus Tigers come within a point of tying the Bears. Again Red's fans were disappointed—not so much because Red was unable to score as because a sandlot player named Rapp outplayed their hero in nearly every department—outrunning him, and grabbing more passes. Red made a number of good gains—returning one kickoff for twenty-eight yards, and gaining nine yards around end. But there were none of the slippery, ghostly runs from the halfway mark to the goal line that had earned Red's fame.

The real star of the game, Robert Rapp, was a tough little left halfback who could scurry through the line like a spider and could outsprint even the nation's redheaded hero in the open. With the aid of Frank Nesser he very nearly beat the Bears—as he did beat Grange in yards gained and in defensive accomplishments. Rapp, who was also team captain, gained 203 yards to Grange's 138. He made one sixty-yard run for a touchdown, evading tacklers on the snow-covered field with all the slithering grace that had made Grange famous; and he returned one punt forty-two yards.

Rapp was no college hero and actually had never been "coached" in the game at all, except by his playmates and whatever older hands wanted to help him. He did not play football in high school but instead joined a teen-age team called the "Outlaws" and graduated from them to a team of grown-up amateurs known as the Westerns. He was never a big lad—even when he got his growth he seldom reached 150 pounds, and he stood only five foot eight. But his tremendous speed (he ran the hundred-yard dash in ten seconds) and his willingness to accept and to dish out the rough treatment accorded sandlot football players of the day soon made him the best ball carrier in town. He played for a short time with the Jungle Imps, a semi-pro entry in the Columbus Munipical football league, and then accepted an offer from a local cattle dealer to play with the Linden A.C. Bob was to receive five dollars for every touchdown he scored that season and he tucked two or three five-dollar bills into his pants after nearly every game. Then, in the last game of the season, little Bob carried the ball across the goal line nine times. With ten minutes still left in the game, the cattle man decided forty-five dollars was all he could afford to peel off in one afternoon and he sat Bob on the bench.

Bob got more money to play with the West Side A.C. and then was hired by the "big" team, the Columbus Panhandles, home team of the Nesser brothers, and a member at the time (1922) of the new National Football League. The Panhandles became the Tigers and Bob Rapp became the captain. He finished his football career with them. (He starred in minor league baseball a few years longer.) Had he performed today, Bob Rapp would have earned money enough to retire almost as well off as Grange, for he was a crowd-pleasing fellow, always on the go, always willing (he played part of the Grange game with a broken rib), and never afraid to mix it with the monstrous linemen who stood in his path. (One day, playing against the New York Giants, he found stout Steve Owen, the Giants' left tackle, who weighed 265 to Bob's 148, standing in his pathway. He quickly dealt Owen a solid bang beneath the ribs with his fist and before Steve could get his wind and his balance back, little Bob was twenty-two yards away.)

The furor that had arisen when it was first hinted that Red Grange would turn pro was a long time dying. Red at first denied he would leave college for good. "I'll be back," he said, "and get my degree." But coach Zuppke, somewhat soured by all the pulling and hauling, averred: "There's about as much chance of his coming back to college as there is of the Kaiser's getting back his job in Germany." Neither Red nor the Kaiser even tried.

But Red went on to play more and more football, even though Zuppke warned him (at a distance) that he would do better to get into some sound business, like writing, or the motion pictures, or real estate. "I'll play football," said Red, "because that's what I can do best." And in an era when every flagpole sitter or tennis tramp could "become a writer" overnight, by hiring some ink-stained wretch to do the writing, these words had a glad sound to many, notably to one Chicago sportswriter named Pegler. It would have been somewhat less virtuous, Pegler allowed, if Red had become a fake writer or a fake actor rather than a real football player.

Pegler stayed with Red Grange through that winter barnstorming trip, when the Bears played seven games in eleven days. They went to St. Louis, to play a patchwork team thrown together by Eddie Kaw, the old-time Cornell star. The Bears, with only one honest-to-God professional (Jim Conzelman) facing them, just walked through the game. Grange scored all four touchdowns here and the eight thousand fans, having seen what they came to see, it is presumed, went home happy. The real test was yet to come, for the East was hungering for a look at Grange, who had been there only long enough to wreck a Penn team two months earlier. When the Bears got to Philadelphia,

there were thirty-five thousand fans willing to sit out in the wet
to see them play the Frankford Yellowjackets and the hearts of all
football promoters everywhere were lifted up. (Pegler affected
some dismay that football fans should actually be goofier than
baseball fans, who would at least stay out of the weather.) The
game was played in a sea of mud. The Bears won 14–7, with
Grange scoring both touchdowns. He made no really long gains
here, however, averaging only a little over three yards per carry
from scrimmage. He completed two passes and caught one,
earned forty thousand dollars (which he split with Pyle), and
left the field with more mud on him than anyone else.

By this time, of course, the drums had been beating steadily in
New York and despite the fact that Grange as a pro did not seem
nearly so spectacular as Grange the collegian (at Franklin Field,
Philadelphia, in October, he had scored three touchdowns and
gained 363 yards in 36 carries, with just as much mud underfoot
as when he met the Yellowjackets), there were seventy-three
thousand fans willing to pay to watch him against the New York
pros, whom Pegler called "the alleged Giants." (There were uncounted hundreds who crowded into the park without paying.)

Grange by now had begun to feel the strain, not only of the
almost daily scrimmaging but of the everlasting hounding by
newsmen and photographers that made it almost impossible for
him to sleep. Still he managed to lead the Bears to a 19–7 victory
over the Giants before the biggest football crowd New York had
ever known. In the doing of it, Grange took a heavy beating. According to Pegler the officials permitted the Giants to do everything but remove Grange's head from his neck. Once, said
Pegler, a Giant backfield man, after missing connection with a
pass, hauled off and slugged Grange on the back of the head,
actually staggering him. Later another Giant kicked him and one
big lineman, getting Grange around the neck, sat down and undertook to twist his head free from his shoulders.

But Century Milstead, the famous Old Blue, who was playing
tackle that day for the Giants, said pro football was never as dirty
as college play. "I was slugged in high school," said Century. "I

was slugged in prep school. I was slugged at Yale. But I was never slugged in pro football."

Next stop for Grange was Washington, where a makeshift team of college all-stars met the Bears and nearly beat them. "If they had had fifteen minutes of practice together, the All-Stars would have trimmed the Bears," said Pegler, who was impressed by a "quarrelsome, bare-legged party named Lynch" who had played previously for Catholic University. Grange, according to his most critical fan, seemed to dog it a little in this game. Although the Bears won (19–0) and Grange did score a point after touchdown by drop-kick, he gained only six yards altogether. But he brought a badly wrenched arm and a bruised mouth and nose off the field with him, and seemed too used up to play any more. Grange, however, was not going to back out of his commitments. He was never too sure of what made him a great football player— except that he knew it took ten other men to break him free— and he did not know when fame might desert him. A poor boy all his life, with not even a decent suit of clothes to his back until he was halfway through college, he had determined to make what he could while the opportunity offered, to offer his fine father a chance for some security, and even to help kid brother Pinky through the university.

Still the experience that awaited him in Boston, where the Bears were scheduled to meet the Providence Steamrollers, would have taken the heart out of a lesser man. It was the coldest day of the year, in a town where even a warm day might seem chilly to an outlander, yet twenty-five thousand people turned out for the game. On the field, Red was a listless figure, his face drawn from sleeplessness and physical strain, seeming a good ten years older than his twenty-two years. He made only a few short gains through the line, knocked down two passes, and made three tackles. The fans began to boo him early in the game, and at one point, when he picked up the football to toss it back to the referee, the stands roared a derisive cheer to see him "complete" this pass. At the end of the third period, Red withdrew from the game and a crowd of hooting fans followed him to the exit, deriding his appearance, his publicity, his skills, and his ancestry, until one teammate turned around and fetched the leading hooter a solid crack on the mouth. Then a fight started that required the staunch intervention of the police. Red meanwhile withdrew, sorrowing, to his locker.

At Pittsburgh, there were cheers for him, but they came from only five thousand fans, the poorest gate of the trip and, worst of all, the Bears were clobbered 24–0 by a bunch of hastily gathered semipros under the command of Barney Dreyfuss. Grange tore a muscle in his left arm and by nightfall the arm had swollen so that all thought of his playing within the next two weeks had to be abandoned. That meant refunds at Detroit and back home at Chicago too, where the patronage fell off to fifteen thousand as the Bears met the Giants at Wrigley Field. But the crowd that did turn out chased after Grange when the game was over, cheering him and trying to shake his hand. It took a solid wedge of policemen to get him free.

Worn and shaken by the physical and psychological drubbing he had received, Red Grange took comfort in the fat return that commercialization had brought him: $300,000 for the movie that was still to be made; $40,500 for "Red Grange" dolls and sweaters, plus endorsements of shoes and an automobile; $5000 for granting that some ginger ale or other was the best he ever drank; $2500 for lending his endorsement to a cap (his usual headgear) and for putting his blessing on a brand of tobacco, although he did not smoke and did not pretend to.

The football tour was not over, however. There was still a game abrewing between the Chicago Bears and the "Jacksonville All-Stars," a team that was even now being put together by a group of promoters in Florida, where land speculation had become practically a way of life and where nobody, it seemed, would ever be poor, or even have to work again. (One political leader, however, did rather plaintively request that at least *some* of the promotion the state was printing should feature "smokestacks" and not merely the tight-laced attributes of divers wellnourished young ladies in swimming suits.)

The star of the Jacksonville team was to be Stanford's Ernie Nevers, the man Glenn Warner (to poor Jim Thorpe's dismay) named "the best football player I ever coached." This young blond monster, fullback on the football team, star at basketball, speedster on the track, and rugged right-handed pitcher for the baseball team, was guaranteed fifty thousand dollars to play for Jacksonville, not only against the Bears, but against certain other teams that had not yet been scheduled.

Despite the few grievous disappointments that the Grange tour had met, a very fever of professionalism seemed to have seized the campuses of the football universities. Notre Dame's great Four Horsemen hastened eastward to sign for pay with a team named the Hartford Blues (formerly the Waterbury Blues). Some said that at least one of the quartet had signed a previous contract with a league team and league members were warned against meeting the apostate on the gridiron. (The Pottsville Maroons defied the ban and played the Blues anyway. They even violated Frankford Yellowjacket territory to do it.)

The true high scorer of the college season had been Eddie Tryon of Colgate, a small, fleet-footed man who could also kick goals. Inasmuch as he had come out ahead of Grange in the totals, he announced that he too was going to sign a pro contract, with the New York Giants, and play in Florida that winter, where gold, it was presumed, would shower all season long upon just and unjust alike. But when Eddie went home to New Britain, Connecticut, his mother flatly set forth that he was not going to do any such thing, that he would not play professional football at all. Nor did he. (Two years later, he apparently talked mama into letting him play one season with Grange's New York Yankees.)

In Florida the Jacksonville promoters were able to recruit two dozen young men very quickly, most of whom had just finished playing for one or another of the southern universities, but a few of whom had been brought in from far, and some of whom, like the Stein brothers of the Pottsville Maroons, had been professionals for several seasons.

An enormous crowd was forecast, ticket prices were set at
$8.50 and $5.50, which was more than a speculator might get for
an ordinary game, and the local press noted that One-Eyed Connelley, the notorious gate-crasher, was in town—amply proving
that this game was a big-time attraction. Temporary seats were
erected to handle the expected overflow and the city engineer assured everyone that the stands were safe enough to hold an army.
No army showed up, however. There were empty stretches
throughout the stands and the game's drum-beaters had to content
themselves with noting the quality rather than the quantity of
the fans. One-Eyed Connelley did get in, without a ticket, and
he was most conspicuous on the field during intermission. And
seated in the box seats, among other illustrious folk, were George
Ade, Raymond Hitchcock (still famous for his Broadway triumph a few years earlier in *Hitchy-Koo*), and John Golden.
There were also two sets of young ladies to provide each team
with a cheering section.

Grange's performance in the game was far from spectacular.
Ernie Nevers did nearly as well—and earned far more attention
from the newspapers, who were intent on proving that the All-
Stars came within a whisker of beating the Bears (the Bears won
19–7), and that Nevers was worth every penny of his fifty-thou-
sand-dollar guarantee. Red's longest run from scrimmage was a
mere nine yards—and the local sportswriter belittled that by noting how "fiercely" Nevers drove him out of bounds. But Red did
complete some good passes, one of them for a touchdown, and
made one spectacular defensive play when he overhauled Bowser
of the All-Stars on the one-yard line and dropped him from behind.

Between the halves, when the Bears gathered in a private war
council in the middle of the field, a thousand spectators crowded
around them to view the great men up close and to eavesdrop on
the strategy discussion. Then in the fourth quarter the real thrill
of the game developed, after Russ Stein of the All-Stars and Mc-
Millan of the Bears squared off in a fist-fight and hundreds of the
spectators rushed on to the field to have at the foe. The cops

quickly ejected the two players and then they took on the frantic spectators. For some minutes the fight between police and paying customers surged back and forth, while the fans who had remained in the stands yelled in delight.

In the aftermath of the game, the promoters whistled hard to keep their courage up. The draw had been disappointing but Jacksonville "had got publicity." And it was a sure thing now that they had a real football team. There were other teams on the way and, with more chance to practice, the All-Stars were sure to beat some of them. Then there was a tour in the making that might take them all the way to the Coast.

The New York Giants met the All-Stars (who had been strengthened by the addition of a few more experienced pros) the following week and the Giants beat them 7-0. In a belated effort to appease the cold-hearted fans, the promoters had dropped the admission price to $2.75 for box seats, with a general admission charge of fifty cents. But still the crowd stayed home, persuaded by "unthinking people" that professional football was simply not fit to watch. The All-Stars then called off their remaining games. Nevers, who had signed to pitch for the St. Louis Browns the next summer after receiving a "four-figure" bonus, allowed that he would join some of the New York Giants on a basketball tour. He never did play with them, however; and when he came back to professional football it was to play with the Duluth Eskimos and the Chicago Cardinals, where he was named coach. As for Red Grange, he trailed no clouds of glory on leaving Jacksonville. But he did, through a large newspaper advertisement, remind her citizens, who might otherwise have gone all unknowing to their graves, that he owed his stamina to the regular ingestion of Yeast Foam Malted Milk.

Red next visited New Orleans, where a football team had been gathered for the occasion. The Bears beat this crowd 14-0 and Grange got away for a fifty-one-yard punt return that for a moment convinced all six thousand spectators that they had beheld their money's worth. (The run was partially nullified by a clipping penalty.) Red averaged better than four yards a try from scrimmage in this game and once broke loose for twenty yards. The day before the game the auspices all looked most inviting too, for in the "Red Grange Handicap" a horse named Prickly Heat, with a red-headed jockey up, took first money, and the grinning jockey accepted from Red Grange's very hands an enormous pink floral football.

The Bears, with Grange, then traveled clear to California, to play in Los Angeles, and then up the coast as far as Portland, where they discovered a team of pseudo-professionals that they could really clobber: 60–3.

After that, Red Grange made his motion picture—and proved himself a diffident, pleasant, and handsome young man with hardly a trace of acting talent. In 1927 he and Pyle organized the New York Yankees football team, which failed to flourish. Then Red rejoined the Bears and stayed with them for seven seasons.

Grange himself never complained publicly, but there were many close to the game who explained his failure to grow into the galloping ghost of the professional gridiron, or even to resemble the shadow of the college hero, by the reluctance of underpaid linemen to bruise themselves in his defense. Why should they, they apparently asked themselves, accept an anonymous beating for a hundred-dollar check, just so Grange could take home ten or twelve times as much? For that money, they may have muttered to each other, he can do his own blocking.

Thus C. C. Pyle's own failure to cultivate an *esprit de corps* by suggesting an equality of rewards as well as of sacrifices damaged his prize possession so that Red never did return to the glory he had known at Illinois. Men who saw Red in the locker room before the games used to marvel at the yards upon yards of tape that were needed to patch his bruised and aching body. It would have been simpler, but perhaps more painful to old Cash and Carry, if a few five-hundred-dollar incentives had been distributed along the scrimmage line.

But even if Grange never did become the great breakaway runner of old, he did bring to the professional game skills just as valuable even though not so readily convertible to cash at the box office. He was a sturdy blocker and a fine defensive man, still fast and alert, and exceedingly smart in diagnosing an attack. His brain and his determination and his intense love of the game actually proved of as much worth to him as his legs had been. For after he had gone broke in the Depression and had pulled himself back to solvency by his own labors (as an insurance salesman, not as a football player), he became one of the best at reporting a football game over the air, and perhaps the finest at explaining the ins and outs of the play to listeners short on technical knowledge.

And he still remains in the minds of those who watched him devastate Michigan and Pennsylvania, and other great college teams of his day, with runs of fifty, sixty, even eighty yards, the greatest open-field runner the game ever knew—the equal, as Damon Runyon said, of three football players and a horse.

Chapter VI

Football with Wings

The single-wing backfield formation, which eventually supplanted the old-fashioned T as the basic pattern for backs to arrange themselves in before a play began, was originally just a slight exaggeration of the short punt formation. The regular punt formation had a kicker (usually the fullback) ten yards behind the center, with the other three backs—two on the side of the kicking foot and one on the other side—crouched closer to the scrimmage line, so that a string stretched from the kicker's feet, through the feet of the two backs on one side and the single back on the other, then back to the kicker, would have taken the shape of a steep triangle. In the short punt formation the apex of the triangle was some five yards closer to the base. From these positions, coaches learned that backs might run in any direction, and that an end might sweep around and take the ball from the fullback, who was faking a pass or kick. The center could pass the ball to one of the halfbacks, close up, who could then wheel and start around the opposite end, to hand the ball to a back coming the other way, who would himself pound around the end farthest from his original stand. Ahead of him, by this time, would be a formidable phalanx, made up of the other two backs, plus a "running guard" who had pulled out of the line to join the interference.

It took a rugged end indeed, with the aid of an alert tackle, to stop this play. For a time after its invention it recovered some of the overwhelming power of the old momentum plays—the "guards back" and "tackles back" arrangements. Once its advantages over the formal T arrangement and its minor variations had been proved, all the big colleges hastened to adopt it and exaggerate it. The close-up back became a "wing" back—stationed farther out behind the line, even behind the end's normal position. Then both close-up backs moved out along the line and created a double-wing effect, with only the quarterback holding to his traditional position, within reach of the center. Inevitably he too was moved out where he could get a running start and there was a triple-wing formation.

One of the beauties of this formation, from a spectator's standpoint, was that it led sometimes to the naked reverse—after the ball had twice changed hands behind the line—with a ball carrier popping suddenly into sight all alone, hurrying in the opposite direction from the one that all twenty-one other players were moving. All by himself then, without guard, or guide, or interferer, like the Flying Dutchman, he would run like a wraith for the Promised Land beyond the goal line. And from time to time, if he were fleet enough and the ball had been well concealed as it was swapped around in the backfield, he would go untouched for the touchdown.

The effort to get a man out beyond the end, undetected, with the ball in his arms had been the aim of coaches since the rugby game had first been modified into American football. There had been shoestring and sleeper plays—in which a player loafed on the sideline to tie his shoe, or pretended an injury while the rest of the team lined up—from the earliest days. And there had been Glenn Warner's famous "deadman" play that nearly beat Harvard one year in the Rose Bowl. (In this play a halfback, after a feeble effort to run the end, would remain on his back, holding the ball, upon being tackled. The rest of his team would line up, with him roughly in center position, whereupon a teammate would approach and in apparent anxiety ask "Are you all right, Bill?" This was the signal for Bill to pop the ball upwards toward the inquiring teammate, who would then take off for the goal. The play gained eighteen yards against Harvard.)

The pros in this era, conscious now of what crowds could be collected at a game, if the attraction were strong enough, were somewhat quicker to experiment than the college teams. No longer did they need to steal a few hours after work to practice on a tennis court, or in an unmarked lot. Rising pay began to justify a man's devoting most of his time to football, at least for the autumn months, and it was possible to practice complicated pass plays and spinners. (In the wingback formation the fullback, five yards behind center, would often take a direct pass from center and then, while a halfback circled behind him in time to take a handoff, he would spin in a complete circle and plunge into the line—sometimes carrying the ball, sometimes faking a plunge while the ball was still being passed around behind the line.) Now and then a pro team would amaze the spectators, and the opposition, with a spread formation that extended from sideline to sideline, as in the days when the ball was round. Sometimes the ball would be flung forward, and then passed right back from beyond the scrimmage line, for the man who had it first to carry it on a run.

This razzle-dazzle sometimes had no other aim than to excite the spectators, who still seemed largely to agree that college football was the real thing and professional football an illegitimate relative. Great college stars would condescend to play pro football while their luster was still bright, hoping to pick up some easy money on the fame they had earned in college. And a few of them, such as Albie Booth, the miraculous midget from Yale, were startled to discover they could not play in the professional league at all. Even a fierce and reckless competitor such as Christian Keener "Red" Cagle of Army found the going much more difficult in the professional league than he ever had in college. For the pros now were truly pros—or most of them were— able to give as much time to the game as a college boy, and sometimes even more, schooled in all the various murthering devices linemen might use upon each other, and usually, because of the demands of this faster-moving game, combining both speed and size, so that medium-sized men could never prevail against them. The college teams, of course, needed fast-moving linemen too, to pull out of the line and stay ahead of a light-footed halfback; but often in colleges the "pulling" guards would be relatively small men—fast and tough but just not heavy enough to budge one of the professional behemoths from his tracks.

Not that the college game, in the twenties and thirties, was not rough. The rules still permitted the defending lineman to beat his opponent about the head and neck with his hands, and sometimes this employment proved so entertaining to him that he gave little thought to where the play was going. Linemen often devised methods for punishing each other as religiously as a coach might devise his basic strategy. They would burden their forearms with heavy tape so that each arm resembled an out-size blackjack, or would cook up methods for two-teaming an opponent in such a manner as to disable him for the afternoon.

The professionals, however, simply because their jobs demanded it, were generally tougher. While there were hardly any non-college men left in the pro game now, there were many players who still spent their off-season hours in some muscle-toughening pursuit, like wrestling or freight handling, and they rejoiced in the pro game's solid body contact and fierce tackling.

Still there were men in the land who belittled the professional game as an old man's hobby and who contended in the public prints that "any good college team" could wipe the earth up with the best professional team that had ever been spawned. One who offered this opinion freely was Knute Rockne, the great Notre Dame coach (and perhaps the greatest college coach who ever lived). Knute, having played on nearly every professional team in Ohio when the century was young and having recruited tough and agile young men from everywhere to come and play for the "Irish"—who were now mostly Poles and Italians —felt that he had created at Notre Dame two or three combinations that could trim any congregation of professionals in the league.

He had an opportunity to prove his point in 1930, when
athletes and entertainers generally were being exhorted to stage
exhibitions for the benefit of the growing hordes of unemployed,
who held out their hungry hands on every big-city street corner.
The Army-Navy game that year was played in the Yankee Stadium as a Salvation Army benefit, at prices ranging from ten
dollars to fifty dollars a seat. (Be a real sport! Grover Whalen
beseeched his fellow New Yorkers. Get yourself a pair of seats
at the greatest football clash of the year!) And the very day after
that, on Sunday, December 14, the New York Giants were to
meet the Notre Dame All-Stars, Rockne's hand-picked selection
from his stars of the recent past, a few of whom had already
played professional football. All receipts from the game were to
go to Mayor Jimmy Walker's fund for unemployment relief.

His team was sure to lick the Giants, Rockne averred. Professional teams simply didn't have the spirit that was needed to
bring victory on the gridiron. Benny Friedman, former Michigan
star, now quarterback and coach of the Giants, said nothing for
the public prints. But he was not a man to take a licking lying
down, nor had he ever been deficient in spirit.

Benny, the strapping and handsome son of a Cleveland tailor,
had first played football in a Cleveland high school, where his
coach allowed that he would never make the grade on the gridiron. Benny's response to that was to transfer to another school.
But even there he did not immediately develop any devotion to
the game. He was deeply interested in his studies, earned high
grades, and preferred basketball to football. But the coach would
not have him on the basketball squad unless he played football
too. Benny had the "perfect halfback build," the coach decided,
and he was not going to do without him.

In his first season at high school Benny became a star runner,
passer, and kicker. (He was not considered enough of a leader
to be a quarterback, however, and this job was given to a Japa-
nese student.) Benny went on to Michigan to star on the freshman eleven, and to star as a student too. But he found the going
tough, as Jewish lads often do when they forget that what is

deemed self-confidence in a gentile is sometimes called conceit in a Jew. Despite his accomplishments Benny found his first year at Michigan a trial and he considered transferring to Dartmouth. But after working all summer (no one in his large family could afford to loaf) he gritted his teeth and returned to Ann Arbor, where he made his way finally on sheer ability combined with a carefully cultivated (and exceedingly becoming) modesty.

By the time Benny became a pro, he was a seasoned football player, a master of craft, the best passer of his day, and one of the brainiest men ever to play the game. He was also a knock-them-down runner who owned the savage quality (some coaches call it "that extra lean") that keeps a man moving toward the enemy goal even when he is falling down. Benny played professional football first in his home town of Cleveland, put in a season at Detroit, and spent the remaining six seasons of his career in New York, first with the Giants and then with the Brooklyn Dodgers.

When Rockne chose to cross lances with him, Benny had played nearly four full seasons of professional football and had become the coach, as well as quarterback, of the Giants. As a matter of fact he *was* the Giants, for when they were without him they sometimes became, despite the presence of doughty warriors like Red Cagle and Steve Badgro, thoroughly disorganized. (In a game against Stapleton, the Giants, who had beaten Stapleton once and lost to them by a single point later, seemed hardly able to move until Friedman, suffering from a wrenched knee, limped on to the field and pulled the Giants together long enough at least to prevent Stapleton from turning the game into a runaway.)

While Benny made no predictions, it is fair to assume that he and his teammates were panting to show the anti-professional crowd (for whom Rockne was a frequent spokesman) that the pro game was not for small boys. New York was crowded with Notre Dame's "subway alumni," many of whom, having rooted for the Irish all these years, were not too sure but what they had attended the blessed institution themselves—who spoke of the team as "we," and who had not stopped bragging of last year's game against Army, when Notre Dame's Jack Elder had run ninety yards for the only score in a game in which Army (with Cagle) had been heavily favored.

"These Giants are big but slow," Rockne told his charges before the game. "Score two or three touchdowns in a hurry and then just hold them." Alas for Rockne and the pride of the Irish, Benny Friedman and his Giants, before forty-five thousand freezing (and bloodthirsty) fans, thoroughly humiliated the All-Stars. The great Four Horsemen of the twenties—Miller, Crowley, Stuhldreher, and Layden—quickly discovered that they could not knock anyone down with their reputations and retired in favor of a younger group, led by the great Frank Carideo, whom Rockne called the best quarterback alive. But this backfield did no better, nor was the line ever able to move the Giants, or even stop Benny Friedman when he decided to go.

The All-Stars' total yardage on the ground was a dismal minus thirty. They achieved only one first down, completed not a single forward pass (Rockne deplored the excess use of this weapon, as did other coaches of the time), and never crossed midfield into Giant territory. In the opening period the attacking All-Stars were quickly pushed right back to their own goal line, and Stuhldreher was nailed in the end zone for a safety. In the third period, after three successive running plays, the All-Stars wound up with fourth down and thirty-two yards to go.

The final score was 22–0, with Friedman accounting for thirteen points by himself. He was a cool, inspired, and yet furious performer that day. He seemed determined to rub the All-Stars' noses in the mud and make them admit they loved it. Perhaps his most startling and most satisfying deed, and the one that lives in the minds of most of those who saw it, was his twenty-five-yard touchdown run near the end of the second period. He burst off tackle, belting would-be tacklers aside, and ran head-on into the Notre Dame secondary, not veering half an inch from the straight path to the goal. One by one he bowled over the All-Star backfield, Frank Carideo among them, and left them strewn on the hard ground behind him to mark his triumphant way to the score.

The final score might just as well have been 70–0, except that Benny grew merciful and made slight effort to score in the final period. He took himself out (he had hurt his knee) at the half and left the running to Red Cagle, who had a personal score to settle against Notre Dame. Cagle had been on the Army team the year before when Jack Elder made monkeys of them all and he was here to see no such thing happened again. The hard-running redhead got away for several good gains, including one for fourteen yards. But his greatest moment must have come when Elder, with the ball under his arm, finally thought he saw daylight around the Giant end and dared to nose into the secondary. Cagle, breathing fire, roared up from his defensive position and smashed poor Jack to the ground with a tackle that seemed to shiver the concrete grandstand. Run ninety yards, would he?

After this game, a great many New York fans got religion on the matter of professional football. No one could pretend any longer that the game was not played with as much fierceness and flamboyance as the college version nor hold that the pros were not as well-conditioned and as thoroughly versed. Many of the All-Stars profited from the lesson too and no longer told themselves that they could run through a few plays in someone's backyard, then go out and perform as they used to. Only old Knute Rockne refused to strike his colors. "I could still take last year's Notre Dame team," he insisted, "and beat the Giants, if we had time to practice." The charity game, he said, was just a contest between a well-trained team of "ex-collegians" and "twenty-five men who had not practiced." He was right in this respect, of course, for in after years college all-star teams that had taken the time to practice (and had taken the opposition seriously), have put up some mighty battles against the pros.

But Knute had some other observations that were worth a man's time to listen to. While he rejoiced with the rest of the people involved that the mayor's fund had been swollen by

$125,000, he did not feel it was fair to ask college boys to devote their time to trying to alleviate the nation's woes this way—not when there were hundreds of wealthy men in the land who might easily, he said, have done as much for charity without injuring their fat purses a bit, and not when great trusts and industries had failed to donate a single dime to the cause.

It was difficult enough in this and subsequent years just to keep the economy breathing, without having to fret over whether professional football made a go of it. But the game did live, and it lived in New York City largely through the work of Benny Friedman, who is now hardly mentioned in the annals of the professional game. Benny's combativeness, his willingness to put on a show for the spectators no matter what the score, his wild inventiveness, and his determination to bring his team home first drew crowds of ten and twenty thousand out to the park Sunday after Sunday. And once he filled a stadium with a game against the Stapletons of Staten Island, his deadly rivals, played on a winner-take-all basis. Stapleton took it all, chiefly because Benny could not play more than a few minutes—and Ken Strong, of Stapleton, was at his best, running almost the full length of the field with a Giant kickoff to score.

Strong was another New York darling. A star at N.Y.U., in the days when Chick Meehan used the "military huddle," with a cannon to salute every score, Ken had kept many of his fans with him when he joined the Stapletons (and when he shifted to the Giants three years later). A solidly built young man with a generous shock of dark hair and a square-cut face, Strong could run with the speed and power of Grange. He was one of the finest kickers who ever played—and when his college injuries eventually ended his professional career as a ball carrier, he was worth more than his salary merely as a kicking specialist.

Strong was raised in the power football days, when linemen and backfield, like a herd of frightened mustangs, would all come hammering between the opposing tackle and end in a body —with Strong like as not snuggling the ball against his two-hundred-pound frame and ready to sprint for the goal as soon as his escort had disposed of the enemy. Strong could run like an antelope and on his best days seemed as shifty as a hare. He might have been one of the professional game's passers too, except that an operation left his throwing hand nearly useless.

Of course Friedman and Strong were not alone in keeping the professional game alive in New York City, when it was gasping its last meager breaths in other towns. Red Cagle, who never let a mere bleeding injury keep him off the playing field, and Mel Hein, a lineman from the Northwest who became practically the permanent center for the Giants—both these men owned their private devotees who gathered to watch them despite rain, chill, or snow. There was also a sticky-fingered end named Badgro, who came from the University of Southern California to join Red Grange in C. C. Pyle's attempt to set up a second professional team in New York—a venture that was hardly more successful than Pyle's cross-country marathon, or Bunion Derby, that nearly grounded the high-flying promoter for keeps. (Pyle's New York Yankees lasted two seasons, during which they gave away uncounted bales of free tickets, an ocean of coffee, and several miles of frankfurters, all donated without charge, to any newspaperman, or any newspaperman's friends, or any of *their* friends, who could be prevailed upon to come dress up the barren stands with their presence.)

In these hard times the teams from the smaller cities handed in their franchises right and left, or passed them on to some innocent, or resorted to such desperate measures to keep alive (like hiring high school boys for the team) that the league had to put them out of their misery. A story is told of the day that the Brooklyn team delayed its game many minutes to make sure every drop of juice had been wrung out of the gate. Then, as the kickoff whistle was about to blow, some member of the organization risked a gory death by hanging far out over the rail of the upper deck at Ebbets Field, trying to get the attention of the coach. "Hold it!" he screamed. "Hold it! There's three more, just coming around the corner now!"

The smaller midwestern cities, even those that had known

professional football since the beginning of the century, shuffled franchises about in a bewildering way. Sometimes they could be had for nothing, or for the assumption of a few debts. Even in the big cities there were constant changes. C. C. Pyle abandoned his franchise to Stapleton, Staten Island. The Frankford Yellowjackets forfeited their franchise and saw it move a few miles south into Philadelphia proper. Red Cagle and his partner, "Shipwreck" Kelly, after trying for a year to keep a team afloat in Brooklyn, handed over the job to a young sportsman named Dan Topping. Portsmouth became Detroit and Cincinnati became St. Louis. Canton, Dayton, Akron, Duluth, Racine, and Buffalo were long gone.

Yet despite all the failures and the bankruptcies and the shoe-string salvations, professional football through the late Hoover and early Roosevelt years continued to gain strength. In the 1920's it was a matter for comment if a professional football game earned attention from one of the syndicated sportswriters. (When Nig Berry of Rochester scored all the points against Chicago in 1922, with a ninety-five-yard touchdown run, two drop-kick goals and a point after touchdown, Walter Eckersall, writing for the Chicago *Tribune* syndicate, devoted a column to Berry's deeds and his teammates counted this a greater triumph than the score.) In the 1930's, however, the professional game had its own fancy and the great sportswriters often gave it space —if only to compare it unfavorably with the college game. In 1933, the league divided into an Eastern and a Western Division, with a championship playoff between the divisional winners, and this game began to draw a gate at least comparable to what professional baseball was drawing. By 1940, it cost fifty thousand dollars just to join the National Football League. (It had been twenty-five dollars in the beginning.)

Professional football was strongest of all in Chicago, which for more than a decade supported two professional teams and which had long known semipro teams by the dozens. Before Red Grange appeared to bring new glamor to the game, Paddy Driscoll of the Cardinals and the Sternaman brothers (Joe and

Dutch) of the Bears had been able to meet a respectable payroll for several years. And there were games every autumn weekend involving such teams as the Pullman Panthers, the Chicago White Stars, the Mohawks, the Badgers, the Kelly Roamers, the Pirates, the Titans, the Mike Igoe Boosters, the Teddy Bears, and, of all things, the Livingston Tiger Lilies. These in addition to the sturdier suburban outfits, such as the Rock Island Independents and the Waukegan Elks. While the Cardinals or Bears might draw from five thousand to eight thousand customers on an ordinary Sunday, the many other sandlot clubs would sometimes count their own attendance in the thousands too.

The football the professionals played was college football with hair on it—harder and somewhat faster, because the pros had begun to abandon the notion that big men had to be slow. Their big men were fast and their fast men were big—big like Grange, or Ken Strong, or the incomparable Bronko Nagurski. The pro football fans were often not fans of the college game, no matter that nearly all the league teams now were peopled by stars from the universities. Some of the most beloved college stars found the pro game too demanding, or the paycheck not enough to tempt them away from a career; and some of the pro stars had played their first football in freshwater colleges most big-city fans had never heard of: San Jose State; Thiel; West Liberty State Teachers; Chico State; Fort Hays Kansas State Teachers; and Otterbein.

As in every college town there are non-alumni who adopt certain flamboyant favorites in the local eleven, so there developed in the big cities a hard-core group of devotees who made the professional team their own and relished its toughness, its occasional wildly erratic plays, the unusual ferocity of some of its stars, and even its decidedly non-academic atmosphere. As Notre Dame had come to be the imagined alma mater of hundreds of Irishmen and Italians in the big cities of the East and West, so the Giants, or the Bears, or the Steamrollers, or the Lions, or the Packers became the private champions of many a football fan who had always felt like an outsider at the college games—having himself been no closer to college than the nearest streetcar stop.

The atmosphere at the professional games was generally rougher too. Carrying liquor to football games and even drinking one's self into somnambulism had long been the fashion at college games and the pro fan did not scorn to tuck a bottle into his overcoat pocket, against the chill. A few of the pro teams from time to time undertook to recruit cheerleaders and to promote organized rooting of a sort. But the efforts seldom took deep enough root to bear lasting fruit. The pro fan, like the baseball fan, was innocent of the sporting tradition and was as likely to yell happily at a long penalty against the opposition as he was to applaud a long run by one of his own. And it had never been a college tradition to cheer-cheer-cheer for an offside. Coonskin coats, when they were common as crackerjack at college stadiums, were seldom indeed at the pro games, except among the visiting big shots along the sidelines. The pro fans did not often bring weekend dates along, and generally they were an older crowd, more profane, if that were possible, and rather more ready to belittle the referee and howl for the enemy's blood.

It actually cost less to see a professional game, in many cities, than it would have cost to attend the top college contests. Indeed mere attendance at one of the big college games, whether or not you could even follow the play, was itself a status symbol, worth nearly any amount of hard cash or gentle influence. The professional game was left for those who merely enjoyed it.

The professionals were less hidebound than the colleges too and once they began to feel entitled to a life of their own became readier to make rule changes or adopt simple stratagems that may have violated tradition but certainly improved the game.

In 1934, for instance, when New York was treated to a head-on clash between two of the game's greatest—Bronko Nagurski and Ken Strong—the ground, in the nine-above-zero weather, had frozen hard as a wooden floor. Yet the Chicago Bears and the New York Giants, playing for the championship, took the field in cleated shoes that gave them less footing than dance pumps. Between the halves, however, coach Steve Owen of the Giants outfitted his team in hastily borrowed basketball shoes, and they ran away with the game, despite the fact that the Bears had trimmed them twice before in the same season. The Bears, who had won thirty-three games in a row, had been leading 10–3 at the half. The final score was 33–13 in favor of New York. Strong ran forty-two yards for one touchdown, with frantic Chicago tacklers skidding helplessly around him.

Nagurski, when the field was in decent condition, was about as terrifying a runner as the professional game had ever seen. Like all his contemporaries, he played both ways, and was as fearsome on defense (where he loved to throw a body block at a runner) as he was on offense. Indeed, all the great men of this day, because of the substitution rule forbidding re-entry in the same half, carried this double burden. Ken Strong, winded and excited after running ninety-eight yards for a touchdown, would have to attempt to convert the extra point almost immediately. As a result, there were many missed attempts, even by kickers as nearly automatic as he was. And many a strong runner or great pass catcher might take such a beating on defense that his skill would be cut nearly in two before the game was over.

Nagurski, however, was a man who gave out punishment more than he absorbed it. In his day, most coaches could not have named his equal. There were some who said he could have been the world's best at any position he wanted to try—and he was indeed a top-notch lineman as well as a ball carrier. It was his running, however, that earned him his fame, and kept his fans leaping to their feet as they watched him. Bronko ran with his head down and his iron-muscled body straight as a projectile, or nearly so. His knees, as he sprinted for the goal, would lift almost as high as his chest. He often provided his own blocking, using his solid shoulder to flip a tackler on his back as he struck the man.

Like so many players who are solid, big, and fast, Bronko re-

joiced in the direct head-on contact with a tackler and, seldom
went in for the dodging, spinning, and zigzagging that smaller
men relied on. A straight-on tackle was no way to stop Nagurski.
A man who tried to clutch those pumping steel legs, or ram his
shoulder against that driving cannon of a body, would do well
if he carried nothing more than a shoulder separation off the
field. The men who managed to stop Nagurski, once the big
Bronk had gotten into the open, were those who used Bronko's
own pet method: hurling the body athwart the runner's legs.
For Nagurski was the perfect picture of a fullback—a straight-
on plunger who could power through a scrimmage line and knock
a linebacker halfway home by dint of the momentum of his
charge, and the granite solidity of his body.

There has probably never been a football player any stronger
than Nagurski or any who could develop so much horsepower
from a standing start. Had he played in the modern era of
twenty-thousand-dollar-a-season salaries, he might have put
away a competence before age took the spring out of his legs.
As it was he gave his absolute utmost (he always did) for relatively scant wages and was reduced in his middle years to performing as a professional wrestler, where he could exhibit still
his unmatched capacity for dealing out and absorbing bodily
bruises. Nagurski's strength, at which his own teammates used
to marvel, gave rise to a standard joke that writers once liked to
repeat about him: He had developed his muscles, he used to
say, by plowing. But plowing, the listener would protest, was
commonplace exercise among country boys. Every farmer's son
had done plowing. Yes, the Bronk would agree. But without
horses?

Chapter VII

The Green Bay Volunteers

By 1940, when a franchise in the National Football League cost fifty thousand dollars, there was only one "small-town" team left. That was Green Bay, Wisconsin, where the Green Bay Packers had been kept alive for twenty years through the dogged efforts of a few promoters, led by a determined newspaper reporter named George Calhoun. There had been sandlot or semiprofessional football in Green Bay off and on since 1896, but the team that was put together in 1919 was the first one to continue, under more or less the same management, until it attained prosperity.

The promoters, and most of the original team, all Green Bay boys, first met in the editorial rooms of the Green Bay *Press-Gazette*, in the summer of 1919, at almost the exact moment that the National Football League was being born several hundred miles to the east. The meeting grew out of a street-corner exchange between Calhoun and Curly Lambeau—one of those "why don't we start a football team?" conversations such as had taken place a dozen times before in a dozen places, and had actually resulted several times in the creation of sandlot elevens that occasionally lived through a whole season.

This time, however, the participants were not the sort to let go of a good idea just because everyone told them that it would never work. George Calhoun was grim as a bulldog about holding to an ambition and Curly Lambeau, now working for the Indian (later Acme) Packing Company, was Green Bay's greatest football star. He had earned statewide fame at East Green Bay High School, and had played one season under Knute Rockne at Notre Dame, where he starred in the backfield with the glorious George Gipp. Curly was the best football player in town and was itching to extend his domain. These men, and the others who joined them, were not in the game for money. For several seasons they took home far less hard cash and many more bruises than most college stars.

Their team became the Packers because the Indian Packing Company bought twenty jerseys (immediately limiting the size of the squad), a dozen footballs and several sets of shoulder pads, and supplied the practice field. Curly, Calhoun, and the rest persuaded the local high school coach to direct them without pay and secured the use of an area known as Hagemeister Park, where there were neither seats nor fences. Spectators were restrained (in part) by ropes strung around the field and the gate receipts were gathered in Calhoun's hat, passed by George himself, who could wither a man with a single glance who tried to watch the play without dropping a coin into the fedora.

As in all small cities at this time, in Columbus, in Rochester, in Akron, in Duluth, the games developed into haphazard affairs, with spectators sometimes ringing the backfield, so that a sudden reversal, like a picked-up fumble, would send a mob of overcoated refugees tumbling and scrambling out of the ball-carrier's path. Players dressed at home and put on their cleated shoes on the bench. A kid named Jack Rudolph (who became sports editor of the *Press-Gazette* eventually) trotted in and out with the water bucket and the tin dipper whenever time was called. The half-time strategy sessions were held in the open, at opposite ends of the field, with spectators gathered around to watch, to kibitz, even to argue as the attack and defense was planned. The half-time entertainment was supplied by a welter of boys with their dress-up clothes on playing a game that was sometimes called "pick-it-up-and-run"—in which the ball was kicked by the lad who could grab it and get away with it, and in which clothes were torn, caps lost, and noses often bloodied.

In these respects, the Green Bay Packers resembled a hundred other small-time teams throughout the country who grew stronger in the next few years only to collapse at last under the strain of cold rain and dried-up gate receipts. What kept the Packers going was largely the fierce determination of George Calhoun, their volunteer publicist and comptroller. It was George who scouted out new angels when old ones fell and would give no more. It was George who wrote the publicity, browbeat the creditors, and guarded the gate receipts. It was George, even, who ferreted out the gate-crashers (once there was a gate to crash) and hated them to death. A crusty, tough-talking, dour-visaged man with a heart as soft as warm butter, George—called Cal—never for a minute let himself believe that the Packers were not going to be the best football team in the world. They surely became the best known, thanks to the reams of copy Cal would broadcast, and the weekly newsletter he showered on friend and foe alike. Some happy ignoramus in the early days might have thought the Chicago Cardinals a baseball team and the Bears mere denizens of the Chicago zoo. But everyone knew that the Green Bay Packers played football. In fact, no one ever did know what the Packers packed, or perhaps those who did know preferred not to tell.

Cal attended every game the Packers played for more than twenty years (except for an exhibition game in Hawaii when he was too ill to travel), but he used to like to say that for more than twenty-five years he never saw a kickoff. He was too busy at the start of the game sorting friend from phoney at the pass gate. Not even One-Eyed Connelley ever dodged under Cal's iron arm and no newsman's cousins or halfback's hungry neighbors could jaw their way into a free seat when Cal was there.

There is reason to believe, however, that a number of the denizens of Green Bay got a free look at many of the games because they could play, or pretend to play, a small brass horn. One of the features of the team in the early days was its "Lumberjack Band"—a group of local horn-tooters, recruited by a restaurant owner named George DeLair, who first accompanied the team on its trips to Chicago to play the Cardinals or the Bears. Garbed in mackinaws, sixteen-inch lace boots, and wool caps, and garnished with beards, they cavorted about the Loop in Chicago like a caravan of honest-to-God woods monkeys turned loose from a drive. Their antics drummed up trade for the games, brought tears to the eyes of music-lovers, and established a tradition that was finally formalized with the recruitment of a "Lumberjack Swing Band," complete with undressed majorette, in 1939.

There is no question that Green Bay developed the first truly frantic fancy that professional football ever knew. No college rivalry ever grew more bitter or more deeply involved the muscles, minds, and hearts of its partisans than did the feud between Green Bay and Chicago through the twenties and thirties. Nor did any city in the nation ever devote itself so wholeheartedly to following the fortunes of its football champions. Professional baseball, of course, had long known devotion that would keep fans massed around an outdoor scoreboard, or standing hour upon hour in a ticket line. But only in Green Bay, Wisconsin, in the early years of the game, did football players who played for money earn such adulation.

The Packers' original and apparently natural rival was the team in Milwaukee that called itself the Marines. The Packers, however, eventually included Milwaukee in their own fan-shed and, in order to stay solvent, had to play many of their home games there, permitting themselves to be adopted by the very big city folks who had scorned them once as hayshakers from the back country.

The Packers played in Chicago soon after they joined the National Football League and almost immediately developed a grudge against the big city that only the passage of some twenty years could tame. In the earliest games, the Bears' big, tough center, George Trafton, once the pride of Notre Dame, dealt out so much extracurricular punishment that he was more than once ejected from the game, to be marched right out of the park under police guard—with the snarling Packer fans aching to dismember him. For several years then, the coming of the Bears meant a gathering of bloodthirsty natives such as had seldom been seen east of the Little Big Horn. The games were played in a continual uproar and no man could have kept account of the fist-fights. The Bears themselves were originally resentful at the very notion that a small-time crew, gathered from the backyards of Green Bay, or recruited under phoney names from nearby college campuses, could actually score against them.

It soon became clear that the Packers could not only score against the Bears but could lick them. To manage that, they had to reach out beyond the Green Bay area to find players to kick and carry the ball; but still they managed to provide a local flavor to their roster, to the everlasting benefit of the gate receipts. For a time they owned the mightiest kicker in the game —Vern Lewellen, who had been known to boot a ball from behind his own goal line and roll it out of bounds some ninety yards away. Vern was the local district attorney. He was also, like all the backfield stars of his day, an able passer and a mighty runner, who could smash into a line with the authority of a new Ford truck. (Before Lewellen, the Packers boasted another great kicker, also a Wisconsin product, Howard "Cub" Buck, who had served a term with the Canton Bulldogs before the league was formed.)

There was a fierce rivalry too with the nation's other big city —New York—although the feeling never grew quite so bitter between these two. But Green Bay got its back up early in the long series when a New York announcer spoke patronizingly of the "underequipped" boys from the back country—not realizing that Green Bay's Eddie Kotal went without a helmet, not because there were not enough to go around, but because he thought he could run and dodge better without one.

Whenever the Packers met the teams from the big cities in the league, there was invariably a great gathering of the faithful. If the game were not to be played at home, then the fans would jam into a hall to choke each other with tobacco smoke and to watch, on a big green board known as a Grid-Graph, the progress of their heroes up and down the distant field. There was no radio in those earliest days, or at least no public speakers, and the news had to be transmitted through a single receiver, then diagramed on the miniature gridiron. Green Bay was the first city in the whole league, however, that could brag of a public address system in its football park. A young electrical wizard named Pete Platten, without any store-bought parts with which to work, built the whole contraption himself. Speakers were strung at both ends of the field so that all the fans could learn immediately what it was they had just been looking at. There being no traveling microphones then, the single announcer needed a crew of sideline spies to signal him the gain, the carrier, the down, and the yards to go. Meanwhile the real radio announcer, trying to scatter his own description to listeners hundreds of miles away, would grit his fancy teeth every time the homemade squawk box drowned out his painstakingly enunciated vowels.

With a fandom as devoted as theirs, it was inevitable that the Packers should grow mighty in battle. The thirties had not even arrived when they won the professional football championship of the world. On November 24, 1929, in a cold rain on a slimy field, the boys from Green Bay beat the mighty New York Giants into submission, 20–6. The gang that managed this were, one supposes, far superior to the neighborhood lads of a decade earlier, who had gone about slaughtering the likes of Company C of Sheboygan, the Maple Leaf A.C. of Milwaukee, and the Oshkosh pros, by scores of 87–0, 52–0, and 85–0. But they were none of them home grown, except Curly Lambeau, the coach, who, having busted a rib in his final appearance, was permanently sidelined. Even on the sidelines, however, Curly was a prized performer in the show, for he would rant up and down during the play, lifting arms and exhortations to the deaf heavens, and pounding himself on the head with both fists when some precious bit of strategy fizzled. (Later in his career, Curly used to coach from the press box.)

With the Packers in New York was an ex-Giant, craggy-faced Cal Hubbard, who was bent on personal vengeance against the team that had found him expendable while he was still in his prime, and Cal did rack up an uncommon number of enemy ball carriers that day. The Packers were quarterbacked by one of Green Bay's favorites, a football vagabond who called himself Johnny Blood (his real name was McNally), a lanky, tousle-topped young wildman who had earned the fans' devotion by his reckless improvisations both on the field and off and who could run, pass, kick, tackle, turn handsprings and (for all I know) tell fortunes with cards. Green Bay used only one substitute to do the Giants in that afternoon and Curly the coach came up with a defensive stunt that, for the first time in memory, almost completely choked off Benny Friedman's passes.

Lambeau's move, which forecast today's widespread defense and occasional red-dogging of the passer, was simply to pull Cal Hubbard out of the line and let him be the linebacker—middle, left, and right. Cal was delighted at this opportunity to clobber, collectively and individually, his last year's teammates. He dumped massed blockers into the runner's lap, or hustled out to the end to snag a sweeping ball carrier with one mighty paw and splash him on the turf. The other linemen, meanwhile, had been instructed to charge in upon Benny Friedman, who soon began to wonder if the Packers had not lined up with an extra dozen tacklers on their side. Again and again, in today's parlance, he "ate" the football, or heaved it vainly out of bounds. And if he sought some surcease by driving a play through the line, there was the one-man gang named Hubbard plugging up all the holes.

The Packers gloried in their game, yelling with joy and excitement when they scored and almost weeping with rage when their iron-man combination was broken at last, in the final minutes of the game, with the substitution of Paul Minnick for the groggy right guard, Jim Bowdoin. Hubbard rejoiced in every opportunity to wander close to the sidelines and grate the nerves of his ex-bosses, Tim Mara and Steve Owen, by reminding them who was ahead.

While this was not the final game of the season and did not

bring the title with it, it did settle the race as far as the fans were concerned. When the title was clinched at last on a bitter December day, the frost-bitten Green Bay folk jammed the downtown streets from wall to wall to scream welcome to the returning heroes.

From that time on, Green Bay was a mighty force in the league. They won the title in 1930 and 1931, took it again in 1936, won a divisional title in 1938, and took it all again in 1939. In 1944 they won another league championship, with Curly Lambeau still handling the reins. But if it were possible to credit the championships to any one man—and in football that is never possible—that man would have to be Green Bay's great end, Don Hutson. Hutson is still named, by men who recall his greatest deeds, the best end who ever played professional football. Surely no one has ever exceeded him in ability to snag a pass with one hand, with two hands, going away, standing still, falling down—or even, as he did on one occasion, swinging in a vicious pivot with one hand holding the goal post, to evade a defender, while the free hand reached back and snaked the ball out of the air.

Don played both ways, of course. As a defensive end, he was not strong, for he did not have a solid enough build to handle the massed interference of the wingback attacks. But when he was turned into a halfback on defense, as he eventually was, he was wary as a wolf and just as hard to dodge away from.

It was not merely as a sticky-fingered pass receiver that Don excelled. Once he had the ball in his hands—perhaps plucking it out from between the frustrated flippers of a defender—he could streak down the field like a stung greyhound. In college he had run the hundred-yard dash in 9.8 seconds, yet he weighed 195 pounds and was as long-legged as a gazelle. (Sportswriters in Green Bay and elsewhere named him the Alabama Antelope.) In college he was used often as a ball carrier on an end-around play designed to spring him loose at full momentum. A pleasant-looking, curly-haired young giant, Don became the hero of Green Bay and led the team to its league championships in

1936, 1939, and 1944. In this era the forward pass had developed so that some of the older sportswriters and coaches were belittling the professional game as just a combination of basketball and wrestling. A pass now could be thrown from any point behind the line, and as a result passes often developed from running plays, with the ball carrier suddenly cocking his arm, just before crossing the scrimmage line, and heaving the ball thirty or forty yards downfield.

Because there was hardly a defenseman in the league whom Don Hutson could not outspring and outreach, Green Bay's Arnie Herber, a marksman with a football, completed an inordinate number of passes—to the intense delight of the Wisconsin faithful, who cared not at all what the game was called as long as the Bay boys won it. After Herber, there was Cecil Isbell, who led the league twice in number of pass completions (Herber led for three seasons).

Hutson was also a skilled place-kicker and in 1943 was top man in the league in field goals. He never played for any league team other than Green Bay—nor did his pet passers, Herber and Isbell. While there were other mighty men on his side during his years at Green Bay, men like Hank Bruder, Clarke Hinkle, and Buckets Goldenberg, no one can dwell on the great games of that era without envisioning the long-legged Alabama boy plucking fifty-yard passes in one hand (sometimes) and sprinting the rest of the way to the goal.

It may be that Green Bay remained the only undersized city in the league because it was the only city where the team was owned by the fans. In 1923, the Green Bay Football Corporation was formed and stock (promising no dividends) was sold from door to door. The Green Bay populace responded more eagerly than college alumni. Even at that, it was necessary, of course, to beg funds again and again, to supplement the slender gate receipts. But the Packers (who tried out a few other nicknames, such as the Big Bay Behemoths, after the packing company stopped buying the jerseys) persisted while their counterparts elsewhere—often fed by a single hand, or held together by promissory notes and bad checks—were sinking. Indeed, the first set of directors that the Green Bay Packers owned became, through their everlasting efforts to wheedle a few more dollars to finance the road trips, known throughout the city as "the Hungry Five." And they remained hungry for nearly a decade, until the Packers finally began to flourish like a Green Bay tree.

Chapter VIII

Self-made Cowboy

Sammy Baugh, the "Texas Cowboy" who taught the professional football players how to use the forward pass, could not really afford to be a cowboy until he had made enough money at football to buy a ranch. Yet he arrived in Washington, for his first pro football job, in brand new ten-gallon hat and cowboy boots, bought at the urging of George Preston Marshall, the wet-wash king, who had just moved his red-ink Redskins from Boston to the District of Columbia. George thought it would make a good news picture.

Sammy, a lean, leather-complexioned young man from Texas, had always been better at baseball than at football and his arrival to play with the Washington Redskins was strictly an experiment. He had a good offer from the St. Louis Cardinals to come play third base and he had more than half a mind to accept it. All Sammy could do in football was pass and kick. He had made himself into a passer through the most determined regimen of daily practice any football player had ever attempted: He had thrown footballs through a hanging spare tire by the dozens and the hundreds until he could spin one through the wide bull's-eye even when he was on the run and the tire was swinging like a pendulum. No one before Sammy came along had ever attached quite that much importance to passing. Many had been expert at it—like Benny Friedman, or Potsy Clark—but none had concentrated on it to the exclusion of all other skills.

When Sammy Baugh started to play college football at Texas Christian University (his second choice of colleges), his freshman coach, Dutch Meyer, made him practice kicking so that he would have at least two strings to his bow. But the varsity coach did not feel that even an ability to kick would make Sammy into a football player. The flesh was just spread too thinly on Sammy's frame: 170 pounds over six feet three of him. Fortunately for Sammy, he and the freshman coach moved up to the varsity at the same time and Sammy had a chance to edify the Southwest Conference with his new brand of gridiron basketball, in which the forward pass became the central threat, along with laterals and quick kicks, so that the ball was in view of the delighted spectators about 70 percent of the time. George Marshall knew all about Sammy Baugh before he was eligible for drafting. When the draft choices were made (Marshall had second pick) George could hardly believe his luck. The man with first call had not even considered Baugh. Marshall grabbed him before anyone could say another word.

The Redskins (a name chosen to suggest a kinship with the Boston Braves) came to Washington from Boston in 1937, the same year that Sammy joined them. It was Sammy who made the team a success, and gave George Preston Marshall his first pro football profit (about twenty thousand dollars in that first season). Yet even in pro football Sammy had to deal with a prejudice against the pass—or against the "overemphasis" of the pass. Redskin Coach Ray Flaherty, who had been on the receiving end of many of Benny Friedman's throws, solemnly warned the young Texan that he was going to have to learn a lot more football if he hoped to stay in the National League. "You can't get by up here," Ray told Sammy, "by just passing like crazy. You're going to have to learn to run."

It may be that Sammy did learn to run. But it was Ray Flaherty who learned the most. For, working from the tailback position in the single-wing formation, Sammy demonstrated to fan and foeman that the forward pass could sometimes win a ball game almost all by itself. Permitted by the pro rules to pass from anywhere behind the line, he threw passes with a sudden snap of the wrist when he seemed headed full tilt around the end. He threw from deep in his own territory. He threw one, two, three, four, five, even six passes in a row—with the opposition telling themselves that *this* time surely that crazy SOB was not going to throw the ball.

His unmatched timing and deadly accuracy exceeded anything hitherto shown on the professional gridiron. And the success of his style, both at the gate and in the scoring column, changed the whole strategy of the game. Those demigods of the past, who had been triple-threat men, with their passing ability held in reserve as a means of startling the enemy when the ground game was stalled, faded from memory. The mighty powerhouses of the league, even when Sammy had but a mediocre team to support him, many times found themselves outscored and bewildered by this long and lank and brown young man who seemed to have no notion of when was the right time to pass and when it was time not to. With Sammy it was *always* a good time to throw the ball. Yet he sometimes befuddled the enemy by drifting back with his arm cocked and suddenly booting the ball far over the head of the bright-eyed halfbacks who perched ready to grab at his pass.

The quick kick was a favorite weapon of Sammy's and one that developed easily out of the single-wing formation, which was, after all, just a variation of the short punt formation. In the 1942 championship game against the Chicago Bears, the Bears had smothered the Redskin receiver of the kickoff on the twelve-yard line. Backed against the wall like this, Sammy was wont to start throwing the ball immediately, and the Bears were ready for him, eager to pick off a hurried pass and blast their way to a score. Sammy took the direct pass from center and drifted back, the football held between his hands, his eyes apparently seeking receivers. Then, with hardly an extra stride, he laid into the ball with his foot and sent it sailing downfield, out of reach of everyone. It struck about midfield, took a forward bounce, and kept rolling. When the Bears downed it at last, it was at their own five-yard line.

In that same game, with the Bears telling themselves on every down "*Now* he'll throw it," Sammy sent twelve plays in a row right into the center of the line, where the Bears were playing "soft" for fear he might flip one over their heads. On the twelfth plunge, Andy Farkas made a touchdown. The Redskins won the game 14–6, with Sammy scoring the conversions.

But these variations were just the priceless exceptions to Sammy's rule. They were the reward he earned for converting the whole football fraternity to the faith that Sammy Baugh threw the ball at any time and all the time. While Sammy's passing marks, that seemed destined to stand forever, have been matched by others since, Sammy is still the leader. For it was Baugh who first taught quarterbacks they did not need to run, except to get off the field when the whistle blew; and it was Sammy who freed the game from the thralldom of tradition that seemed to have doomed it to remain, especially if the field were wet, a slam-bang, grunt-groan, pull-devil, pull-baker affair that was occasionally less fun to watch than an honest wrestling match.

The brutal scoreless ties that Fordham played with Pittsburgh in the thirties were prime examples of single-wing football at its deadliest. When the heart was bound up in victory, as the college devotee's was, then these unresolved wrangles could deeply stir the blood. But they provided little satisfaction to a man who liked to watch football. Much of the great work was done in the line, where some granite-legged guard might pile up a whole phalanx of plungers—and where there was none to see and applaud beyond one's teammates and the referee.

A muddy or a snow-covered field in the pre-Baugh era might mean an aimless slithering about, with only an occasionally juicy (and wobbly) punt to indicate that the men were playing with a football. But not even snow and ice could convert Sammy to conservatism. The Redskins won the championship the first season they had Sammy with them and the game for the prize was played on snow, at Wrigley Field in Chicago. It was not a gentle snow, but an icy one on which a man could break his fingers, and the players, unable to get a footing with cleats, all wore canvas rubber-soled sneakers. This was the first snow that Sammy Baugh had ever played in and it took him the better part of the game to get adjusted. But in the final quarter, with the score 21–14 against the Redskins, rookie Sam let go with a pass to Wayne Millner that covered seventy-eight yards. The next time Sammy had his hands on the ball he passed it thirty-five yards to Ed Justice and won the ball game.

After Sammy had played eleven seasons in Washington, a writer in *Sport* magazine suggested that this year (1948) might be Sammy's sunset season. He was thirty-four years old and had taken a fearful beating from tacklers who earnestly slammed him to the ground every time he passed—often beating into him seconds after the ball had left his hand. But Sammy was not even close to the end. He had always stayed in top condition, his weight never varying, his muscles never growing soft in the summer. He gave up baseball when, after a tryout with the Cardinals, with Columbus, and with Rochester, he found he could not hit a curve ball often enough to make it count. While the salary that George Marshall paid him would hardly tempt even a small-time politician out of the ways of righteousness, Sammy did earn enough, what with bonuses and payments for advertising endorsements, to afford a Texas ranch, where he could practice flipping the lariat. He amused himself and kept his muscles tough by rodeo calf roping and even by the milking of wild cows.

Sammy was not a drinking man, and he lived by the clock, not only keeping regular hours but dividing his day into definite sections for play, practice, and diversion. His one "sin" was a devotion to playing pinball machines for money, a pastime that was not designed to lead him among evil companions or even keep him up late at night. (It was whispered, or even said out loud on occasion, that Sammy had been known to lay a sizable bet on his own team in a football game, thus adding weight to his own incentive just as professional baseball players often did before salaries and bonuses began to swell.)

Sam stayed with the Redskins through 1952, and played a great deal more fine football, even though the Redskins by then had fallen on evil days indeed. (Ironically, they might have prospered in Boston, had not Marshall thought to spite the Boston sportswriters and fans by taking his team away just when it was playing championship ball. The fans and writers had turned on him when he suddenly raised his prices one day because the upcoming game looked like a sellout.) Coach Flaherty, Baugh's first pro coach and the best the Redskins ever hired, had been let go and Marshall appointed himself (unofficially) the real coach of the team, by reserving to himself the right to order shifts in strategy and to scold players who did not live up to their notices. Marshall did hire some able coaches after Flaherty but could keep none of them long for he sometimes undertook to call the major moves in a game through the walkie-talkie radiophone in his private box. He unleashed his temper often on coaches he deemed disobedient. He lost the services (and the friendship) of his good friend Curly Lambeau, whom he hired as coach with much fanfare, when he engaged in a childish fistfight (in which no real blows were struck) with Curly in a hotel lobby, after Curly refused to fire two players who had smuggled beer to their rooms.

But Sammy Baugh remained the team's bread and butter through good times and bad, through the war and even through the coming of the "new" T formation, which one might have thought would have spiked the guns of a man brought up on the single-wing. In 1943, Sammy became a T-formation quarterback and learned to fade back, to stay in the protective pocket, to fake and bootleg with the best of them.

Even in his final year, 1952, when he was nearly forty, wearing half a hundred sore spots and dormant charley horses from much walloping, and still wearing the flimsy little shoulder pads he had bought from Ernie Pinckert in 1937, Sammy could put on a show that would send fans home with their throats sore from yelling. In that year, he closed out his passing career in a game against the Chicago Cardinals, whose linemen seemed determined to divide Sammy into pieces before shipping him back to Texas to grow old. Sammy had had a poor season in 1951, with only 67 passes completed out of 154 attempts and with a higher percentage of interceptions than he had ever suffered before. He had broken his hand in training before the 1952 season began and the Cardinals, scenting blood, seemed intent on getting him down and keeping him there. The big Chicago tackle, Don Joyce, devoted himself to Sammy with the fierceness of a dog worrying a cornered bobcat. No matter that Sammy had long ago unleashed the ball, big Don would pile into him and beat him to the ground, just as if the skin-and-bones Texan might get up and run another thirty yards. With not a complaint or a sign of flinching, Sammy called pass plays —one after another, completing every one, seven, eight, nine, ten, eleven! On the eleventh Joyce belted him again and slammed him earthward. This time Sammy rose and celebrated the end of his passing career by pasting the monster from Tulane right square on his chin. (He was thrown out of the game then, and Joyce with him.)

Sammy returned to professional football in his "old age" (he was past forty-five) as coach of the American Football League's New York Titans, owned by Harry Wismer, a former associate of George Preston Marshall. But Harry and Sammy could not seem to agree on which one of them was to coach the team, or who was *really* to blame for the Titans' rather dismal showing. Sammy, still lean and tough as a trailworn steer, thereupon hied himself home to Texas again.

Chapter IX

Last of the Full-time Footballers

Whoever the little leather-girded god may be who has in his keeping the rules to regulate the names that football players wear, he seems to have had a secret appetite for alliteration. As Green Bay had its "H" boys (Hinkle, Herber, and Hutson), the New York Giants had Filchock and Farkas, and the Chicago Bears in the 1948 season had Luckman, Lujack, and Layne. The trouble with this trio, however, was that they could not all play at the same time—they were all quarterbacks and all most able, although not entirely equal in their skills.

Sid Luckman got there first and in 1948 was starting his tenth season. Johnny Lujack and Bobby Layne were just beginning—but Layne was destined to stay in the National League for more than a dozen seasons himself. Luckman was one of the first, and surely the best, of the T-formation quarterbacks, for George Halas of the Chicago Bears was the man who popularized if he did not actually invent the "man-in-motion" T that was to turn football upside down in the 1940's.

The T-formation, as revived and refurbished by the pros, had hardly anything in common with the "old" T-formation, which was the original football formation of the 1890's. The quarterback in this new T-formation kept his hand in contact with the center. The center, through a rule change, no longer needed to crouch and peer back through his legs to spot his target: he could shove the ball into the quarterback's hands while never taking his eyes off the opposition. He could hold the ball, not flat on the ground as he had to do in the old days, but almost perpendicular, so that only one end of it touched the turf and he could handle it with one hand. Linemen were not required any longer to drive their shoulders or heads into the opponents and half-lift, half-shove them back. Now they just "brushed" them back, using forearms and chest rather than shoulder, long enough to permit a fast-driving ball carrier to slide by. The linemen could then hasten on to provide downfield blocking.

The quarterback in this style of play was more important than ever. An ability to "hand off" without shoving the ball in the runner's neck and causing him to fumble, to fake to one or two other backs before delivering the ball to the proper carrier, to conceal the ball while hastening back to pass, to remain cool and safely in the protective "pocket" provided by linemen who had dropped back for the purpose, to "roll out" to one side, carrying the ball, ready to lateral it to a trailing back or to drive quickly through a hole in the line, and to throw the ball sharply, accurately, either long or short—this was what a T-formation quarterback needed. In brief, he had to be a man who could handle the ball deftly and deceptively, and could turn in either direction without stumbling over himself.

The development of these skills took more doing than some coaches realized and it was necessary therefore to have a couple of good substitutes ready if the number one man were disabled. The T-formation attack without a first-rate quarterback was a complete catastrophe in the making. (Many prep school and college coaches, who were always eager to stay in fashion, learned this to their dismay after they had instituted the "Modern T," with only one boy really able to pivot without falling down.)

The "man in motion," according to the current legend, was discovered rather than invented, when one Chicago backfield man took off for the sideline, in accordance with the prescribed pattern, before the ball was snapped. The manner in which this disrupted the opposition, causing it to spread out haphazardly to make sure this man was "covered," prompted George Halas to keep this bit of business in—as a good stage director learns to retain some accidental bit of business that adds zest to a scene.

It had always been the aim of the attacking team to spread the defense so as to have openings through which to run the ball. This had been accomplished from time to time through various spread formations—sometimes stretching the whole width of the field. (Navy, in the 1930's, had an assistant coach named Cliff Schwab who was a great improviser. He taught his second team a whole series of plays from a widespread formation, until his crew became known as "the spreaders." The head coach put "the spreaders" in against Yale one day, to rest his regulars, and the second string gave the big Blue fits.) The single-wing formation had employed an unbalanced line as one means of getting an angle on a defender so as to open up the line—that is, the attacking team shifted into a formation that put two guards on the same side of the center, with a resultant confusion in assignments on the other side.

But the man-in-motion opened up the opposition as nothing before had done. Against the standard six- or seven-man defensive line it sometimes pulled an end right out into the open field, or it left the man-in-motion wide open to receive a toss and run at least until the defensive halfback could get up to him. And because the heart of the new T was deception—with the ball offered to and sometimes even "given a ride" with one or two backs before the real carrier took it, the linemen often had no notion of where the play had struck until the ball carrier was already loose behind them, with only three or four defenders left to deal with. The defense eventually learned to cope with this advantage by using a five-man, or even a four-man line, so that the secondary defense, who got a better view of the backfield shenanigans, could outnumber the attackers at the point of attack. But in the beginning, the attack had a sudden edge.

This unexpected and undue advantage was never better exemplified than on the day Sid Luckman led his Chicago Bears against Sammy Baugh and the Redskins, in the championship game in 1940 at Griffith Stadium in Washington, D.C. Of course it was not simply the difference in formations that made one team so much the superior of the other that day. (The Bears had met the Redskins earlier that season and had lost, 7–3.) But there was a wide difference in preparation, with the Bears taking swift advantage of all the potentials of their own attack and the Redskins sticking to the stolid defense they had used in beating the Bears previously. But this time the Bears were destined to come out so far ahead that Redskin fans were shaken as if by a dynamite explosion. The final score was Bears 73, Redskins 0. (Some numbers player may have read a significance in the way the 7 and the 3 "jumped out" again.)

The Bears, led by Luckman, a solid and handsome young man from Brooklyn who had nearly played all the football out of his system while directing a succession of losing teams at Columbia, had dedicated themselves to evening the score with the Redskins. They had grown red-eyed from studying motion pictures of the game they lost; and they had learned the defensive habits of the Redskins so that you might have shaken any one of the Chicago team awake at 2 A.M. and he could have told you how the Redskin secondary would move to meet an end run.

There was no guarantee, of course, that the Redskins would repeat all their moves from the previous game. But it seemed likely that they, having won the game, were not dwelling on their errors with quite so much religion as the Bears were. The first play of the game, a slant off tackle, was designed by Luckman to probe the enemy defenses. It gained eight yards. Better still, it indicated that all the Redskins were behaving just as they had in the motion pictures. When the Chicago end moved out fifteen yards the Redskin halfback on that side moved out with him. And when Nolting, the Chicago halfback, went in motion to that side, the linebacker trailed him, leaving the alley wide and free.

The next play started in the same way, and in the same direction, and the Redskin secondary reacted in the accustomed manner. This time, however, Luckman, after faking to Nolting, pivoted completely and gave the ball to fullback Bill Osmanski, who could get off the mark like a cannon cracker, and Bill started

for the wide open space between tackle and end. But the outside proved more inviting and Bill swept all the way around,
while the Redskins rushed over to intercept him. They never
made it. End George Wilson, when Bill was partway home and
suddenly cornered by two big Redskins, removed both of the
enemy with one roaring block and Osmanski ran the whole
sixty-eight yards to the touchdown. Jack Manders entered the
game to make the conversion. It was 7–0 and the game was
less than a minute old.

The Redskins, though shaken, were by no means subdued.
George Preston Marshall had been telling them, and telling the
press, and telling anyone else who would hold still, that the
Bears were a "first-half team" who would fold as soon as someone
got ahead of them. And the Redskins had just the man to put
them ahead in a hurry—Sammy Baugh, the best forward passer
in football.

On the next kickoff, Max Krause of the Redskins, to the
howling delight of their paleface customers, smashed back down
the middle of the field for sixty-two yards, to the Bears' thirty-
two-yard line. Then the Redskins drove to the twenty-six. With
second down and four to go, everyone in the park must have
known that Baugh would throw a pass. The ball came straight
to his hands and he moved back a step or two, babying the ball
into position as he sought downfield receivers. He and the fans
and the outwitted Bears all spotted the same one at the same
time: right end Charlie Malone, all alone on the two-yard line.
It was money in the bank. The frantic spectators screamed happily as they saw the score about to be evened. Sammy who, it
was said, could break a bone with one of his passes, or could lay
it in a receiver's hand like a turkey feather, sent a perfect peg
into Charlie's ready arms. And Charlie, blinded by the sun,
dropped it.

This, it developed, was the real turning point of the game. The
Bears, who were supposed to be the front-runners, and the team
that lost heart most easily, accepted this bit of Luckman luck as
a portent, while the Redskins felt the heart go out of them.

After "Bat" Masterson missed a field goal, Luckman drove his inspired Bears from their own twenty-yard line to the one-yard Redskin line in sixteen ground plays. Although many a fan had come to the game expecting a throwing contest between Sammy and Sid (who were best and next best in the league), Luckman never let go of the ball at all, except to slip it into the arms of a ball carrier. When his team reached the one-yard line, Sid took the ball himself on a quarterback sneak and made the second touchdown.

The Bears after that could not discover a way to lose. Ground plays, passes, pitch-outs, and pass defense all operated as they do in a coach's daydream and every player seemed above himself. The hapless Redskins, even including the mighty Sammy Baugh, never could get their feet set. At the half the score was Chicago 28, Washington 0. While this is hardly a hopeless margin, especially in professional football and most particularly when you have the world's best forward passer on your side, it struck the Washington fans dumb. They had come to see a smashing victory over a team they had been taught to call "the crybabies" (George Preston Marshall did not care for the way the Bears appealed to the rule book when a tricky decision went against them). Now they were viewing an utter rout. The worst, had they only known it, was yet to come. In the Bears' locker room, George Halas, who had been "inspiring" his team by pinning up quotations from Marshall's predictions to the press, merely reminded his sweating charges that Marshall had called them a "first-half" team. So now it was the second half.

The effect on the Bears was to send them roaring out to the last half as if they were two touchdowns behind and had bet their equipment on the game, right down to the aluminum. Where they had been cool and efficient before, they were now red-hot and indomitable. At the start of the third quarter, Hampton Pool, the Chicago end, leaped up to punch a Baugh pass into the air, then grabbed it as it fell and carried it all the way across the Washington goal line. And this indignity was the least of it. The Bears made four touchdowns in the third quarter and three more in the fourth. George Halas had a hard time finding a man who would miss a point-after-touchdown. It was not until the third quarter, when Dick Plasman tried to convert after Pool's touchdown, that anything went wrong for the Bears. Plasman was the fourth man to attempt a conversion.

The nightmarish quality that the game acquired is best indicated by the fact that the Bears eventually kicked away all the footballs. It was standard by this time to use a new football whenever the first had become badly soiled; and it was accepted practice in championship games, at least, to allow the customers to keep as souvenirs the balls that were kicked into the stands on conversions. The Redskins had brought along six new footballs—enough to last through a couple of ordinary games—and a supply of practice balls. Before the final quarter was over they were down to the last ball, and the officials asked the Bears please not to kick any more conversions. So the Bears tried forward passes for the final two, and completed one of them.

During the game, the Bears had accomplished everything. Luckman had carried to a touchdown and passed to another. Hampton Pool had "read" a Baugh pass into the flat and had been there to swat it into the air and intercept it. Osmanski had gone all the way around end for a touchdown. On exactly the same play Joe Maniaci had gone forty-two yards for a touchdown. George McAfee had intercepted a LeRoy Zimmerman pass for a touchdown and center Clyde "Bulldog" Turner, a 240-pounder who could outrun most backs in the league, intercepted another and carried it twenty-one yards to score. Turner also recovered a fumble by Frank Filchock on the Redskin two-yard line and Gary Famiglietti scored on the next play. Sixteen different Chicago players had gotten into the scoring column. The Redskins gained exactly three yards on the ground.

That game is probably the one that Sid Luckman remembers best. But he did have another day when he performed more spectacularly. In 1943, at the Polo Grounds in New York, Sid's fans, many of whom had cheered for him at Erasmus Hall High School (in Brooklyn) and at Columbia, provided a "day" for

(1) The first football pro. Lawson Fiscus, known as the "Samson of Princeton," signed to play for Greensburg, Pennsylvania in 1893 at twenty dollars per game plus expenses. Fiscus had been a star halfback at Princeton in 1891 and 1892 and was noted for his tremendous strength. In this picture he is wearing the "tiger" uniform of the Princeton eleven.

(2) The Latrobe (Pennsylvania) professional football team of 1896. Marcus Saxman, extreme left in first row, holds only headgear, the rudimentary sort used by boxers. This is one of the first instances of its use and Saxman's lack of a good hair-cushion may have prompted it. In center of middle row is bearded David J. Berry, the true "Father of Professional Football" and owner of the club. Second from right in back row is Ed Abbatticchio, who earned fame later as an infielder with the Pittsburgh Pirates. Seaman, third from left in front row, became coach of Massillon Tigers in 1905.

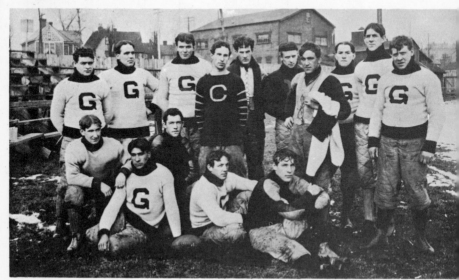

(3) Greensburg's greatest. This 1900 squad was the last professional team to represent Greensburg, Pennsylvania on the gridiron and it featured the first Indian ever to be named to a Walter Camp "All-American" team, Isaac Seneca, reputed to be greater than Thorpe. Seneca, with a big "G" on his sweater, is seated second from the left in the front row.

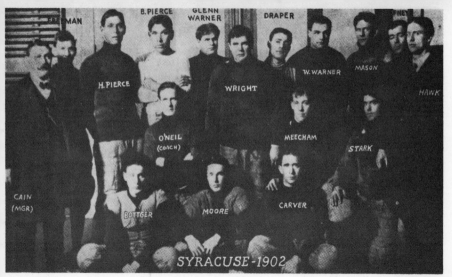

(4)   This is the Syracuse club that won the "indoor championship" in 1902 at Madison Square Garden. The Pierce brothers, the Warner Brothers, and the great Phil Draper of Williams are all in the back row. *(Pro Football Picture Service.)*

(5)   Massillon's first pro football team, recruited to fit their jerseys and to beat Canton. Two of the great Nesser brothers of Columbus played with this squad. Salmon was the finest kicker of his day. *(Pro Football Picture Service.)*

(6) The Bulldogs in their second year, with Blondy Wallace, eventual "King of the Bootleggers," as their coach, and with Pop Sweet, the forward pass expert. The Thorp is no kin to Jim. "Schrontz" is also the "Shrantz" of the Massillon Tigers of the previous season. (*Pro Football Picture Service.*)

(7) The Rochester Jeffersons of 1911, long before there was a league. Some men still wore the "smocks" of the 1890's, with pants attached. There were few helmets. Fourth from the right in the back row is Henry McDonald, probably the first Negro pro and one of the greatest, a sprinter and an accomplished boxer. In the front row with the football in his lap is Manager Leo Lyons, who played end. (*Pro Football Picture Service.*)

PAN HANDLES - 1911

8) Named for the Panhandle Division of the Pennsylvania railroad, this club, built around the six Nessers, could travel free on the railroad, for they all worked there. Their manager, Joe Carr, became president of the National League and was the man who held it together until it began to prosper. *(Pro Football Picture Service.)*

9) Jim Thorpe in Canton, Ohio. He has just kicked a football ninety yards through the air. The man in the long coat is a photographer with an old Graflex, who has just recorded the deed, while the man beside him notes it for posterity. (About 1917.) *(Pro Football Picture Service.)*

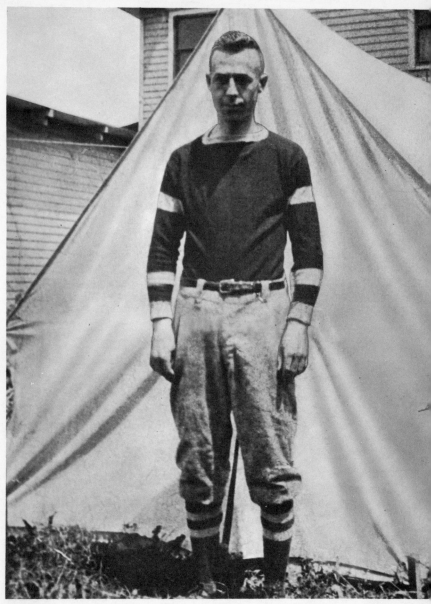

(10) Leo V. Lyons in 1917 was still playing end for his Jeffersons. He kept [i]
trim by running the roads and circling a nearby park in this approximation of h[is]
football uniform. Also, when it was too dark for anyone to notice, he tried [to]
build his strength by setting his shoulder to the portable bleachers and trying [to]
budge them over a foot or two. *(Pro Football Picture Service.)*

(11) A good study of the greatest football player who ever lived—Jim Thorpe, first president of the professional league and leader of the revived edition of the Canton Bulldogs. *(Pro Football Picture Service.)*

(12) Ben Lee Boynton, the triple-threat man from Williams, seemed too slight to be a football player. The old-fashioned pads protect him also to his shoulders. Before he joined the Rochester team, he was working in a steel mill. *(Pro Football Picture Service.)*

(13) Elmer Q. Oliphant of Purdue and West Point was chosen for the All-American team six years in a row. He needed no silk pants nor spaceman helmet to adorn his great ability. He played fullback for Rochester in 1919, the first year of the American (later National) League. (*Pro Football Picture Service.*)

(14) Red Grange's face shows the strain that even college football placed upon him, when his fame cost him needed sleep and stole his study time. *(Brown Brothers.)*

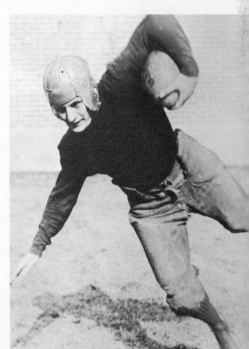

(15) Grange exhibits his drop-kicking form. *(Brown Brothers.)*

16) Grange tries to show the photogra-
her the secret of his elusiveness. *(Brown
Brothers.)*

(17)   Red Grange displays his great prowess in being able to pass the fat football of the 1920's. His torn pants and ripped jersey indicate how little pampering he received in school, hero or not. (About 1925.) *(Brown Brothers.)*

(18)   Here (at right center) is Joe Guyon, Indian teammate of Jim Thorpe's at Carlisle and Canton, an iron man who stayed in the game twenty years. At the right is Joe Griggs. (About 1920.) *(Pro Football Picture Service.)*

(19) At the extreme left of the middle row of this picture of the 1925 Rochester team (the last pro team from that city) is Eddie Lynch of Catholic University. He is the "quarrelsome character" (so designated by Westbrook Pegler) who almost ruined Red Grange's first pro appearance in Washington by fighting the Chicago Bears nearly to a standstill, with a pick-up team of semi-pros. In the center of the row is Hank Smith, named on first "all-pro" team chosen by the Cleveland *Plain Dealer* in 1920. (*Pro Football Picture Service.*)

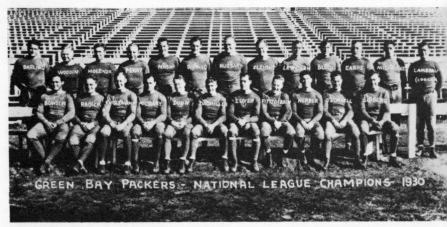

(20) The Champion Green Bay Packers of 1930 were big and tough, and several of them were hometown boys, notably Lambeau and Lewellen, the great kicker. "Blood," who started out with a partner called "Sand," was really named McNally. Cal Hubbard, in the back row, became a baseball umpire. (*Pro Football Picture Service.*)

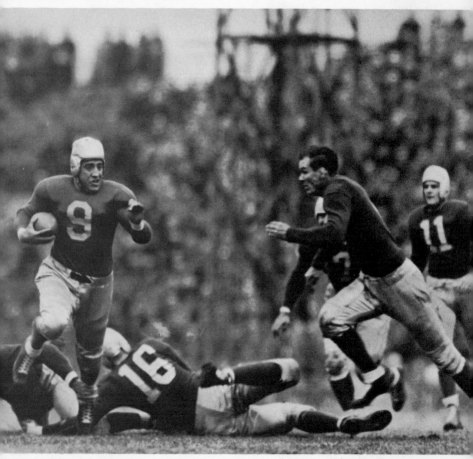

(21)   The pros in the 1930's still played without helmets if they wanted to. Here Bill Sheperd (9) of Detroit gains four yards against the Brooklyn Dodgers before the hatless Dodger (unidentified) downed him. *(Wide World Photos, Courtesy of Detroit Football Company.)*

(22) When the Lions played Pittsburgh in September 1940, Cardwell of the Lions made thirteen yards on this run. And A. B. "Happy" Chandler gained added renown as the referee. (*Detroit Football Company.*)

(23) The greatest pro passing combination in action. Cecil Isbell, being wrestled to the ground, has sent a scoring pass to Green Bay's all-time hero, Don Hutson. (Green Bay vs. Detroit Lions, 1940.) (*Detroit Football Company.*)

(24) This typical scene in prewar pro football is notable now because the man who has just let the forward pass go is Byron White, recently appointed to the United States Supreme Court. He did not like his synthetic nickname, "Whizzer." (Detroit vs. Cleveland, 1940.) (*Detroit Football Company.*)

(25) This apparent invitation to the dance is the sort of oddity that football photographers often come up with. Here a Detroit defensive man performs a square dance figure with Fiske of Pittsburgh before dumping him to the ground. (Pittsburgh at Detroit, 1940.) (*Detroit Football Company.*)

(26) This is the day Y. A. Tittle beat the Green Bay Packers, November 18, 1956. Tittle, a 49er then, is shown here scoring for San Francisco on a dive over the line, while Jerry Helluin

(27) Three great football players converge on the same point. Paul Hornung of Green Bay, escorted by guard Fred Thurston, hastens downfield while Robert Lee (Sam) Huff of the New York Giants picks out the spot where (he hopes) he will bring their journey to a violent end. (New York at Green Bay, 1961, regular-season game.) (*Vernon J. Biever.*)

(28) A strategist at work. The last play having fallen dead at his feet, with Green Bay's defensive linebacker Ray Nitschke (66) and defensive end Willie Davis (87) nailing Baltimore fullback Mark Smolinski almost before he got under way, Johnny Unitas (19) gives thought to his next play selection. (Baltimore at Green Bay, 1962.) (*Vernon J.*

(29) A unified charge by Green Bay's excellently coached line makes a highway for Tom Moore (25) straight through scrimmage. (Baltimore at Green Bay, 1962.) (*Vernon J. Biever.*)

(30)   The only sure way to stop John Henry Johnson of Pittsburgh is to take hi feet from under him with a block. Jimmy Harris of Dallas is shown doing it a Pittsburgh on November 12, 1961. (*Wide World Photos.*)

him—the typical ceremony whereby certain fans indicate their devotion through lavish gifts and tiresome speeches, requiring a stumbling, and becomingly modest speech of acceptance from the blushing recipient—to be followed customarily by a miserable performance on the field of play. Luckman, however, besides being one of the best football players alive, was a highly articulate man and a good student. His acceptance speech was modest enough but anything but stumbling. And his performance on the field was nearly miraculous.

A few moments after the game began he threw a touchdown pass to his left end, Jim Benton. At the end of that quarter, he threw a forty-four-yard pass for his second touchdown to substitute end Cornelius Berry. There was a third scoring pass to Hampton Pool and then Luckman drove his club overland to get the fourth. After Sid had thrown his fourth scoring pass (for the Bears' fifth touchdown) thirty-three yards to halfback Harry Clark, the writers and announcers began to wonder aloud about Sammy Baugh's scoring record: six touchdown passes in the same game. Could Luckman tie it? Luckman could. He completed a fifteen-yard pass to Benton for his fifth score and soon thereafter tossed a short pass over the middle to George Wilson and made it six.

But there was still time now. Could he possibly set a new record? Seven touchdown passes? Even the Giant fans began to pull for him now, as the fourth quarter faded. And sure enough, before the gun was sounded, the mighty Luckman, onetime touch football star on the streets of Flatbush, drew back his arm and fired a pass that the inspired Hampton Pool seemed to catch with his eyebrows and his fingernails, then hold it long enough to make the score. That left Luckman holding at least one passing record that the great Sammy Baugh did not have a paw on with him.

Luckman had never played T-formation before he joined the Bears and he learned the art from George Halas. He had developed one skill, however, that made his new job more natural to him. At Columbia, where he had led some valiant stands against stronger opponents, Sid had never owned much protection. He had grown used to seeing opposing tackles and ends lumbering around in his own backfield and he had become adept at darting about to escape them, always with his eyes on the watch for receivers, but picking up in his side vision the clutching hands of the enemy. So he had become really skilled at scrambling about, as every pro quarterback must, because a stationary target to a charging lineman is like a prostrate matador to a bloodthirsty bull. Of course, Sid was beat to the ground many times (he had his nose broken often), but was far better than most of his contemporaries in dodging in and out of the pocket or taking off on a dead run to get throwing room. (Some of his frustrated opponents used to snarl scornfully that Luckman never had to have his football pants laundered from the start of the season to the end.)

The T-formation spread throughout football during World War Two and afterward. Before the forties were over, some coaches had developed variations of the T, with the quarterback still handling the ball, but with a back on the wing again, where the advantage of that running start might be gained.

Bobby Layne and Johnny Lujack sat and watched Sid Luckman for most of their first year with the Bears. Then the Bears let go of Layne who, despite his admitted addiction to late hours and uproarious company, and to looking upon the wine when it was red and bubbly, eventually became one of the top signal-callers and forward passers in the game, a wrathful competitor and a man impossible to scare. Lujack, after one great season when he seemed the peer of Luckman, and possibly destined to outlast and outluck him, slowed down until he could no longer hold his place on the team. (His football genius, however, found a far more remunerative outlet in television.) So, in a sense, Luckman was never replaced; and nowadays there is no more need for a man who can only run, pass, kick, block, and call signals and also bar the gates to the enemy offense. While men do play on both offense and defense still, they do so spasmodically. And a T-formation quarterback who carries the ball regularly is not only an anachronism but an extravagance. A modern professional quarterback gets punishment enough merely holding his ground to find a pass receiver, and accepting the organized pounding, kneeing, slugging, and scratching that are his weekly lot, without courting torn ligaments by dodging goalward through a battalion of hairy-armed tacklers. As a twenty-game pitcher is not to be run ragged on the basepaths, so a top forward passer has no need to exhaust himself by sprinting downfield on every third or fourth play. In the words of the old hymn, which I once thought must have been written for pitchers or forward passers, "sufficient is thine arm alone, and our defense is sure."

Chapter X

Football, Both Ways

In 1950, the professional game divorced itself forever from the college game that gave it birth, by adopting permanently the unlimited substitution rule that had been a temporary dodge in college. From that time on, with the game able to afford squads that would be three teams deep, every professional club began to develop a distinct and separate defensive team that would march into the game en masse when the ball changed hands and that never needed to run the ball except on interception or the recovery of a fumble. And with this rule, the full-time football player, the man who had to tackle as well as block, began to dwindle like the dodo.

One of the last to retire was the best of them all—the only man alive who was ever named Most Valuable Player in all three sectors that had employed him: college, armed services, and professional league. He was Bill Dudley of Bluefield, Virginia, another one of several great stars who was first deemed "too small" to play the game. Bill played high school football as soon as they would let him have a uniform. (He tried out for two years before they did that.) He weighed 136 pounds when he first started at left halfback for Graham High School in Bluefield. Two years later, when he was ready to look for a college, he weighed 152 and had attained his full growth of 5 feet 9. The football coach at Virginia Polytechnic Institute turned Bill down when he looked for a scholarship there; but Frank Murray of the University of Virginia, impressed by Bill's ability to kick extra points (he had never missed one in high school), decided he might be worth a small investment. Bill received five hundred dollars a year to attend Virginia, and out of this he was to buy room, meals, and books. The university earned a fat return on that investment, for Bill was a star from the first moment they handed him the ball. He was never a real speedster, but he was quick off the mark, fearless, and determined that no one should stop him. Football seemed to lift him out of himself, so that he always played over his head, in a sort of frenzy. He was a full-time football player in every way: he not only played both defense and offense, he played with every ounce of his strength every moment he was on the field, and he was often carried to the sidelines exhausted.

Bill joined the Pittsburgh Steelers in 1942 to play under Dr. Jock Sutherland, the stern and dedicated Scottish gentleman who had created invincible football machines at the University of Pittsburgh, then resigned in protest when the university decided to "de-emphasize." When he reported for work that fall, Bill still had a bad ankle, earned in his last year at Virginia. But bad ankle and all, Bill played the first game against the Philadelphia Eagles and broke away in the opening minutes to run fifty-five yards for a touchdown. Against the Redskins, the next Sunday, Bill's ankle gave way and he had to be carried from the field; but in the second half he was back in the game, at his own insistence, his ankle taped up tight. He took the kickoff opening the second half and ran all the way to the other goal line with it. Nothing short of knifing, it appeared, was going to stop this solid little character from the Virginia hills. For Bill took football seriously and, no matter that he was not earning the highest salary on the team, he felt it was his duty to give out with every ounce of his energy just as long as he was able to totter.

But Bill thought everybody else should do the same and he was no man to hold his tongue if he felt that some player was dogging it a little—as football players sometimes do when the play seems headed the other way. For this he was occasionally dubbed "Beefy" by his teammates and occasionally accused of trying to coach as well as play. But he owned the admiration of all his mates, just the same, and could sometimes lift the whole team right out of itself on the wings of his own inspiration.

Bill's willingness to speak his mind, even in the austere presence of tight-lipped Jock Sutherland, who was never known to tolerate any intimacy by his charges, gave rise to a rumor that he was "hard to handle" and would probably be a headache to any coach who hired him. But Sutherland was the only coach who ever had any fault to find with Bill, either on the field or off; and the dour doctor might more properly have blamed himself. The trouble began when Bill, still unlearned in the ways of professional players, reported for practice at noon rather than at nine in the morning. (Wartime football, still starved for money and still not organized to the extent that it is today, operated on a rather haphazard schedule—with brief morning practice and only one or two meetings a week during the season.) Jock Sutherland assumed that Bill was playing the prima donna (having been Most Valuable Player in college) and took the first opportunity to snarl at Dudley when the young man, practicing forward passes in scrimmage, missed connections on three or four in a row. "It would be a damn sight easier," said Bill, in his mild Virginia voice, "if you'd use different colored jerseys so I could tell the receivers from the defenders."

Lèse majesté of this sort had been unheard of, all through the doctor's coaching career. A frightened hush fell over the field, the rugged pros all gazing fearfully at the coach like little boys in Sunday school when someone has dared talk back to the preacher. Sutherland's eyes were aflame but his voice was icy: "Are *you* coaching this team?" he demanded. "No, sir," said Bill, still unperturbed, "I am not." "Then you take orders like anyone else," the doctor snapped.

Later, when Bill undertook to apologize to Jock and suggest that if there was any dissatisfaction he be traded away, the coach tried to imply that it was the players who were dissatisfied with

Bill. But Bill knew better. The only players who ever resented having Bill Dudley on the team were the ones who thought that a professional football player had a right to loaf through most of a game, as long as he gave the appearance of activity. Dudley had simply been brought up differently. He did not know what it was to loaf, or to let a teammate down, or even to take it easy when the going seemed hopeless.

His apologies to the grim Scotsman did not make Bill's life with the Steelers any easier and he soon decided that, much as he admired Jock as a coach, he could not put up forever with the good gentleman's icy sarcasms. His contract expired two years after his return from service and he declared he was through with pro football. "I'm too small for the game," Bill said. But what he meant was that he could not play ball with a coach who, out of spite, would force him into a game when he was badly hurt. Bill took a job as coach at the University of Virginia but the Detroit Lions that summer received permission from Pittsburgh to deal with Dudley and their emissaries trailed him to Los Angeles (where he was honeymooning). Bill finally agreed to a contract discussion. He flew to Detroit then to sign for the highest salary in pro football at the time—twenty thousand dollars a year.

Coaches and fellow players in Detroit watched Dudley uneasily at first, expecting him to strut about giving instructions rather than taking them. But he buckled down to practice as if he were just trying out for the team and set even the recruits an example of how to keep the mouth shut and the ears open, and work every minute. By the time the season opened (in Forbes Field, Pittsburgh, of all places), the Detroit team met and, by secret ballot, elected Bill Dudley captain. He received every vote except his own. Everyone on the squad knew, as even old Dr. Sutherland must have known, that Bill was the one player who could be counted on to put out his full effort with every tick of the official clock. He was not inordinately fast, yet he was the most feared kickoff returner in the game, averaging some thirty yards a try. He passed "sidearm," yet he had a high percentage of connections. He was "too small," but he was hardly ever hurt too badly to play. He was the league's top ground-gainer, yet he was also one of the fiercest defensive tacklers and the best in the game at interceptions. He was *always* trying to gain.

It was part of Bill's creed, for instance, that when he played safetyman, as he usually did, he should catch *every* punt and try to run it back, especially if grounding the punt was going to cost his team severely. If a kick seemed headed out of bounds, Bill, if he felt there was the least chance of his catching it, would give it a try and endeavor to recover at least a yard or two of the ground the kick had covered. And it was this determination that led to what was perhaps Bill's greatest run, and the one that will stay in the record books a long time.

Bill made the run in 1950, when he was playing for the Washington Redskins against the Pittsburgh Steelers on a muddy field on a wet December day. Joe Geri of the Steelers had boomed a towering punt diagonally across the field for some sixty yards. It was clearly going to bounce over the goal line, or more likely, sail across the sideline in the coffin corner. Everyone on both teams, acknowledging these possibilities, seemed to have frozen into position to watch—everyone, that is, except Dudley, who was on the dead run to his right to try to nail the ball before it could set his team back practically on its goal line. He kept his feet inbounds but had to reach out of bounds to make the catch. The ball landed in his hands and he clutched it to his chest, then look inquiringly at the nearest official, who stood silently only three or four yards away. The official nodded, meaning yes, you are still in bounds, and Bill, after one brief glance at the stock-still figures far up the field, took off for the Pittsburgh goal. There was one potential tackler who had come within ten yards of Bill, but Bill quickly faked him out of position by pretending to cut back into the field, only to return to the sideline and pound along in the mud. Now Bill's teammates came to life and gathered to clear the way. The Steelers were just too slow to realize what had befallen them and by the time they started after Bill he had a phalanx of blockers to guard him—and he himself was speeding down the sideline like a thief. He went ninety-six yards to a touchdown and not a hostile hand was laid upon him. "I still don't quite understand it," says Bill.

One thing that everyone understood about Bill Dudley, however, was the quality of his effort. It was *always* his utmost, no matter what the score, the weather, or the tactical situation. He could not even quit if he wanted to, and once took his place in the huddle when he was completely unconscious and only failed to go through the play because his muscles would not respond to his befuddled will. He had just completed a punt return for a touchdown; his team (the Detroit Lions—this was in 1947) led the Chicago Bears 14–0 and were starting to move again. Bill started around left end with the ball, eluding tackle Fred Davis of the Bears. Davis, enraged at this added indignity and unable to grab hold of Dudley, swung a heavily taped forearm that caught Bill just above the ear. Bill went down, got up, took his place in the huddle, heard the play given, then just stood there, swaying like a small tree in a rising wind. His teammates looked back and called time, then led Bill to the sidelines, where it took him some minutes to come to his senses.

"Where am I?" he whispered to the attentive trainer.

"Chicago."

"What's the score?"

"We're ahead, 14–0."

Bill digested this intelligence slowly, and shook his head a little to reawaken his memory.

"Am I married?" he whispered.

He was. He had been married the previous July, to his school days sweetheart.

Bill had made an even longer run for a touchdown one day with an intercepted pass; but that was in a post-season game in 1942 between the champion Redskins and the pro All-Stars, after Bill's first season in professional football, and just before he entered the Army Air Corps. It will not, on that account, live in the record books. The All-Stars that season were mostly Chicago Bears, who had lost to the Redskins in the championship playoff. This was a benefit game, had no effect on team standings, and the only real motivating force the All-Stars had was to square things with the Redskins.

Most of the players being far from home (the game was played in Philadelphia), they put in more time exploring what dim oases of drink and dalliance had managed to persist through the wartime blackout than they did in running through plays and pass defenses. Part of the kick had gone out of the game anyway, even for the vengeance-seekers, when it was learned that Sammy Baugh, the natural rival of All-Star Sid Luckman, had packed up and taken off for Texas. But Bill Dudley was out to give his utmost, and his determination seemed to infect his temporary teammates. The All-Stars beat the Redskins 17–14, and one of the touchdowns was supplied by Bill, who picked off a Redskin pass on his two-yard line and took it ninety-eight yards the other way for a score. Again he required the help of his mates and because he had never let them down, they did not fail him now. Big George Wilson, permanent end with the Chicago Bears and never a teammate of Bill's before, got him off to a running start by violently erasing a tackler who almost stopped Bill before he started. Some forty yards later, Dudley was in trouble again, for there were plenty of men on the field that day who were faster afoot than he was and one of them had caught up with him at midfield. But lo and behold, here was George Wilson again, who had risen up from his first effort on the two-yard line and had caught up with Bill. With another mighty swipe of his body, he took the last tackler off his feet and let Bill become a hero. It was the least he could do for a guy who would put out the way Bill did.

Bill Dudley earned the highest salary of his day, yet he did not grow rich, nor did he ever sample the sort of wealth and glory that accrued, even in those days, to the top baseball players. The game of professional football was still struggling and still haphazardly organized. Chicago had two teams, where there was really patronage enough for only one. And Boston, where George

Preston Marshall had left a bad taste in the mouths of many football fans by his shifting of the franchise some years before, could hardly support any team at all, and certainly not one that could never win as many games as it lost and seemed doomed to dwell in the cellar of the league forever.

Times were getting better nevertheless. The 1946 championship game between the Chicago Bears and the New York Giants at New York drew the fattest gate since the day Red Grange had come to town and all the participating players pocketed well over one thousand dollars each. And the creation of a new "major league," the All-America Conference, despite hungry days for the club owners and acres of empty seats, meant competition for players and higher salaries. (Even in the forties there had been men who would take home only $150 a game.)

But franchises were abandoned or declared forfeit, owners lost heart, and new teams were born and buried in the same season. Owners fired their coaches in despair, or hired famous names in the fond belief that fans would come flocking to observe the hero in action. Owner Dick Richards of the Detroit Lions reasoned that fans would like to have something to watch between the halves other than some kids chasing a football, or some cops chasing kids, so he hired the director of the Wayne University band, Graham Overgaard, to create half-time entertainment for the Detroit customers. Before long every other owner in the league had adopted the custom of putting on a show of some sort during the half-time interval. They had to imitate Richards in other ways too, for he clothed his players in matching uniforms and headgear of spectacular shades, so that the hand-me-down appearance of some of the opposing teams' outfits shamed the wearers and the watchers both.

Richards was the first man to put a professional football game on radio (in 1934) and he was ready for television with a team that made a smart appearance even on the bench. (Dick used to make sure the illusion was sustained off the gridiron too, by supplying made-to-measure outfits of sport jackets and slacks to the entire clan.) Under the influence of Richards and a few others who had seen the value of showmanship in the big college games, the pro game grew out of its sloppy, sandlot past. Soon every player was required to wear a helmet and a pair of socks as part of his uniform. (There had been a fad, beginning in the late twenties, for college players to go stockingless, regardless of temperature, in imitation of some of the daredevil vagabonds of the southern gridiron.) The demands of television meant prompt starts too, and well-dressed officials (and occasional long time-outs to work the "commercial" in). There were faster substitutions now and quicker lineups, so that spectators at the professional games might actually see more football plays in the same period of time than a college fan ever saw.

In some parks spasmodic efforts were made to synthesize the rah-rah spirit, through the employment of short-skirted cheerleaders and the creation of "fight songs" (some of which may eventually prove useful for sending our grandchildren into paroxysms of incredulous mirth). But the pro football fan, who was beginning to evolve now as a separate phylum, had no rah-rah in him, raucous as he could become, and he was not to be regimented into celebrating the glories of Victory with Honor, with or without music. It was not the lack of college spirit that had kept fans away from the football parks. It was mostly sheer ignorance, too often fostered by certain sportswriters, who did not believe the professional game could be as thrilling as the college version. When television began to allow fans to see for themselves, they recognized that they had been missing a great spectacle, and one in which it was easy to involve one's self, heart, soul, voice, and paycheck.

The game had always been tough and it remained tough, even when it began to prosper. But it was no longer ragged, or sloppily equipped, or given to dreary pulling and hauling.

Improved scouting and the general improvement of the breed increased the supply of young giants who could run fast and hard. But in the teams in the early forties they could not yet afford the type of organization they now own. The team worked out together briefly each day during the season and once or twice a week the coach would gather them all together to make diagrams on a blackboard and generally face up to the prospect of playing a football game come Sunday.

After the war, as patronage, under the beneficent influence of the "52–20" system that gave hundreds of thousands of young men the time and the spare cash to attend ball games, began to swell, professional football clubs went on a year-round basis, with full-time staffs and offices that rivaled those bragged about by the big universities. Exhibition games proved attractive to fans and more and more of them were scheduled, until professional football had its minions all suited up in midsummer (for early practice) and kept them occupied until the following January, when there were always post-season games to drain out a few more dollars from fans before the long dry season set in.

In the late forties, all the professional clubs were spending far more money than they wanted to. The new All-America Conference forced the National Football League to bid up its salaries, to increase its scouting staffs, and to improve the plants they operated from. Soon the professional football player was averaging about six thousand dollars a year—with a few of the lesser lights, of course, still getting barely enough to justify their staying away from a year-round job—and most of the major stars getting at least a respectable full year's salary. Football players in the off-season still wrestled professionally, or coached or officiated, or delivered bottled soda pop from a truck. But at least while the money was coming in, they began to live like professional athletes in other lines. No longer did they cram themselves into second-hand limousines to make their road trips. While they often rode day coaches still, there were occasional pullmans. And the quick-and-dirty sandwich bar and the milk in a cardboard container yielded to the tablecloth dining room and the chrome coffeepot.

Men still saw their clubs go broke in the game, as the Lyonses and the Berrys had in earlier days, but now they were men who could afford it—millionaires who were looking for ways to enhance the "public image," with now and then a random son of the rich who wanted to make a name as a "sportsman." For four years the two football leagues ran their shows in bitter opposition to each other. Chicago during this time had a third team (the Rockets, later renamed the Hornets) inflicted upon it; and only the perennially successful Bears made a profit there. Of the seventeen teams in the two leagues, only two were safely in the black for the season of 1949. Others came out even or were grateful for only small losses, while a few reported disasters.

The game that had been able to subsist two and a half decades earlier on gates of five to ten thousand now needed steady patronage of thirty thousand at every game. Only in Chicago and Washington was this assured. New York had too many teams, with the Giants and the Yankees, the Bulldogs and the Dodgers all at one time or another trying to secure all the customers there were. The Cleveland Rams gave up before the Cleveland Browns (the best and most exciting team in the new conference) and fled to Los Angeles, where monumental expenses made them wish they had stayed home, or had merely dropped dead. Buffalo, despite a rugged line and a wonderfully ingenious quarterback named George Ratterman, could neither win consistently nor draw consistently, and Boston was simply lucky that owner Ted Collins had all that cash to spend.

The only two winners, in the ledger warfare, were the two who fought most earnestly against the inevitable peace treaty that would bring the two leagues together, divide up the market, and make possible the "normalizing" of wages for the hired hands. George Preston Marshall of Washington and George Halas of Chicago would have much preferred to see the new league tumble into the nethermost deeps of bankruptcy. Marshall even invited the gasping owners of the Los Angeles team in his own league to go down for the third time and get it over with. But eventually everybody saw the light and a pact was signed that finally set up the "natural" inter-city and inter-region rivalries that have long been the life-source of professional sports.

Marshall had fought bitterly against the amalgamation because it would legalize the invasion of his private preserve by

the Baltimore team. But that team folded after one season of the
new combined league and when it came back it was listed in the
"western" conference (and thus did not play a conflicting schedule), while George Marshall's Washington team continued in
the "eastern" grouping.

Chapter XI

Brown of the Browns

The new league prospered through more than the simple pooling of lean purses and the injection of hot rivalries. The All-America Conference contributed to the new league one of the true geniuses of the game, who had made professional football into a contest between wide-open offenses, as stirring as "firehouse" basketball had been when it first broke out its five-man attack. So enormous was the influence of Paul Brown that it might truly be said (as Otto Graham, the Cleveland quarterback, did say at a "peace banquet" one night) that the All-America Conference really absorbed the older league. Certainly it was Paul Brown strategy and the Paul Brown pass patterns that soon prevailed and that helped to prompt the sudden upsurge in attendance.

Paul Brown, as seems entirely fitting, won his first fame as a coach in the very seedbed of professional football—Massillon, Ohio, at a high school where it was whispered there was as much football recruiting as there was at Ohio State University, where Coach Brown also served a successful term. He had coached for a while at Severn Academy and later at the Great Lakes Naval Station too and never ran into any opposition he could not surmount, nor any experience that suggested to him he could not operate a football team better than any other man in the business.

A slender, balding, and cultured man who talked football with a religious intensity, Brown had a brain that worked every minute on the numberless possible maneuvers offering to a man who had eleven players to move about on a hundred-yard field. The game he played against his rivals became a form of chess with muscles and the manner in which he flouted the moss-grown orthodoxies of the game enlightened his followers and his foes —and enraptured the fans.

But before his influence on the playing field came to public notice, Brown wrought a wholesale change in the organization of the game. In an effort to recover the cohesiveness and the *esprit de corps* that had long seemed the peculiar feature of the college game but often withered quickly away when the players turned pro, he put an end to the loosely programed practices and random skull sessions, in which the better-paid stars sometimes doped off to dwell on the money they might have to spend on payday. Brown, not the least bit abashed by their size and maturity, regimented his grown-up charges like schoolboys. No more did they ramble about town in their off-hours seeking non-football companionship, or picking up extra dollars in part-time jobs. No more did they doze through skull sessions on the theory that they had heard all this stuff before. Paul Brown football was a full-time job that paid a full-time salary. Anything short of complete involvement, Brown held, was semipro football and not to be tolerated on his team.

The Cleveland Browns, of whom Paul Brown became manager and part owner as well as coach, lived together at the practice camp and on their travels, obeyed a curfew, avoided heavy drink and light ladies, ate the same food, and carried college notebooks and pencils to his lectures. If they needed time off for anything—from an ailing aunt to a tooth extraction—they had to ask for it. And sometimes they had only their lunch hour to perform their private business in. This sort of regimentation being the common lot of nearly every man who worked for wages, it hardly scandalized any of the fans who learned about it. But there were sportswriters and some well-publicized players who viewed the whole business with open scorn.

This was schoolboy, pencil-and-notebook football, they averred, and damn poor business for a grown man with football talent. But the pencil-and-notebook business was only a small part of a carefully planned and well-reasoned program based on teaching methods that had produced results in a half dozen fields of human endeavor. The scholars at the Paul Brown football school learned football as some men learned sciences. They saw it demonstrated or diagramed, they heard it explained, they wrote it down, and then they did it. And they did it and did it and did it, until every move in every mass maneuver had become instinctive as walking or swimming.

No matter how long a man had been with the team, or how often he had listened to the lesson on which opponent the guard was to trap, or what move the end had to make on a screen pass, he was required to write it all down again on a fresh page in his notebook. Every man on the squad had to be able to diagram every detail of every play in the book. And in practice each man performed and repeated his separate part until he meshed with his teammates like a ratchet wheel in a complex machine.

A member of the Cleveland Browns was a member of the Browns all the year round, no matter that he might find temporary employment in the late winter and early spring. He reported for training at Hiram, Ohio in the heat of summer and lived like a soldier preparing for a special mission, with calisthenics, signal practice, drills, and dummy scrimmages every day, early bedtime and special diet. This developed, of course, especially among the old-timers, many strong resentments and muttered threats to tell the "goddam tyrant" to take his whole team and commit it to some unmentionable fate. But it also developed the sought-after *esprit de corps* (with the coach sometimes as the necessary "common enemy"), and a feeling of belonging together that would save many a yard on the field of battle. Men with a real sense of unity always seem less likely to let the unit down.

Brown developed strong organization in other ways too. The front office became a full-time job for a number of men and ceased being a pleasant fall hobby for a man with money to waste, or to hide from the tax collector. Scouts were employed who had some sense of what the team needed in the way of strength or speed and they ranged all over the continent, no longer depending on sports publicity to guide them to the top players. They would recruit men from campuses most city sports-writers did not know existed and had no shame about offering to public view at high admissions "stars" that had never shone in but the smallest and most distant skies. (Curly Lambeau and George Halas had all along been signing players who had not even made an "all-county" eleven, but Paul Brown systematized the cultivation of these remote garden patches.) Brown himself had a sharp eye for football talent and often developed it where others hardly noticed its existence. Marion Motley, the first in a series of piston-legged Negro fullbacks who would make yardage records with the Browns, came from the University of Nevada, where All-America selections had been somewhat thinner than snow, and he had no publicity fanfare to precede his professional career. Indeed, when Paul Brown first noticed him, at the Great Lakes Naval Training Station, Motley was something of a for-gotten man, who was not even carried along when the team left town. The Browns' most sensational pass catcher, Mac Speedie, was recruited from Utah, and Ray Renfro from North Texas State.

Conversely, Brown had no compunction about passing up a highly-touted star who did not seem destined to fit into the Brown complex. A few years after Motley had joined the Browns, Ne-vada produced a thoroughly publicized passer and runner named Stan Heath, the country's leading ground gainer. He signed with the Browns but immediately scorned the notion of carrying a notebook and pencil to "class" just as if *he* had more to learn about football. Brown turned him loose at once. He was ob-viously not going to adjust to the boss's ways and Brown wanted Heath to have a chance to sign on elsewhere without delay. (Heath joined the Green Bay Packers and lasted but one sea-son.)

Paul Brown was devoted to offense. The free-substitution rule of 1950 permitted him to concentrate on this aspect of the game as no one ever had done before. It was only natural that his choicest players—men who in an earlier day could have starred on defense too—played only one way and came into the game, whenever Cleveland took the ball, all rested and ready to roll. Brown's offense seemed based so thoroughly on the forward pass that some casual observers felt he had forgotten about the running game completely. He had not made any such error, of course; indeed, he always maintained an even balance between passing and running plays, stressing whatever part of the game best suited the players currently enrolled. But he did have his quarterback throwing passes when old-time coaches would have brained a man for even suggesting such a move. Once when Cleveland was two touchdowns ahead, with the ball on their own one-yard line, Otto Graham, the quarterback, faded into his own end zone, shot a short swift pass to Mac Speedie on the one-yard line, and saw the man who was paced to fit his name scamper the remaining ninety-nine yards for a touchdown. Such a move was bughouse! It was immoral! At least in 1948 it was. Perhaps that is the chief reason why it worked.

In the early 1950's, as other coaches tried to imitate Brown's heart-lifting style, the free use of the forward pass—which some thought was Brown's real secret—did seem in a fair way to be turning professional football into a form of basketball-with-body-contact. Now and then a spectator might see a football team drive the whole length of the field without once running the ball. Experts of the day (but not Paul Brown) taught recruits and observers that "passing is 75 percent of the game." And some mighty passers did evolve and perform some exciting feats. But once Sammy Baugh and Sid Luckman had grown older, there was none for a long time who could match the great Otto Graham—a thinker, an improviser, and a daring strategist, perfectly suited to the type of football Paul Brown taught. Graham was a big man—212 at his best playing weight—and was surprisingly fast and light on his feet. He also possessed a gift that most great football backs and all great basketball players (Otto was a basketball star at Northwestern) have owned—remarkable peripheral vision, the ability to spot moving figures and to gauge speed and distances without looking directly at the target.

Paul Brown first saw Otto Graham when Northwestern played Brown's Ohio State team before the war. Graham played tailback in the single-wing formation that day, not calling plays but running, passing, blocking, and doing much of the tackling on defense. What impressed Brown most, however, and what stuck in his mind from that time forth, was a single pass that Graham made. Running out to his left, while his receiver moved across the backfield on a dead run in the opposite direction, Otto turned and drove his pass on a trolley wire straight into the arms of the receiver, who did not even need to break his stride to take the ball and keep going with it. In the better part of two seconds Otto had timed the man's speed, timed his own speed that was stretching the gap between them, and had put the ball exactly where it had to be. This converted Brown. And it moved him a few years later, when both he and Graham were still in service, to sign Otto to a professional contract. After Otto's first great season had gotten under way, Brown tore up the contract and substituted a better one.

At this time the Cleveland Browns were still in the All-America Conference and still hampered somewhat by the rule that allowed only three substitutes in any series of downs—just enough to rescue the kicker or other key player from defensive play. Graham usually played both ways then, for he was the strongest defensive man on the team. His remarkable wide-angle vision served him well on interceptions and he did not often meet a man who could outrun him, or one he could not stop dead in his tracks if he got a clear shot at him.

Graham's passing eventually became his trademark and he was named Automatic Otto because of the frightening precision with which he hit his targets. Brown's pass patterns, which were causing the game of football to flower into something altogether new and inexpressibly thrilling—like the symmetrical and unpredictable explosions of color in a kaleidoscope—provided all types of targets for Otto. First a back might "come out," then another, then a third, then an end might flare to the sidelines or, on what became known as the "fly" pattern, sprint out beyond the safety-man.

Other coaches had sent several potential receivers downfield and had worked out plays in which decoys might dodge and fake about in one zone while the receiver was shaking himself loose far away. But before Paul Brown's day, passing was a man-to-man affair—Isbell to Hutson, Herber to Hutson, Filchock to Farkas—with the receiver selected in the huddle and the other eligible men merely exhorted to stay out of the way. When the pass went to some man other than the first choice it was often an act of desperation.

In Paul Brown's patterns, however, every eligible man had a complete job to do, with the common aim of opening up one area where the prime target would appear. The number one receiver was still selected in the huddle. But Brown would rejoice if the pass went instead to some other man who had done a better job of getting a lead on his defender. And every eligible man had a path to pursue in which he was well rehearsed. If the prime receiver were to be sent behind the defending halfback but in front of the safetyman, then there would be another eligible receiver to draw the safetyman further downfield and still another to pull the defending halfback in close, so that the target area would be made as wide-open as possible.

Every man on Brown's team, thanks to his patient drilling, knew in exactly what order the receivers were to "come out" and where they were meant to appear. But only Otto could hold them all in his view at once, so that, if his number one target were well covered, the man who had a step advantage on his defender, or better still the man who had found open pasture far downfield, would spring instantly into focus.

Some of Brown's detractors liked to say that he gave his quarterback no option, and that his receiver was always chosen in advance with no alternate permitted. But this is just the opposite of Brown's aim in working his patterns out so completely. There were no "decoys" in a Paul Brown pass play. Each man had a set task to perform which might have as its primary aim the luring of a defender away from the target area. But he was still a potential receiver, fully prepared to shake loose from the man assigned him and take the throw himself. The quarterback could still make his choice of receivers if the number one man had run into trouble. The only stratagem Brown deplored was the panicky flinging of passes out into the flat, or side area, when the target did not open up and the enemy crowded close.

Of course no quarterback, not even Otto Graham, performed a pass play by himself. The rest of the team had to provide the protective pocket from which Otto could look out upon the field and select his target. Most valuable of all in keeping Otto unhindered long enough for him to get the pass away was Marion Motley, the explosively fast fullback who was so shifty, so quick on his feet, and so alert that, big and fast as the man might be who would first come barreling through to destroy Graham, Motley could still get his shoulder on him and run him in a helpless semicircle, out of reach of his target, while Otto coolly picked out the man to deliver the football to, ten yards or fifty yards away.

In the early years of football's golden decade—the 1950's—the quarterback became the most valuable man on the squad, as priceless an asset as the pitcher is to a baseball team, or even more so, because he often directed the strategy in detail as well as performing the feats of strength and accuracy that would propel the ball deep down the field. Defense weaknesses that might permit a score could be remedied in two or three swift blows by air as soon as the ball was recovered. The quarterback therefore was withdrawn immediately when the team went on defense and deposited on the bench, lapped in warm wool, to be rushed back to the battle line only when the moment returned to attack.

But Graham, big as a fullback, fast as an end, and light-footed as a tennis player, was often used on defense even when the rules allowed any player to be freely shuttled in and out. There was no man on the squad better as a safetyman—the final defender of the goal and the man who was charged with halting the long touchdown pass that might spoil a victory within ten seconds. Otto did more than pass on offense, too, for he excelled at the "quarterback draw"—the most devastating play in football, the dropping back of the quarterback as if to pass, and his sudden reversal and plunge down the middle, along the very path of his retreat. On this play (which Otto called only when the coach insisted on it), often the whole center of the line has charged in upon the passer to be nudged aside by blockers, and the center linebacker has picked up a potential receiver and trailed him to one side, leaving most of the field open ahead of the quarterback. Spectators are sometimes prone to interpret this play as a haphazard decision by the quarterback, for it does seem as if he had planned to pass, then suddenly changed his mind.

The free substitution rule permitted Brown to adopt one method that became his trademark, his glory, and finally, in the eyes of his critics, his chief weakness. Every time the ball was whistled dead with Cleveland on the offense, Brown would send a guard or an end racing in from the sidelines to tell the quarterback what play to call. In the beginning, he allowed Graham, who was one of the few football strategists equal to Paul Brown in knowledge and in craft, to call plays on his own, especially when some daring innovation was called for, or when the defense seemed confident that they knew what was coming next. But ultimately Brown took all the basic brainwork upon himself, despite occasional gripings from the locker room or from the stands and frequently doleful comments in the press, where one or two writers brought up on college football still held that the game should be left in the hands of the "boys."

The professionals were not boys, however, but men who were playing their game for a living. The immediate object of their efforts was to win ball games, that the hearts of their followers might be made glad and the gate receipts wax great. The ability of Paul Brown, once a 152-pound quarterback at Miami of Ohio, to win ball games for the Browns needed no elucidation, because the Browns, after having taken first prize in the All-America Conference in all four years of its existence, took the regional title six times in their first six years in the National

League. In that period they also won the top title in 1950, 1954, and 1955.

The title game in 1955, played against the Los Angeles Rams in Los Angeles Coliseum before eighty-five thousand spectators, was the last game Otto Graham played for Cleveland. He won it for them 38–14, scoring two touchdowns himself (he was never a rocking-chair quarterback) and throwing to Renfro and end Dante Lavelli for two more. Out of the lavish gate, each member of the Browns brought home thirty-five hundred dollars, as compared to the eleven-hundred-dollar check they each earned in the title game played against the same team five seasons before.

It was only natural that many a graduate of the Cleveland Browns should carry away resentments against the boss that had never been charged off, just as many baseball players who had suffered under John McGraw's tight discipline and strict control of the game's strategy could be expected to go home and dream (as one star once confessed he had) of beating the Little Napoleon over the head. Paul Brown is no John McGraw. Indeed, he seems more like a school superintendent than an athletic coach; in manner he is often gentle and even withdrawn (although fierce as an eagle when aroused). But he does resemble McGraw in his insistence on calling all the pitches and in his burning determination to win.

But when you look at the matter calmly, as no one could ever do during a football game, there is no reason why a football coach, bearing the ultimate responsibility for the winning or losing of the game, should not direct his team just as closely as a baseball manager does. Much fairy tale is preached concerning the quarterback's greater knowledge of the immediate tactical situation—of his ability to survey the defensive formation, detect their moves in advance, and call the "automatic" (one of an agreed-upon group of check-off or alternate plays that can be rung in by an audible signal after the teams have lined up), but actually such plays are used less than many people imagine and are often disastrously unsuccessful. No quarterback can really count on a modern defensive player's giving his moves away in advance. Some linebackers like to pretend they are about to "blitz"—charge in upon the quarterback—on nearly every play, so a check-off call may be made upon fake evidence and lead to a loss. And there are quarterbacks who just do not own the mental agility to diagnose a defense at a glance, yet who can execute their own required moves with consummate skill. The automatic is really a salvation play to call when a sudden change in the defense promises disaster.

Bobby Layne, a tough, dedicated, and generously gifted signal caller, is often pointed to as a man who uses "automatics" consistently. Yet Bobby, out of sheer impatience and fighting spirit, most often starts his plays on the "first audible"—the very first number he calls aloud after the huddle, so it would hardly be possible for him to signal a change in plans as frequently as people say he does.

Paul Brown himself insisted that he did provide check-offs to be called by audible signal in certain circumstances and he gave the back of his hands to his critics, including his quarterback, Milt Plum, whom he traded to Detroit for a lad named Jim Ninowski—himself a former Brown. When the 1962 season began, Brown suddenly abandoned his continuous messenger system and let the quarterback call many of the plays in the first part of each ball game. This, said Brown, was merely because he decided that it helped Ninowski assume leadership. (Some skeptics did whisper that owner Modell of the Browns had grown restive under the criticism from fans and sportswriters and asked Brown to modify his system.)

Of course Brown was not the only coach to send plays in from the sidelines. Before the unlimited substitution system permitted the use of messengers, Greasy Neale in Philadelphia was employing baseball-type signals—movements of the hands, arms, and legs—to tell his quarterback what to call. And Curly Lambeau of the Redskins, unfamiliar with the T-formation and so reluctant to send in plays, still, among his many sideline gestures, included waves and postures and movements that indicated the type of defense he wanted. In 1962, Tom Landry of the Dallas Cowboys, when he had two sound quarterbacks, used to alternate them from play to play, sending each man in all primed with the play and its alternative.

One consideration that the critics of the messenger system do not often deal with is the responsibility accepted by the coach. Many a pro coach, including some who join with outside commentators in tut-tutting Paul Brown's tight control of every play, secretly wished he had the courage to imitate Brown. But when you frankly make the moves yourself you had better be right. It is easy to recall a quarterback and let the catcalls bound off his back. But not many coaches are ready to expose their own tender flesh to the heat that is visited upon the man who makes too many wrong decisions.

Paul Brown, however, never blamed his players for poor play call, but only for failure to "execute" properly. He could be bitterly sarcastic at failure and did not always remember to butter a man up for doing well; but if the fans wanted someone to yell at, Brown was willing to let them yell at him. And they did indeed on many occasions yell their derision at him, sometimes even ridiculing his play calls by predicting them aloud from the stands, particularly when his hotfoot messengers seemed to be bringing in plays right out of the book, rather than the dazzling strokes of genius the situation appeared to cry for. Yet season after season there are relatively few observers ready to bet that Paul Brown, wherever he may be, will not once more take it all.

Chapter XII

The Grown-up Game

Professional football never extensively degraded itself by trying to keep colored men out of the organized game, even though occasional Negro players in the early days ran into rough treatment at the hands of opponents or fans. There were Negro stars, however, from the very earliest times. Fritz Pollard, Brown University's All-American ball carrier, who used to run so close to the ground it was said that tackles would actually slide over him, starred with Akron in 1920 and played in Milwaukee and in Providence as well as with the Hammond Pros, who also carried on their roster another great Negro from Brown, Jay Mayo (Inky) Williams. But before these men had even entered college there was a professional colored star in Rochester named Henry McDonald, who first played football at Canandaigua Academy and joined the Rochester Jeffersons in 1912.

Henry, a handsome, long-legged man, played for Rochester in one of their first games against the Canton Bulldogs where he found himself face to face, early in the game, with one of the unreconstructed Confederates then working for Jim Thorpe. The Confederate, instead of tackling, or trying to tackle McDonald, stopped dead in his tracks and drew back his fist. "Black is black," said he, "and white is white. Where Ah come from, they don't mix!" McDonald, an accomplished boxer, also stopped dead and faced the white man, still holding the football, but quietly awaiting whatever might betide. Fortunately Jim Thorpe, who, being part Irish and part Sac and Fox Indian, might be said to have been racially neutral by heritage, hurried up and laid hold of his southern cohort. "We're here to play football," he growled. "So let's play football." The game went on then, with no further unscheduled violence.

What might have followed from that incident had the fight been allowed to flare, no man can say; but it is possible that the trouble might have spread the taint of Jim Crow so that it lasted into the league—both Rochester and Canton being among the league's charter members.

It never did, however, and nearly every team eventually carried Negroes on its roster. There was bound to be dirty work, of course. Southern men new to the league sometimes dealt out an extra wallop to a Negro opponent when the play was over, or managed to employ a closed fist during a tackle of a Negro runner, and the colored men were not above getting a little of their own back when the chance was offered. But the pros were proud of their toughness and hardly anyone ever complained or ever carried the matter away from the field of play. And because every Negro star had big tough white players on his own side too, the roughhouse did not develop along racial lines.

Negro stars at the eastern universities could always find a professional team to play for. The salaries offered them were not in the beginning as high as those given to white men, because their bargaining position was not as strong. Away from professional football the work that awaited the colored man was always manual and sometimes menial and invariably low-paid. He had no stockbrokers beckoning, nor telephone company soliciting him with talk of the big future, nor insurance companies promising him untold thousands in commissions through inveigling his "college contacts" into insuring themselves for more than they were worth.

Still, while the game was on, they were accepted as equals by their teammates, who often found it easy to forget in the heat of play that there was any difference in skin color at all. Paul Robeson of Rutgers, an All-American like Pollard, played with Pollard on the Akron Steels and the Milwaukee Badgers. Iowa sent their All-American tackle, Duke Slater, into the professional game where his exceptional leg drive and quick-charging style excited fans for ten seasons. In the modern game, Slater, who was rangy and fast, might have played fullback and possibly have been rated near the greatest of them all, Jimmy Brown of today's Cleveland Browns. But Duke Slater would have been required to wear a helmet today. In his best days at Iowa, in the 1920's, he and two of his white teammates, Leo Kriz, right guard, and Craven Shuttleworth, halfback, preferred to play bareheaded. Nor was any of them ever removed from a game because of injuries.

The last holdout against the hiring of Negro players was, naturally, George Preston Marshall of the Washington Redskins, who for a long time made a special promotion of the fact that his lineup was lily white. All the Redskins' games were broadcast on a Dixie circuit and they counted on their Confederate fans to keep the cashbox full even long after they stopped winning championships. Consistently Marshall passed up great Negro players whom he might have chosen in the draft and who might have won some titles for him. His team were Redskins, and his half-time entertainment was provided by a band in Indian costumes, but it was a strictly whiteskin patronage that he sought and there were more Rebel yells than Indian war whoops from his grandstand. Marshall liked to pretend in public that it was mere chance that left his team the only one in the league with never a Negro player; but privately he vowed he would not be "pushed around" by the forces that were trying to get the Redskins back into the Union. When finally he sought the use of a federally financed stadium, he was required to put an immediate end to his lily-white policy and, despite the many letters and calls he received, and the pickets who appeared to exhort him to remain a secessionist even though the team might go broke in the process, Marshall surrendered. In 1961 he made a deal that brought Bobby Mitchell, sprinting halfback, from the Cleveland Browns to the Redskins. Nor was the thoroughly mongrelized human race set back a single century thereby. To some people it seemed

that the Washington Redskins, or their owner, had achieved
adulthood at last.

Bobby Mitchell, with the Redskins, has seemed to become
twice the player he was with Cleveland. This was chiefly because Washington could use him as a flanker, where his chief
task was to catch passes and where he did not have to subject himself to the smashing gang-tackles that had so often caused him to
fumble when he was trying to "go inside" as a running back with
the Browns. Thanks to Bobby, and a few others, the Redskins in
1962 lifted themselves from the cellar of the league to near the
top and looked at the start as if they might even run off with the
Eastern Conference crown.

The game of professional football by now had grown so great
that some writers were predicting that it would supplant baseball as the national game. It had already developed adherents as
fanatic as any who had ever pranced howling down the main
street of an American city to celebrate a World Series victory. By
the mid-fifties the crowds at the major professional football games
were larger and more wholeheartedly committed than those that
appeared at any baseball game other than the various crucial
ones involving the top contenders. In Chicago, in Detroit, in
Green Bay, in New York, and in Baltimore, it became nearly
impossible to crowd into any game on the schedule unless you
had bought your ticket well in advance. (In Baltimore, when the
Colts were at their best, even the intrasquad practice game,
staged for charity, would draw forty thousand fans.) The temper
of these crowds was violently partisan and devoutly involved.
They did not wander about in search of hot-dog vendors during
the play, nor go visiting among friends in other sections, as baseball fans do. They yearned openly to participate in the struggle
and would invariably jump to their feet whenever a particularly
long run or forward pass seemed about to erupt.

Where a few years earlier it might have been difficult for one
of the pro football fancy to find another of his kind with whom
to share his wisdom, it was now possible to overhear men on the
streets of the big cities shouting back and forth the virtues of the

local quarterback or the sins of the coach. And one might mention "the game" to a doorman or a cabdriver or an elevator man on Monday morning and not have him look back at you goggle-eyed and doubtful.

Television was mostly to blame for this widening circle of interest, for the game of professional football had become a prime television spectacle, and knowledgeable commentators like Red Grange, and Paul Christman, and Johnny Lujack had elucidated so many of its apparent mysteries that housewives, and small girls, and men who had never even seen the game in high school became adept at all its intricacies, could keep a mental note of the number of the down and the yards to go, and could even, in the acquiescent atmosphere of their own living room, presume to damn the quarterback for doing what they would not have had him do.

There is no doubt that professional football is often easier to follow on television than it is from a distant seat in a park planned to house a baseball team. But the home team in pro football always takes care to black out the area within fifty miles or more of the park so that no television signal can tempt a devotee to stay home on a wet or bitter day and view the game with his shoes off. Games are played in snowstorms, on icy surfaces, in pouring rain, even on top of tarpaulins that have frozen to the turf and gathered snow and in temperatures so bitter that fans are led to light fires in the stands to keep from freezing.

Psychologists and other professional or amateur thinkers-aloud sometimes ascribe our devotion to football to the lurking beast within us all that takes a grinning joy at the sight of physical suffering inflicted by one man (who might be us) upon another (who could be some universal Foe). But this, like so many of those ten-cent theories that bloom in the tangled brush of the conventional wisdom of the age, makes sense only if you carefully limit your knowledge of the subject. Football fans are out to see victory and will rejoice as wildly over a fifty-five-yard field goal that brings victory without drawing a drop of blood as they will over a smashing block that sets a runner free to carry the ball over the goal line. Indeed, the screams of delight that follow an interception and a long run, when hardly one man lays a hand on another, would drown out the yells and groans emitted when some potential tackler is utterly demolished in the open field.

Still, men who play football do usually discover the extreme delight of being able to beat a foe to the ground with the strength and weight of one's body. Boys who have just gotten their full growth and who suddenly outweigh their fellows sometimes learn in football that one need not cringe from contact—that the joy of belting into an opponent at top speed and seeing him go over like a tenpin without even causing one to break stride is greater by far than the satisfaction that comes from slipping or dodging away untouched.

The 1950's really marked the era of the linebacker, when the big, fast-moving men who took a special pleasure in the solid body contact that good blocks or tackles provided finally became as famous, or as notorious, as the passers or ball carriers might. Television, with its increased understanding of the game, its crisp explanations of the defensive maneuvers, and its close-up focusing upon the gang-tackles, the blocks, and the pileups, did most to lift the linebacker out of the near-oblivion in which he had long dwelt. There were men now who could count on their box-office value to help improve their earnings, even though they never made a single score.

Of all the mighty men who back up the line on the defensive units of the professional football clubs, best known to fame in the past few seasons has been Church Bednarik of the Philadelphia Eagles, an All-American center at the University of Pennsylvania in 1948 who became center on the offense for the Eagles and then decided to join the defensive team as well, where he really found more fun. His name came to full national notice, and became a dirty word among New York Giant fans in 1960 when he rendered halfback Frank Gifford of the Giants unconscious with a vicious blindside tackle. It was a deed, incidentally, that frightened the fans more than it exhilarated them. It was thought for a time that Gifford might be dead, or dying, or crippled by the blow, and the New York fans, who are as quick to fight for their heroes as they are to revile them when they lose, roared with anger when big Chuck, knowing his deed had ended the Giant threat, did a little dance of joy beside the limp body of his victim.

The pleasure of belting a man full strength when you know he does not see or expect you is a thrill Jim Thorpe used to savor and probably every pro football player since that day has known some of it. But watching a man poleaxed all unawares this way is not a sight that fans take pleasure in. That it is "part of the game" they are sure to be reminded and they are ready to acknowledge. But it always causes a gasp of fear rather than of vicarious delight in the grandstand.

Football players fresh from college who stand relaxed to watch a play pile up when they have no part in it are deemed fair game in professional circles, if they can be dynamited to the turf before the whistle blows. Ever since the beginning, the Chicago Bears, for instance, have made it a part of their program to punish the opposition whenever it can be managed legally. Wingbacks who dawdled in the backfield before engaging in some fake or other would be belted across the thighs by solid bodies until they seemed to sprout charley horses at every stride. Secondary defenders who decided to remain spectators when the play developed far from their domain might find themselves sliced almost in two by a body block that left them chin down in the mud with 250-pound linemen atop them. Slippery runners who dodged away from a tackle might still be clouted with a forearm heavy as a blackjack and twice as big. This was all part of football and if any man was such a sissy he could not stand it, then he had better seek the sidelines.

Nearly every team will develop a play that includes catching a linebacker unawares, in a sudden block-from-behind that would be called clipping if it were done beyond the scrimmage-line area. Bednarik had been nailed on such plays often enough to know what such an unexpected "clothes-lining" might do to a man. But he never complained or asked to be relieved. He just set out to return the muscle double when his time came.

He hit Gifford instinctively, wild with joy at the chance afforded him when handsome Frank, the triple-threat man and the movie hero, ignored Bednarik and tried to fake his way past another tackler to gain a first down. Then he jumped with delight and congratulated himself because his tackle meant that the Eagles had gained possession of the ball. He did not even see for a moment whether Gifford had gotten up or still lay where Chuck had stretched him.

After the extent of Frank's injury had been borne in upon Bednarik he sent his apologies to Gifford's bedside in the hospital. Gifford, in public at least, laid no blame on Chuck. But he did declare soon afterward that his playing career was over. (It was actually only suspended for a season.) And despite much bloodthirsty talk in the press and in bar and locker room, the Giants did not ambush Bednarik when next they played the Eagles. Fifteen years before they might have. But now they had their eye on the championship, which could mean five thousand dollars a man. So they concentrated on playing football. And they lost once more to the Eagles.

In an earlier day, when the players worked for smaller wages, at least a share of their pleasure lay in the charging off of grudges and the squaring of a previous defeat. Also, less rigid officiating made for more rowdy play in the line and often left room for the cultivation of some private feud. But when there was flagrant and definitely dirty play, as opposed to plain rough treatment, teams had been known to lie in wait for the culprit and deal him out a collective beating under the stands. This for a time was an effective substitute for fines and suspensions. But even as the game became more dressed up and rules were more promptly enforced, there still remained a lot of punishing play that could not properly be called "unnecessary roughness," and a number of plain dirty tricks that could be applied out of sight of the officials —especially in dealing with a quarterback who had already let a forward pass fly. In theory such a man cannot be knocked down, but when a tackler starts his charge before the ball is thrown, or when a defender's momentum seems to carry him into the quarterback willy-nilly, no official flag is thrown. And often, because there is so much for an official to keep an eye on downfield, there are several moments when it is possible to wallop a quarterback from behind, or even dig fingers into his face without any notice from a referee or an umpire.

Deeds of this sort, however, despite the frequent growls from the victims or their teammates, the dire decisions to settle the score, and the obscene name-calling, practically never lead to open warfare. The other team just dishes it back when the opportunity offers. (Under the unlimited substitution rule, however, the attacking team never gets a chance to switch sides with the defending team and so is seldom granted a chance to square matters on a man-to-man basis. On this account, some observers used to hold, the unlimited substitution system made for dirtier play.)

There are always certain teams and certain players who wear a name for roughhouse tactics. George Trafton of the Chicago Bears was once well hated throughout the circuit (and especially in Green Bay and Rock Island) for his rowdy manners on the field, where he seemed determined to leave a mark on at least one opponent that would last until the next time around. Chuck Bednarik was called a "cheap-shot artist" by some of Gifford's teammates, meaning that he specialized in belting opponents when they were looking the other way or could not defend themselves. (Chuck did delight in blindside tackles, but was a clean player all the same. Once, in a Pro Bowl game, he knocked Los Angeles star Dan Towler loose from the ball and temporarily loose from his senses, by blasting him from behind just as big Dan gathered in a pass from Bob Waterfield in what he dreamed was "open" territory. And this time too, Chuck walked off laughing.) It is doubtful, however, if Chuck was any rougher or took any more delight in roughness than many another linebacker—a breed of wildcat that began in the late fifties to develop its own culture, its own standards, and even its own vocabulary. Sam Huff of the New York Giants is himself a slambang tackler and a dealer in high-powered body contact. He became nationally notorious when a television program wired a microphone into his shoulder guard so viewers could hear as well as see him in action in a game. The show, called "The Violent World of Sam Huff," helped increase fans' understanding of the perils and satisfactions of modern football defense, in which the center linebacker sometimes finds himself as prime a target as the quarterback. The fierce threats that Sam offered, in the hearing of thousands, to opponents identified only by number who dared transgress the proprieties of public manhandling, were perhaps slightly exaggerated for dramatic effect and somewhat purified to suit them to general broadcast.

But Sam, when he was at his best, was a dauntless and violent man indeed who, some wryly admiring opponents used to declare, wore shoes only because four or five men held him down and put them on him. Like every linebacker in the game, he varied his tactics, either charging in upon the quarterback in what was known as the "red-dog" or "blitz," or playing soft, to avoid being trapped on a draw play—a play designed to draw the defense in after the retreating quarterback, and turn a halfback or fullback free, with the ball in his arms, after the chief defenders had gone by him. On the frequent occasions in the late fifties when Sam would barrel into the backfield and knock a quarterback nearly loose from his teeth, or pounce upon a ball carrier like a rabid gorilla dropping from a tree, the home fans would hail his accomplishments by yelling in unison: "Huff! Huff! Huff! Huff! Huff!" as if they were imitating a monstrous donkey engine engaged in pulling a city down.

On the West Coast, the man whom opponents most desired to see dismembered was Les Richter of the Rams, whom many victims accused of delighting in doing bodily harm to ball carriers. He was another big strong hearty man who, like all the best of his tribe, took a special joy in using his extraordinary weight and strength against human targets. He did not confess, or even believe, that his tactics were dirty or his aims illegal. But he made no secret of the fact that he was prepared to hand out punishment far beyond the actual requirements of the immediate play to any who stood against him.

Joe Schmidt of the Detroit Lions, a graduate of Pittsburgh, was another stalwart who helped make the job of middle linebacker the most important assignment on defense. The middle linebacker, who was still listed as a "guard," actually became the defensive quarterback, the chief strategist and the key to every formation. He could often by himself wreck a pass play or pile up a drive into the line. He was consequently the prime target of the attacking team, who would dream up pass patterns to surround and confuse him, or assign blockers to "get an angle" on him and lay him low before all else. Conversely, the defense began to protect him as if he were indeed the ball carrier. Often it would be one defensive lineman's job just to protect the middle linebacker, to spot the villain assigned to do our hero down, and to intercept, delay, or eliminate that man without concern for where the ball was going.

It being the middle linebacker's usual task to pick up and cover the "second man out" when a pass was in the making, the strategists who sat up nights to draw pass patterns on paper developed a scheme designed to immobilize the crucial linebacker and leave one receiver always available in his territory: they sent men out together to overload his zone, or to sweep around him so that whichever he chose to pick up and follow he would be wrong.

These stratagems, however, served only to bring out the best in the professional game's mightiest defenders. Outnumbered as they might be, or outrun by sprinting halfbacks, or bewildered by new methods of attack, the Schmidts and the Huffs and the Bednariks and the Richters and the Campanellas were always alert to "read" plays as they developed and be ready for them. Joe Schmidt—who, according to the standard tactics of the Detroit club would be "blitzing" most of the time anyway—would, on the occasions when he did not charge in upon the quarterback, use the attacking fullback as his key, and depending on which way that man might run or block, he would retreat into one corner of his zone and cover the first pass receiver to get there alive. These were the "hook zones" in Joe's vocabulary—the zones in which a receiver would turn and hook back toward the scrimmage line to receive a pass.

The use of keys in this manner, or the reading of blocks, became a feature of modern defense, which must always expect the attacking team to engage in deception even when, or especially when, the play choice seems obvious. The corner linebackers, who would have been the defensive ends in the old-time football, feel even more pressure than the middle linebackers, for there is no one assigned to protect them. They are always faced with the problem of whether to play the end close or loose, whether to lay back for a pass or charge in to break up a sweep or to drop the quarterback in his tracks. Invariably, if the chance offers, they will at least delay an end who starts past them, yet they must not leave him room enough to slip in behind them and catch a short pass. So they endeavor to read the line blocks or look for telltale and habitual motions by the end or backs in order to pick up a clue as to whether the ball will be passed or carried, and in which direction.

Defensive linemen, charging in upon the quarterback, will read "screen pass" whenever they find that all opposition melts before them and they will yell their discovery to the linebackers. It has long been the defenders' creed that a man should move against opposition—to go where the blockers don't want him to go, and to avoid going too far when there is no effort being made to stop him. Modern linemen have refined this doctrine to the point where they can often anticipate which way the attackers would like to have them move.

The intricacies and refinements of defense, once understood by the watcher, become nearly as thrilling as the carrying or pitching of the ball. Defensive stars, particularly the tackles and linebackers, earn almost as much fame as the ball carriers and many of them carry rooting sections of their own. Gino Marchetti, defensive end of the Baltimore Colts when that team won its first championship, had Baltimore fans on their feet yelling

"Gino! Gino!" even when Johnny Unitas, the Cinderella quarterback, was fashioning a miraculous victory and Gino was laid out on the sidelines with an injured leg. New York Giant fans in the fifties never failed, when the opposition held the ball on the Giant five-yard line, to stand up and remind the coach it was time to put in the stoppers—tackle Roosevelt Brown and guard Jack Stroud, two mighty men, quick, strong, and nearly immovable, who ordinarily toiled in the anonymity of the attacking line. (A few centuries from now perhaps, if nothing remains to tell our story but the records of a few football games, historians may decide that some man named Roosevelt must have been a folkhero of the American Negro, inasmuch as two colored men on the same team were named Roosevelt Brown and Roosevelt Grier while indecipherable records in the same city also revealed the name of a Negro named Jack Roosevelt Robinson. What reader of obscure rolls could ever persuade his disciples these three were not all named after the same Roosevelt?)

Robert St. Clair, defensive tackle of the San Francisco 49ers, built a political career upon his fame, and football fans throughout the nation knew him as the strongest man in the game, an eater of raw meat (out of simple preference), and a man who took pleasure in brutal physical contact.

There still were, of course, strong men in the line who went unnoticed, or violent blockers who earned only minimum pay—lost as they were to public notice on the kicking squad, or the offensive line, or the kickoff squad, which was sometimes called the suicide squad. And these earnest and wholehearted men, some of them built like oxen, but still alert and fast on their feet and nearly impervious to pain, made liars of the commentators who still averred that no one played professional football for anything but money. There were players in this nearly nameless group who could be counted on to deal with the enemy as violently and as valiantly as a foot soldier at the walls of Rome, and to do it for no more pay than they might draw as salesmen or machinists in a mill. Among them there were blockers who took as much pride in their wounds as a Prussian duelist ever did, who gloried in the flaming scar tissue atop their noses, indicating that their plastic helmets had often been jammed down hard enough to cut the flesh as they charged into an opponent head-first. It being nearly futile sometimes to attempt a body-block against an opponent, the approved method, in modern times, has been to aim one shoulder at the victim and endeavor to engage his midsection that way and thus remove him from the path. But the truly fierce blocker, who has no fear of injuring his skull or tender neck, will use his head rather than his shoulder, and will sometimes butt the wind clear out of a man and leave him helpless. This form of attack, called "spearing," long known to rough-and-tumble fighters on the American frontier, is as instinctive as biting or scratching, but like those stratagems, is seldom "coached" by the professional game's pedagogues.

There are some coaches who maintain that defense is the real feature of modern professional football, and that until its development as a separate art the game was bound to languish. It is true that, after the revelation of the marvels of the new T-formation and the man-in-motion, and the variants that grew from that, along with the sudden stress on the forward pass, professional football teams, or those who led them, overstressed the attack so that it seemed as if either team could score almost at will, and the victory would go to the men who managed to control the ball the longest.

Today this is no longer so. Indeed, one of the finest games every played was actually a victory for the defense, and fans in every city will stand and offer the defensive unit a roaring ovation sometimes when the ball changes hands and the defenders return to the bench.

The New York Giants in 1959 defeated the Detroit Lions 9–7, in a game in which the New York attack was, in the vernacular of the Manhattan streets, strictly nowhere. The Giants' top quarterback, aging Charlie Conerly, was laid up at the time and the attack was engineered by his stand-in, Don Heinrich. Heinrich's efforts were of so little avail that the fans were howling "We want Shaw!" whenever the Giants had the ball. (George

Shaw was quarterback number three, and when he did enter the game his efforts to dent the stalwart Detroit line, outwit their ends, or shoot forward passes into their secondary were just as futile as Heinrich's.) The ball-carrying unit of the Giants was seldom in Detroit territory and only once penetrated past the thirty. Yet they held the ball long enough for Pat Summerall, the New York place-kick specialist, to boot three field goals—two from beyond the forty-yard mark. And the mighty New York defensive unit wrested the ball away from Detroit every time but once—when Detroit's John Henry Johnson took off near midfield and made it all the way to the goal line, with a Giant defender riding his back part of the way.

Each time the attacking team took over in this game and the hulking New York defensive team, dangling their battered helmets in their grimy paws, plodded grimly back to the bench, the entire assembly stood up and rendered them a wild, yet respectful salute that must have echoed like musketry across the Bronx and partway downtown.

Chapter XIII

Of Backs, both Full and Quarter

Through professional football's earliest "golden years"—golden in that they began at last to show profits for the game's promoters and even full-time salaries for its players—the performer on whom the weight of the whole game seemed to rest was the quarterback. At least he was the man best known to the fans, most counted upon by the coaches, and made the full-time target of the opposition. And his sole job, it sometimes seemed, was to throw passes.

In fact, of course, he had to do far more than that. He had to be decisive and even inspiring in the huddle—not a hem-and-haw'er, nor a man who did his wondering out loud, and not a man who let others tell him what to do. He could, and usually did, take advice from the men just returned from probing the enemy defenses. But he had to make the decisions quickly and forcefully and invite no backtalk, except when the coach took the major decisions out of his hands.

There were some men close to the game, and even some quarterbacks, who allowed that a T-formation pro quarterback had a rocking-chair job, with no part to play in the game except tossing the ball to someone else, or slipping it into another man's belly to carry down the field. And all the great quarterbacks, from Sid Luckman on, have been accused of taking care never to get their pants dirty. A pro quarterback, it was said in the late 1950's, doesn't need to run.

As the 1960's opened, however, it became clear that a quarterback who could occasionally carry the ball was more than a luxury. The defense could unload quickly on a quarterback who had no dangerous runner at his side, and could not himself do any more than fake and fade and throw the ball. Some of the supposedly "great" quarterbacks looked mediocre indeed when they could not get their passes off—for, as the old rhyme had it, how the hell can you pass when you are flat on the seat of your pants? A fast halfback who could pick up a blitzing defensive man and run him around the quarterback until the pass was in the air could keep a quarterback looking good. But if there were no fullback who could really scare the opposition—as men like Jimmy Brown of Cleveland and Jim Taylor of Green Bay have done—then the defense could fire its blitz at the quarterback with such fierce concentration that no man in the world could withstand it.

Red Grange, in all his comments on his skill at getting away from tacklers, never failed to remind his inquisitors that football was played by eleven men and that without good blocking he never could have gotten past the scrimmage line. But in appraising quarterbacks, many spectators, some sportswriters, and even a few coaches, have been guilty sometimes of awarding the signal caller sole credit for what a whole team has accomplished. It is said, for instance, that there are never enough good quarterbacks to go around in football—only half a dozen really great ones, and that every team is in the scramble for those. Yet there have been occasions when some of those numbered among the "great" have performed on a level hardly worthy of the third substitute in line. Even Charlie Conerly, counted in his day among the truly great ball handlers and signal callers, knew days when he had to eat footballs enough to nourish a stable of goats and when his ears have ached with the howls of the many thousands who were begging the coach to get him out of there.

Bobby Layne, another man who long ago earned ranking with the best, has also stormed off the field more than once, cursing himself aloud for all the things he had done that he ought not to have done, and the many things he could not do at all. And he has been subjected to so much abuse on his home field that he was actually withdrawn from the lineup to spare him.

The Los Angeles Rams, who, beginning with the great Bob Waterfield, have owned some of the fleetest and smartest quarterbacks alive, have frequently set fans to wondering if the whole Ram team had not been eating stumble pills, so often has their line failed to contain the surge of the enemy blitzers toward the quarterback, and so many times have their wing-footed backs been cornered and nailed to the ground within their own backfield.

With all that is due having been rendered to the rest of the team, however, and to the coach who often originates and prompts the play that takes the ball across the goal line, there still remains more than a modicum of honor due the successful signal callers in modern pro football. There is a wholly bald gentleman named Yelberton Abraham Tittle who is not often a ball carrier but who is acknowledged by mates and rivals as the most accurate passer since the days of Luckman and Baugh. Charles Conerly, who retired from active service not long before his real age had caught up to his uniform number (42), was known as a quarterback who could breathe life and desire into an offense that had begun to turn faint and dissolve. And while Conerly, some people said, ran like a duck, and had less speed afoot than a pregnant woodchuck, he left no doubt in the huddles that he was in command and that he intended to win, and he could, when desperation demanded it, get a pass off with a man on his neck and spin it through an opening no larger than a porthole.

Bobby Layne, with fourteen campaigns behind him and a freely confessed addiction to all the indulgences of the flesh that were supposed to rot a man's bones and render his heart too flabby to carry him up the stairs, with even a small potbelly to announce his age, still had to be counted with the most aggressive, the sharpest-eyed, the most fiercely competitive, and the most relentless in fledging his teammates and their ancestors with quill-sharp epithets when they failed to fulfill his hopes. His passes were wobbly and his moves in the backfield often lackadaisical, but he breathed confidence (and owned the confidence of his coaches) and on that account commanded the confidence of his mates. But Layne, laboring with the Pittsburgh Steelers, could win no championship and not too many ball games—not merely because he was older or because he looked too long upon Pennsylvania liquor when it was red, or because he refused to wear a face guard, but because, until the 1962 season, he had no man beside him in the backfield who would consistently frighten the other side into leaving him alone lest all hell break loose off tackle.

Norman Van Brocklin, who was often acknowledged, even by men whose beaks he had threatened to punch, as the smartest quarterback in football, left his job with the Philadelphia Eagles to become the coach for the Minnesota Vikings (the only pro football team named after a state). He had been a coach even as a quarterback, for he was one of the few in the profession who refused to let the real coach call his plays for him, and he participated directly in plotting the strategy of the games. A hot-tempered man, who could not stand even the sort of polite but useless questions that sportswriters often feel constrained to ask after a game (What are your plans? What does it feel like to be . . . ?), the Dutchman, as he was named in print, was no fool. In command of his eleven-man army, he was cool and quick. At calling automatics, which nearly everyone but Paul Brown accepts as the mark of ye Compleat Quarterback, Norman had no superior. And as a passer he had long known that the men to watch were not the receivers but the defenders, who would reveal by their characteristic moves whether or not they were about to leave their area open. The receivers he hardly watched at all, for he had them all in his peripheral vision and could nail whichever one he knew was going to burst free.

Van Brocklin knew some bitter afternoons, as all quarterbacks do, but most of the Dutchman's must have been compensated for by the glorious day on which he led the Eagles to their first 1960 victory over the New York Giants—a victory that practically secured the conference championship for Philadelphia, by putting them two up on New York, who were supposed to smother him. The fact that the great Giant defense did smother him for the first half, allowing him to complete only one pass, and granted his club a total gain of only thirty-one yards, made victory all the sweeter, and gave a good sample of how hard it always had been to put the Dutchman down and hold him there.

This was the game in which Chuck Bednarik of Philadelphia knocked New York's Frank Gifford clean out of football for a year, and which caused some New York fans to suffer from hallucinations—for there were some who swore they saw Bednarik punch his foe, although he never punched anything but the November air, and that out of sheer delight.

The man the New York Giants most feared that day (they said) was Tommy McDonald, the Philadelphia halfback who could outrun a race track rabbit, and they kept a man named Lindon Crow on Tommy's back most of the afternoon. But Van Brocklin, undaunted in the second half, kept throwing to Tommy and hit him at last on a thirty-five-yard pass for a score. The ball whistled past Crow at the goal line and Tommy took it over his shoulder, jumping, and carried both the ball and Lindon along to make the touchdown. Altogether in the second half Van Brocklin completed twelve passes out of the eighteen he attempted. And while he won the game largely because of a fumble by fullback Triplett of New York, who only half held the ball as he came snorting through the line, still Van Brocklin did what he had to do, and did it after he had been thoroughly beaten through the first two periods. Stubbornness being nearly half his nature (he was accused sometimes of using a play over and over again, despite constant failure, just to prove he was right the first time), the big Dutchman must have tasted a deep satisfaction to rise up off his bruised haunches this way and demonstrate that he was still, in trade language, a "maximum" quarterback.

(The vicissitudes of a quarterback's life were never better exemplified than by the fact that, in the game against New York the following Sunday, Van Brocklin was nearly at his worst, heaving passes here and there as if he were asking kids to scramble for the ball, and three times "completing" passes to men in the uniform of the New York Giants. The Eagles won the game, however, because the New York quarterback, George Shaw, was equally skilled at dropping his passes into the arms of the opposition.)

There is probably no such thing really as a "maximum" quarterback, for nearly any one of the best can occasionally match the worst. And some of the worst, once they have good blockers and runners at their side, can suddenly blossom into maximum performers. Ralph Guglielmi, one of the most talented and aggressive ever to steer the Notre Dame eleven, looked no better than anyone else while he was with the sorry Redskins. And Bart Starr of Green Bay, who was supposed to be too scatterarmed on the "fly" passes (the long-long touchdown throws) to rate with Tittle and Conerly and Layne and the other aging leaders, made all the other quarterbacks in the league, particularly Tittle, look like nervous bridegrooms in the 1961 season, when he coolly and forcefully guided the Packers to their first National League Championship in Lord knows when. But riding at his side in this campaign were Paul Hornung, who had been a quarterback himself once and who could pass or kick, or run the ends, or blast a hole off tackle, and rugged Jim Taylor who, in carrying the ball downfield, knew only to knock men down and run over them.

The San Francisco 49ers in the same year seemed to have three maximums at once, or each may have been one-third of the maximum, for through the first part of the season at least they won games they were not supposed to win—and did it by rotating three quarterbacks, Brodie, Waters, and Kilmer, not one of whom had ever been listed by the sages of the game as among the honored few. Of course, they operated with the temporary advantage of an "unorthodox" formation, named the "shotgun" because it threatened to scatter runs or passes in all directions, and which was really nothing more than a resurrection of the short punt formation, a favorite passing formation of the twenties. The league at first seemed unable to handle this cross between a triple wing and a kick, but Jim Thorpe, Leo Lyons, George Halas, and all the students of old Pop Warner could have handled the "new" lineup in their sleep.

In the shotgun formation the quarterback had to be a threat to run, and he often did run, so this sort of play was hardly tailored for the older and slower man, who still wore the badge of "maximum." And the constant swapping of quarterbacks, each one with his private style of stepping, pivoting, or selecting plays, made it difficult for the defensive team to find the "key" they relied upon to tip off the play a half-second in advance.

Inevitably the defense caught up with the shotgun and managed to spike it (George Halas's Bears, naturally, did it first), but it perhaps gave the game a foretaste of what sort of attack lay beyond the T, and it may have forecast too the eventual end of the rocking-chair quarterback, be he maximum or minimum. For, in the short punt setup the quarterback was expected to run whenever the defense started to play soft for a pass and even to quick kick when he caught the safety man up too close to the line and felt that a good long punt was in order.

But coaches and players in the late fifties and early sixties generally agreed that if any single quarterback were to be named the greatest, the truly maximum of all those still unspavined and unretired, it would be Johnny Unitas of the Baltimore Colts, who had been fired with ten dollars bus fare by his hometown team (Pittsburgh) when he first tried to turn professional.

Unitas had his own peculiar weaknesses, as every player has (Benny Friedman said Unitas turned his head too much, failing to keep the whole field in his vision), but he owned as well all the vital qualities that a T-formation quarterback among the pros was supposed to possess: leadership above all, which was closely allied to utter confidence. Quarterbacks who are afraid of interceptions do not usually last through the training season with the pros. In prep school or in college a quarterback may pray his way through a game, with never a pass attempted except the long pass far over the receiver's head, or the sideline pass that has to be caught out of bounds, if at all. But the pro has to throw his passes as if he were spotting his receivers by radar and using a ball that only his side could see. In short, he must *know* he will complete the pass. He must ooze that knowledge in the huddle, when he calls it, in the pocket, when he calmly awaits the opening, and at the moment he lets the ball go—toward a receiver who may at the second seem to be looking and running the wrong way.

A "chicken" quarterback will never throw a pass into the flat, or side zone, where interceptions are sure death, inasmuch as the passer cannot get over in time to bar the way to the goal. Unitas would throw flat passes as if he were home in his own back yard. He never questioned his own ability to finish what he had started and no amount of bruising by the blitzing defenders, or even interceptions by lucky halfbacks, ever shook his confidence in his arm or his aim.

This burning inner conviction that what he was about to do was right and was bound to succeed must have been what kept Johnny Unitas going when everyone in the world seemed determined to keep him from playing football for money. Unitas, at an age when his playmates were dreaming of growing up to be firemen or aviators or cowboys or millionaires, had already set his young mind on becoming a professional football player. He attended a small-time college, the University of Louisville, and in 1955 was drafted by the Pittsburgh Steelers. Walter Kiesling, coach of the Steelers, who had started his professional career some twenty years before with the Duluth Eskimos, had brought along to Pittsburgh a favorite of his own, Ted Marchibroda, whom he had coached at St. Bonaventure, and he had no eyes for any other who might aspire to quarterback. It was said by some that because Johnny Unitas was small, only a little over 160 pounds, and because he had no college reputation to peddle and no records in the book (he broke both ankles while in college and never realized his full potential), Kiesling gave him no opportunity to show his wares.

But Johnny and Marchibroda were almost the same size. And Johnny did have opportunities to display his skill. In fact, he completed every pass he threw in the exhibition games. But

Kiesling had his mind made up and no mere act of brilliance on the playing field was going to move him to alter it. So he turned John loose with just his bus fare home.

When he joined the Baltimore Colts (who had passed him up in the draft in order to get George Shaw of Oregon), Unitas had been earning six dollars a game playing with a sandlot football team in Pittsburgh known as the Bloomfield Rams. He got his job with the Colts on the long-distance telephone and became their quarterback when Shaw was injured. Once in the Baltimore backfield he stayed there, and men who have played against him say he will stay there forever.

His greatest season, of course, was 1958, when the Colts won their first championship. But in his first season as top quarterback, in 1957, Unitas performed a series of minor miracles that came within minutes of earning the Colts at least their conference championship a year earlier. Johnny was best, it seemed, when the pressure was greatest—when it was pass or lose the ball and when the defense was stacked against him. In their first game with the Chicago Bears that year, the Colts, working up from a 10-0 deficit at half time, won the game 21-10. Two of the touchdowns came on passes by Unitas and both passes were thrown on fourth down, one from eight yards out with three yards to go for a first down and the second to fullback Alan Ameche, on a flat pass, with nine yards to go for first down. Unitas made the play choices himself and calmly dropped his passes into his receivers' arms as if he had been in the league for ten years.

Unitas nearly won another game for the Colts in what was probably the most hair-raising contest ever presented in the Baltimore park. With the Green Bay Packers leading the Colts 17-14, and less than a minute to play, ice-cool Johnny, having driven his club from its own twenty-yard line into the depth of the enemy preserve, let go a long pass to his hot-footed halfback, Lenny Moore. Lenny stumbled as he turned to take the pass and fell flat in the end zone. But as he was falling, the ball nestled gently as a toy balloon into his arms and he squeezed it tight.

The Baltimore applause was like a bomb going off. There were just twenty-nine seconds left to play! And Baltimore had done it! The point after touchdown was automatic, and the score was 21–17. But in the remaining twenty-nine seconds, the Packers ran two plays. The second play, from the Packers' twenty-five-yard line, found the gleeful Baltimore defense completely out of position, with the safeties pulled up close even though a "fly" pass was a certainty. Quarterback Babe Parilli of Green Bay called the obvious play and Bill Howton, the Packer end, who could hardly believe there was not some trick to it, seeing the defenders playing so shallow, gathered in the ball as if in practice and ran all the way to the goal line. It was as if someone had unloaded a tank of ice water on the rollicking Baltimore stands. Some of the spectators, grinning like happy idiots, had already started for the exits when the checkerboard was suddenly upset, and they stood gaping for several seconds before they could believe what the scoreboard was telling them: The game that had been theirs was theirs no longer. And their lithe-limbed heroes had become a collection of stumbling fools.

The previous season, in the final game, Unitas had pulled off a similar miracle, built largely out of luck, and had won the game, and kept the coach's job for him, so it was perhaps not ordained that he should get away with the same thing twice. In the final game of the 1956 season, against the Redskins, Unitas, then the second-string quarterback, having done most of his professional playing for the Bloomfield Rams, where he had to sell raffle books to finance his own uniform, had thrown the winning touchdown. It was another come-from-behind gesture in the last few minutes of the game. Washington was leading, 17–12, and a few of the fans were telling each other "Same old Colts!" when young Johnny faded far back to fling a long, long pass that seemed nearly as high as a punt. Hecker, the Redskin safety, settled under the ball and should have had it. But it had beef enough behind it to bounce off his chest and land in the hands of the man for whom it was meant—Baltimore end Jim Mutscheller, who bucked like a demon into the end zone.

Both of these exploits finally turned pale when matched to the game that won the title for Baltimore. This was the championship game against the New York Giants in 1958—the first sudden-death game in league history and the game that has been hailed, even by men who never saw it, as the "greatest football game ever played." It was certainly the greatest for Baltimore and for Johnny Unitas. It was a tragedy for the New York fans, who could count over half a dozen play choices or ball bounces, or measurements that might have brought *them* the title.

The buildup to this game had much to do with its tension, for it followed upon two wild wins by the Giants, who had been practically counted out of the race earlier in the season.

The Giants managed to thrust their big feet in the door by beating the favored Cleveland Browns in a game the Browns were not supposed to lose, and then by beating them again in a game many people who courted pneumonia in the stands perhaps thought they should not have played. Yet play it they did in bitter cold and through a howling blizzard that obliterated the yardlines. The frantic fans, many of whom had lit fires in the stands to ward off certain frostbite, at one point surged on to the field and caused the outnumbered Browns to take quick refuge in their dressing room lest they be done in and left to rot on the icy field. This game, which the Browns had but to tie to capture the conference championship, was won by Pat Summerall of the Giants, who kicked a field goal (to make the score 13–10) from what was supposed to be the Cleveland forty-seven-yard line but which later turned out to be, when the snow was brushed away, the forty-eight-yard line of the *Giants*. When that wild and desperate kick spun safely across the goalpost bar the fans, who had already screamed themselves hoarse, leaped into a frenzy. One hysterically happy colored man, standing up behind the grandstand seats, turned and grabbed the nearest person to him—an Abercrombie and Fitch type returning from the men's room—and the two leaped about in each other's arms like drunks at a Polish wedding.

The conference playoff, also played in Arctic weather, was

almost an anticlimax. But the ardor of the Giant fans burned just as hot as the football fever did in Baltimore and there were no empty seats in the park. Indeed, many fans, to gain entrance to this suddenly scheduled game, stood four and five hours in line while others tried to bribe elevator operators or adopted divers disguises to get up front in the line-up for tickets at the New York Giants' offices. When the Giants won it 10–0, the fans actually beat the police into submission so that they might take their own goalposts down.

The Baltimore Colts came to the championship game in a state of similar ecstasy, even though they had lost the two games preceding. They had actually clinched the title in the third game from the last, when they beat the San Francisco 49ers 35–27, coming from behind once more through a fierce stop-start, twist, cut, zigzag run by Lenny Moore, seventy-three yards from scrimmage line to goal line. (Johnny Unitas, having thrown at least one touchdown pass in each of the twenty-two games preceding, threw one in this, but it was not really needed, for Moore's run had made victory certain.) The hysteria in the Colt dressing room following this win forecast the letdown in their final two games, played in Los Angeles and San Francisco. But when they got back to Baltimore they found the hysteria was still abuilding among the fans. No college kids had ever prepared for the final assault on a rival with more frenzy than the whole city of Baltimore did in December 1958.

The mob that descended upon Yankee Stadium on the final Sunday in 1958 were mostly gathered to hail the Giants and confident they would trim the Colts in this game as they had earlier in the season. But the Baltimore contingent was ablaze with banners and hats and pennants that proclaimed their devotion to the Colts (a name the team had won in a contest) and their conviction that they were going to ride the Giants into the ground, even though Baltimore had not beaten New York since 1954.

In the earlier game against the Colts, New York had won by the margin of a field goal, kicked, as always, by the matchless Pat Summerall. But this playoff game, played in fine, brisk weather before a crowd that jumped to its feet on every play, started as if neither team were going to yield a single inch. Almost ten minutes of the game had been used up before either side made a first down—and that was made at last on a pass from Johnny Unitas to Lenny Moore, for a sixty-yard gain. The fierce defensive unit of the Giants, sparked by Robert Lee Huff (who was always called "Sam" for short), dug in on the twenty-five-yard line and folded the Colt attack back upon itself until fourth down brought in the place-kicking team, with Steve Myhra wearing the shoe. The place kick from the thirty-one-yard line was not even close and the Baltimore fans groaned aloud. Flags had been tossed out before the kick was ever in the air, however, and the penalty was against the Giants for offside. This brought the ball five yards closer and Myhra tried again. He and everybody from Baltimore wished he had not bothered, for, of all things, the kick was blocked by Sam Huff and the cat-like Jim Katcavage was there to pounce upon it for the Giants.

It looked again as if the defensive units were eventually going to have to slug it out. Charlie Conerly's passes were being smothered, or hurried, and once even blocked by Gino Marchetti and his fellow blitzers, while Huff and Katcavage and Dick Modzelewski and assorted others were smashing into the Colt backfield and just about shoving the football down their throats. What really cost the Giants the ball game at last were the fumbles, credit for some of which could be awarded to the Colts' defenders. One or two of the fumbles, however, were the sort that have no excuse at all and that have caused coaches since the game's beginning to howl blasphemies at the skies.

The first score of the game was a field goal by Summerall, and it did look for a time as if place kicks might account for all the points. But the second quarter opened with a fumble by Frank Gifford, the first of three he was to make in that same quarter. Baltimore recovered them all. They turned the second one into a touchdown after ripsnorting runs by Lenny Moore and Alan (The Horse) Ameche.

Four points down, with the end of the half approaching, Conerly of the Giants dodged and ducked the blitzing Colts often enough to get off a pass that gave him first down at midfield. Here he was dumped upon his pants for a nine-yard loss and could earn only three with one of his favorite running plays— Alex Webster on a reverse. With the "impossible" situation coming up—third and long yardage, a pass was almost the only choice—and everybody on the field would be looking for it. But big Charles Conerly, never faltering, found Gifford wide open in the space left empty by the blitzing Marchetti and rifled the ball into his very arms. Gifford, however, to the howls of his fans, once more found the ball too cold or too slippery and let it trickle through his hands. This did not count as a fumble but it surely made Giants' fans begin to suspect that they were watching not the greatest game ever played but one of the worst. And almost immediately afterward, when safetyman Jackie Simpson of the Colts, trying to grab a Don Chandler punt, found the football had neither ears nor tail and dropped it, the Colt fans would have agreed with them. For Melwood (Buzz) Guy of the Giants dropped on the ball and the hungry New York attacking team came slavering in for the kill. It was just eleven yards to the Baltimore goal line.

On the first play, the Baltimores nailed Gifford in his backfield with the ball in his arms and Gifford dropped it like a cornered thief, for fumble number three. The Colts, starting on their fourteen-yard line, with about two minutes left in the half, hustled down to the Giants' fifteen and Johnny Unitas laid a pass in Ray Berry's arms for a touchdown.

When the team trooped off the frozen field at the halftime gun, the Colts were leading 14–3 and if you had tried to tell any of the gloomy New York fans that they were in on the greatest game ever played they might have provided you with a fat lip. How could the Giant offense have been worse, they asked each other: dropping the lousy ball three lousy times when they had a lousy touchdown in the bag!

But the second half provided an exhibition of Giant defensive football that had their fans almost tearfully grateful. Early in the third quarter, the Colts brought the ball right down to the New York one-yard line, with four downs left to travel those thirty-six inches in. Alan the Horse, Baltimore's fast-starting and hard-hitting fullback, gave it a ferocious try. But the Giants' line rose up and bounced him right back into his backfield. Then Unitas, always ready for anything, decided to "wedge them out" with a quarterback sneak—a play that has no particular plan to it, except that everybody jams in the center and tries to pry the enemy apart so the ball-carrier slides through. But the Giants' line, snarling like cornered beasts, yielded not even room enough for Johnny to poke his head across the neutral zone. It was time to let the Horse hammer at them once more, but he hammered in vain. He might more easily have bucked the entire contents of the centerfield stands. And when Johnny sent him around on a sweep, with a chance to flip the ball to Mutscheller, the Giants downed him in his tracks, four yards behind the line, and it was New York's ball.

Thereafter came a play that was one of the craziest, luckiest, and most spectacular ever seen, and that had the New York fans screaming in alternate joy and agony for the better part of two minutes. First Charles Conerly, back behind his own ten-yard line, let fly a sharp straight pass to the cutting flanker, Kyle Rote, who took the ball in stride at the forty-five-yard line and lit out for the other end of the park. Alex Webster, the Giants' running back, pounded along behind him but could not keep safetyman Andy Nelson of the Colts from slicing Kyle down. As Rote hit the hard ground, the ball spurted up out of his arms and danced crazily down the field in the direction it had been going. Webster hardly faltered. Even as the curses and groans of his fans and teammates desecrated the air, the hard-driving redhead scooped the ball up on a lucky bounce and half ran, half stumbled toward the goal line. The groans all changed to screams of incredulous joy. Impossible! It couldn't have worked better if it had been planned!

One of the Colt defenders, quickly back in the play, leaped after the staggering Webster and caught him almost at the goal line. Down went Webster and there must have been fifteen thousand spectators ready to swear that he went down in the end zone. But the officials said no, his knee hit the turf at the one, and so it was on the one-yard line that the ball was placed for the Giants to work out a way to take it further. They solved the problem immediately by sending the fire-breathing Mel Triplett, who really had a gait like a small horse—galloping, chug-chugging, and snorting along in a way no man could imitate—right through the Colt line to make the six points. Pat Summerall, who could do it with his eyes closed, made it seven, and the Giants were only four points behind.

From that time forth, Charlie Conerly and his cohorts played like men inspired. They were really, in a sense, playing over their heads—or perhaps finally playing up to their full potential. They had had some good days before but never this good. And they had had some miserable failures. But now when Charlie faked and ducked and spun around he found his receivers popping out into the open as if the whole thing worked on the same wire. He ended the third period by passing to Bob Schnelker— the Giants' good-catch no-run wide end—for a first down in Colt territory. They changed goals then and Charlie immediately threw to Schnelker again, who once more leaped into the air with no Colt near him and snared the ball. Then Frank Gifford made up for all his fumbles by taking a Conerly pass on the run and driving in his own beautiful manner right down the sideline for a score. The screaming and celebrating in the stands now was indescribable. There were men and girls in "Colt" hats, with Colt banners spotted all through the seats and they had to shrink into themselves as their gleeful neighbors howled the score into their ears. Stampede, was it? It looked more like a round-up, with the tame Colts all trussed and helpless and the Giants on the long end of the score at last.

It was dark now and the lights went on as the Colts accepted the kickoff. But how could they hope to budge those fighting Giants, who had belted them dizzy at the goal line once before? This was where Johnny Unitas began to exhibit the coolness and skill that mark him the best in his trade. Despite the obvious fact that the Giants could read his passes as if they were listed in the program, Johnny turned to the fly pattern and fed a long, high one to Lenny Moore, on the Giant four-yard line. The horrified gasps of the Giant fans were quickly stilled when the officials ruled that Moore had been out of bounds when he took the ball. That was enough to chill a man's resolve. But Unitas tried again and settled for a short pass to Ray Berry on the New York thirty-one-yard line. The Colts made four on the ground, to keep the defense honest, and then Johnny went back to the pass pattern. But the Giant defense was thinking right along with him, allowed him to fake his hand-offs, and bored right in to set him on his tail eleven yards behind the line. Johnny arose, brushed his tight trousers, rubbed his fingers together, and called for another pass. Again the Giants read his intent perfectly and this time they set him nine yards back. Ah, that Giant defensive unit! There was no out-thinking them! Now the Colts had to kick and all the Giants had to do thereafter was control the ball a little while, with Charlie Conerly eating up all the time they'd let him have in the huddle.

The Baltimore punt went to light-footed Jim Patton, who carried it back fourteen yards, almost to the Giant twenty. Then Charles Conerly and his battered gladiators came back to keep the ball on the ground. Alex Webster blasted at the line and earned only a yard. The Colts' defense were stacking up now, confident that Charlie would not pass. Frank Gifford, however, with his quick cut and hard leg-drive, got through the right side for five yards, to make it third and four. This, in pro football, is the crucial down. But four yards seemed no great distance to make right here. Gifford, who had just done better than that, undertook to repeat. I know there is at least one man present in the park that day who will insist under torture that Frank did repeat, that he made four yards and some to spare before the Baltimore gang-tackle brought him down. But it took some time to untangle that pile, and underneath it all lay the mighty Gino Marchetti of Baltimore, whose leg was so badly twisted he could not rise. The referee set the ball where he thought he had found it, at the upper end of Gino Marchetti, while Giant partisans howled that he had not given Frank his forward progress.

Still, the failure to make first down hardly seemed disastrous. The Colts, if they did get the ball, would still have to cope with the Giant defenders, who had throttled Unitas' passes completely the last time out. There were some moans of dismay when the Giants elected not to go for the foot or so needed to make first down. But when Chandler came in and boomed one of his mighty punts down to the Colt fourteen-yard line, not even the Colt fans held much hope. There were hardly two minutes left in the game and the hulking defensive unit, with Katcavage and Modzelewski, and Andy Robustelli and Rosey Grier and violent Sam Huff all there to forbid the way.

Johnny Unitas did what everyone thought he would do—he tried a long, long pass for the first prize. But Mutscheller never reached the ball. He tried a short one then, to "Long Gone" Dupre, and Dupre, with the ball in his fingers, let it drop. Then Unitas did what no one expected at all, with third down and ten to go, he asked Lenny Moore to run for it and Lenny obliged by making the whole ten and a yard to spare.

Now he had four more downs to operate in and Johnny, cool and determined, undaunted by the pounding he had received, set out to pass again. He missed connections three times in a row. On the fourth down with little more than a minute left to play, he finally fed a pass to Ray Berry, who carried it from the thirty-five-yard line to midfield. The Colts stopped the clock immediately with a time out.

On the new series of downs, Johnny was invincible. He reached Berry safely and Ray carried to the Giant thirty-five, where it was first down again. Again Johnny called a pass and this time, while the Giant safetymen were frantically covering the long receivers, he found Ray Berry open ten yards out and Ray cradled the ball in his arm and took it to the thirteen-yard line.

With the final few seconds whispering away, Steve Myhra

rushed in to try for a tie with a field goal. The whole team hustled. But George Shaw, replacing Unitas for this play, was cool and deliberate as he set the ball on its end for Steve to kick. And Steve made it good. The score was tied.

To describe the Colts' fans as delirious at the moment would be to suggest that they had been in full possession of their senses as the team had rolled down field. Actually, the screams had been so continuous and the scenes in the stand so frantic that all some fans could do when the kick was called good was gape voicelessly at each other and dance like maniacs. There was a kickoff to come and just nine seconds to run one play in. The Giants made but one yard on that play.

Now the first sudden-death period any of the fans had ever seen in a football game was about to begin. There would be a toss to decide who would receive—and everyone in the stands felt morally certain that the winner of the toss would take home the ball game. The Giants won. The cheers at this intelligence, however, were strongly tempered by the cold chill that Johnny Unitas had struck into the hearts of the New Yorkers. What if there was a fumble?

There was no fumble. Don Maynard, a dashing runner who had fumbled several kicks during the season and who seemed to slow down sometimes when tacklers approached him, squeezed the ball tight on the eight-yard line and returned it to the twenty. The first play saw Gifford sweep out to the right, on a maneuver that sometimes led to a pass. But this time Frank was hit before he could get under way. Ordell Braase, the man who had replaced Marchetti, proved just as hard a fellow to shave—at least on this play—as big Gino had been. Well now it was time for Conerly to unleash the artillery. With excellent deception, he won time enough to spot Bob Schnelker in the open. But Conerly missed him completely.

It was the moment of truth once more—third down and six yards to go. It had to be a pass and it had to connect. Conerly took the ball from center and faded back. But so did all the Colts, playing soft now in the conviction that Charlie had to pass. And

Charlie, seeing the open boulevard ahead of him, turned the play into a quarterback draw and ran for the first down. His running had neither drive nor deception. He just ran until someone caught him and then he turned and tried to shove his way a few feet further. He did not shove quite far enough, for when the ball was downed and the sticks brought out to measure the distance, there was still a foot lacking. The grandstand quarterbacks beseeched the Giants to go for that extra foot, to retain control of the ball at all costs. But even with the whole package going to the first side to make a score, the Giant brass still decided to play the "percentages." (Actually, who could tell what the "percentages" were in a sudden-death period, which none of them had ever played before?) So the Giants called in Chandler to bang the ball as far as he could with his mighty foot. He banged it to the Colts' twenty, and there it was that bristle-headed Johnny Unitas donned his casque once more and trotted back into the fray.

Johnny did not pass right away. Instead he outwitted the Giants by letting Dupre cart the ball off tackle for a first down. Johnny did pass then but lanky Lindon Crow of the Giants beat the ball to earth before Lenny Moore could grab it. Still it had been close enough to give the Giant secondary defenders religion and they hung back an extra second on every play now lest slippery Lenny should get the ball and run off with the ball game. So Johnny moved the ball on the ground until suddenly it was third and seven. It was too much distance to cover in a run and pass receivers would be covered like partners at a dance. But Johnny passed anyway, in the most dangerous pattern of all—the flat pass, where interception would mean good-bye championship (and good-bye a thousand dollars a man). But Johnny never considered an interception. He flipped the ball out to Ameche and The Horse plugged for the needed seven. He barely made it—the measurement this time showing the nose of the ball just past the point to be gained.

New York hearts were sinking now. A man who would dare a flat pass in this situation and make it work might do nearly anything. And just about anything was what the Giant defense had to prepare for now—sudden dives by Dupre, long passes, or one of those dodging, spinning runs by Moore. Unitas stayed on the ground until he had the ball at his own forty-four yard line. Then he faded back at last for the clincher. This time Modzelewski had outguessed him, however, and the big rough tackle drove straight into the pocket and laid poor Johnny low. Johnny got right up and tried again.

This next play, for some reason, has been marked as the really crucial play of the game and it is memorialized in a series of photographs that show Johnny at his best. He first faded to pass, then broke to his left as if to skirt the end, then pulled his arm back and faked a pass, then ran further out. Raymond Berry, running down the sidelines, was doing his best to fake his defender, halfback Carl Karilivacz, out of position. Johnny, just as cool as if he were playing touch football in a Pittsburgh backyard, watched Berry work. Berry faked, turned, and started in a new direction and this maneuver caused Karilivacz to get tangled in his own feet. Down went Karilivacz and Berry was free. Johnny, however, with no Giant close to him yet (the famous picture sequence shows one Colt protector with his arm out across the chest of Giant end Jim Katcavage in what most people would call "holding"), stood and motioned Berry even deeper down the field. When Ray had gone far enough Johnny let him have the ball and that made it first down on the Giant forty-four.

The Giants were beginning now to feel the pressure. They had to watch Moore, blitz Johnny, and make sure, for a change, that someone got that guy Berry under a blanket. What they did not consider at the moment was Alan the Horse, who was champing at the bit in the Colts' backfield. On the next play Modzelewski, who had been harrying Johnny pretty successfully, charged in again and did not take heed quite fast enough that he found no pressure awaiting him. Before he could awaken to the fact that a draw play was in progress he was clouted by the Colts' guard and removed from the play completely, while another Colt lineman drove through and caught Sam Huff off guard, too.

This left Ameche a wide street to gallop down and he got as far as the twenty before the law caught up with him.

Nothing had happened yet to diminish Johnny Unitas' confidence. He tried the ground again and, gaining nothing, he tried a pass. This time he reached Berry moving diagonally across the field toward that demon interceptor Jim Patton. Patton nailed Berry after he had caught the pass but Ray's momentum carried him down to the eight-yard line.

All the Giants could do now was pray. A field goal would be practically automatic and a field goal was all that was needed. Reacting perhaps to this certainty that the game was in the bag, a wayward fan jumped down out of the behind-the-goal-line stands and started toward the play. It took a minute or more for the police to persuade him that he should come to the sidelines with them. Johnny watched this byplay without emotion. When time was in again, Johnny gave the Horse another try with the ball and Ameche this time took it to the six. How much surer could you get? Was there anyone on the field who couldn't kick a field goal from here?

But Johnny Unitas was positive about just one thing at the moment—his ability to put a pass where he wanted it to be. So he flicked a flat pass (was he daring the gods, or what?) to Mutscheller and the big end carried it right to the one-yard line. Another step inbounds and the Colts would have had it all. Well now, for sure, the field goal team would come in to win it.

But the field goal team did not come, and some people wondered if perhaps the smart money had bet a wider spread than three points. Else why go on tempting fate this way?

But Coach Weeb Ewbank may have told himself that a field goal attempt, with its long direct pass and its charging defenders, could mean a fumble. But with Johnny he was sure at least that Baltimore would hang on to the ball.

Johnny himself could have been a hero here, by lugging it the final yard or tossing it into the end zone. But instead he whistled up the Horse once more for the play that had worked so well before—popping the fullback right up the middle. With lots of wallop, and a quick charge, they ought to get a yard at least. But everything worked like the movies. The charging ends were neatly blocked out of the play. The linebacker was knifed off his feet. And Alan the Horse sped through a hole so wide he could have dragged a cart behind him. The first hands to touch him were the hands of the joyous fans who had poured down out of the field stands to hug and kiss him. (At the other end, they had destroyed the goalposts before the play had ever started.) The fans took the ball away and the Colts had to fight to get it back. Then they went howling into the dressing room to pound each other's backs and to shout into each other's ears how wonderful, how incredible, how magnificent each one had been, and to dote on the fat checks that awaited them—$4718.77 apiece.

For days afterward everyone, pretty near, was a hero or a goat or a villain but it had to be granted eventually that the man who had won the game was the man in the saddle, Quarterback Unitas, with his stylish fakes and his beautiful timing and his icy nerves. On the flat pass to Mutscheller that preceded the touchdown, Cliff Livingston of the Giants, having "read" the play, made a break to intercept the pass, and could have intercepted it and taken the championship along with it except that Johnny pumped a fake pass directly at him and froze him in his tracks for the split second needed to make the connection with Mutscheller. On the supposed key play of the game, the pass to Berry where Unitas calmly waved him down the field before letting him have the ball, it was Johnny's unmatched skill at scrambling—that is, getting out of trouble by himself—and his convincing fakes that gave him the time he needed to shake a receiver clear.

On every play, Unitas, unlike some of the older quarterbacks, who just hand off the ball and watch it go, would fake so convincingly that at least one end would always be held up for a second lest a sweep be in the making. And his constant threat to let go a long one to Moore, or to send Ameche up the middle, kept the Giant defensive backfield in a state of confusion, so much so that, at the end of the game, they had abandoned their famous (and effective) man-to-man coverage, and were playing a zone defense against passes.

Of course, the protection Unitas received helped him immeasurably. The Colt pass patterns usually offered only three receivers, which meant that there were two backfield men, in addition to the linemen, to remain behind and help form the protective pocket for Johnny. Troop concentration like this served to discourage the blitz by making the charging tactics vain—and this, of course, meant more time for Johnny to await an open receiver. His passes themselves—low and fast—were extremely difficult for a linebacker to intercept, and his "fade"— i.e., his dropping back after taking the ball from center, was surefooted and swift. In short, his own technical excellence, as well as the abilities of his teammates to protect him, to control the ball, and to get the ball back when the other team had it, earned, and deserved, the championship.

There are other quarterbacks who will profit no doubt by the addition of a fire-eating fullback to the roster—as Bart Starr became a star with the aid of Jim Taylor—but no one deserves rating with the best—with the Luckmans and the Waterfields and the Baughs and the Friedmans and the Grahams—unless he can perform his appointed tasks with the technical skill Unitas and a few others, notably Sonny Jurgenson, display. Brilliant young men like Norman Snead and Don Meredith own the potential and need only perhaps an infusion of the calm self-confidence that seems to come from having fought one's own way out of trouble. But the old tobacco-chewing, lazily moving pro who hands a fullback the ball and waves him good-bye has no job waiting him, even in the new American Football League, where standards are not so high but where youth and style are sought after.

Quarterbacks are still too valuable to use as ball carriers—unless you are ready to carry two of equal skill and shuttle them throughout the game as the Dallas Cowboys did for a time. But the new quarterback who hopes to attain maximum rating will in all likelihood be a man who is at least a threat to carry, and who is fast enough on his feet to scramble safely out of difficulties and dodge the enemy long enough to find a receiver of his own.

Of the modern fullback one can only say that he must be heavy and fast and strong. There was a day when a fullback was a sort of human piledriver—a stocky young man with a wrestler's neck who would not quail at putting his head down and butting into the enemy's scrimmage line like a maddened bull. Often when a fullback in the old days broke through the wall, he was stumbling wildly, off balance from the momentum of his drive and the fact that the upper part of his body was parallel to the ground. But the professional fullback today is expected to pop through the line swiftly and fight, squirm and dodge, or bang his way as far as the foe will permit without losing his balance or slowing the pace of his feet. He does not often pass or kick, as all the old-timers did, and is required only to try for a touchdown every time he takes the ball. Great leg-drive is required, as well as a willingness to go where the enemy is massed most thickly, and where a man is sure to wind up with four or five, or even seven tacklers atop him.

Football may develop greater fullbacks than Jimmy Brown of Syracuse and of the Cleveland Browns. But if it ever does, they will have to be built in his image. Jimmy, who weighs about 230 pounds, is perhaps the most solidly muscled and beautifully built paid athlete of the mid-twentieth century. People who watch him on the field may imagine his uniform is well padded to protect him from the fierce pounding he receives from three-hundred-pound linemen and two-hundred-pound linebackers who always seem to hit him two at a time. But his uniform actually has almost no padding at all. His shoulder pads are trifling and the bulges that stretch his trousers are but the solid muscles of his powerful legs.

Jimmy is fast off the mark and fast down the field. For a time he played as a teammate with Bobby Mitchell, a man who could run the one hundred-yard dash in very close to world record time. But there were some players who watched them both in practice who would insist that in the first fifty yards, Jimmy Brown could beat Mitchell. Because a professional ball carrier cannot, as a college man can, jiggle back and forth for a second or two before heading for the right hole in the scrimmage line but must explode off the mark with the starting signal and never let up until the whistle, such "early foot" is important.

Jimmy had another skill that used to leave new fans goggle-eyed: He would often find himself laid hold of by three or four tacklers, and so tightly boxed that a normal man might forgivably have surrendered. But Jimmy, by letting his magnificent body relax for a tenth of a second, would prompt an answering relaxation in the foe. Then Jimmy would turn on the full power of his amazing leg-drive and would burst out into the open again, occasionally to go all the way without ever again being slowed.

It was not that Jimmy was unstoppable, for of course he was often stopped. (Several teams in 1962 held him almost to a standstill.) But it always took more than one man to stop him. And many a defensive unit assigned a couple of strong-armed heroes to stay on Jimmy from whistle to whistle, and do nothing else. Even Big Daddy Lipscomb, the 285-pound defensive tackle, could not bring down Jimmy singlehandedly, but was carried right along on Jimmy's back.

Jimmy Brown's first coach in pro football, Paul Brown, will tell anyone who asks, and many who don't, that Jimmy is the greatest ball carrier he ever knew. Nor does he pretend he ever "taught" Brown anything about his job. Jimmy always knew, says Brown, just what had to be done, and he always did it. In Jimmy's first year as a pro, 1957, the young man from Manhasset, Long Island, led all the ball carriers in the National Football League with a total of 942 yards gained. And he led the league in ground gained for the next three seasons too, the only man ever to accomplish that. The Cleveland command does not waste Jim's muscle in blocking jobs, but sets him to faking a line plunge on nearly every pass play. He is valuable as the safety valve on pass plays and more than once the quarterback, vainly seeking downfield receivers, and nearly swamped by the inrushing defenders, has flipped a last-second screen pass to Jimmy and Jimmy has run for a touchdown. (In such a play against the Chicago Bears in 1961, Jimmy took the short pass and ran seventy-seven yards to score.)

The presence of dashman Bobby Mitchell in the backfield helped Jimmy by providing an extra threat, both as a pass receiver and as a runner. But even when Mitchell went into the Army in 1961 and, playing on weekend passes, operated at something less than his maximum skill, Jimmy still managed to break through the ganged-up defenders often enough to keep the opposition thoroughly respectful.

Respect was one of the things Jimmy wanted most when he was a boy, living in a high-income neighborhood, where his mother worked as a domestic and his father was long gone. He earned it primarily through athletics in high school, where he played baseball and basketball as well as football and where he was a runner and a high-jumper. Jimmy, like most truly great athletes, was devoted to conditioning right from his boyhood, and would run for hours on the back roads or practice his jumping or shooting baskets until darkness stopped him. He was not an aggressive boy, however, and let his ability speak for itself. Always well-mannered and soft-spoken, he hardly seems the type to move into the scrimmage line like a goaded war horse or to battle for footage with five opponents trying their wild utmost to hurl him back. But no one can view his amazing physical development—shoulders wide as a doorway, a size eighteen neck, a thirty-two-inch waist, and long, leanly muscled legs—without spotting him at once as an athlete.

Jimmy Brown, at this writing, is probably the highest paid professional football player, in keeping with Paul Brown's system of paying a man in accordance with what the man is asked to do. Jimmy has grumbled briefly in the past (prompted sometimes, one suspects, by his interviewer) at the number of times he is asked to carry the ball in a ball game (in 1961, he set the league record by carrying the ball 305 times); but he cannot say that his hourly rate is substandard.

Rated close to Jimmy Brown as a fullback is Jim Taylor of

Green Bay, who is twenty pounds lighter than Jim and not nearly
so tall. He seems indeed, in the company of other footballers, a
squatty sort of man whose muscles are made in chunks. But he is
actually reckoned to run with more power even than Brown. He
is not an elusive, dodge-and-twist runner of the Lenny Moore
school. He is closer to the old notion of a fullback—a head-down
runner who plows right into his opposition. His body is always
wonderfully balanced, however, and he is difficult to knock off
his feet. And he takes an obvious delight in belting into the safetyman who may try to stop him when he is getting away for big-
time yardage. Once when he approached the Giants' goal line,
with only lightweight Jimmy Patton to halt him, and Jimmy so
situated that a simple cut would have taken Taylor around him,
Taylor chose instead to lower his shoulder in Bronko Nagurski
style and buck Patton flat on his back.

But unlike the old-time fullbacks, Jim Taylor does not blindly
smash into the line regardless of what stands there. He can cut
swiftly to take advantage of the moves of his blockers, for a really
good runner must help his blockers by luring the tacklers to turn
the wrong way, until the blockers can get the "angle" they need
to slice the men down. And Jim takes pleasure too in blocking
for his talented teammate Paul Hornung, last of the triple-
threats, who has made many a long slanting run off tackle after
being turned loose by means of a shattering block on the tackle
by hard-shelled Jim Taylor.

Fans in St. Louis will often argue that their John David Crow,
even if he does fumble the ball a little too frequently, is as hard
a back to bring down as either Jim Brown or Jim Taylor. With
a stronger lineup to help him, John David might prove his
fans correct, for he is even shiftier than Brown and has a short,
vicious stride that makes it practically impossible to bring him
down with a "form" tackle from the front. One of Crow's special-
ties seems to be bouncing off a tackler or a group of tacklers and
taking off immediately at top speed in another direction. His
ability to let go an accurate pass while he is on the dead run has
made tacklers more wary of him and less likely to drive straight

in to bring him down, for an early commitment by an end or linebacker when John David has the ball may merely mean that the big Texan will flip a pass over the man's head.

Alex Webster, who turned into a fullback for the New York Giants after a leg injury had almost finished his career, is not nearly so speedy as Brown and probably not so fast as Taylor or Crow, but he *seems* fast sometimes because he knows how to turn on his speed at the crucial second, to cut sharply into an opening and blaze away. He has often been the single most dependable man on the field for getting the yard or two needed on third down, because he will keep digging his cleats into the turf as long as he has his feet under him, and no matter how many tacklers are riding his back or shoving at him from in front. His ability to fake and to change direction swiftly have made him a valuable pass receiver, nor does he ever count himself out of the ball game, no matter where the play has gone. His presence right at Kyle Rote's elbow when Rote lost the ball in the "greatest game ever played" enabled him to nail that hair-raising fumble and practically turn it into a touchdown.

The average size of a modern pro fullback can be best understood when you consider that Los Angeles' Dick Bass, who weighs one hundred and ninety pounds and stands five feet nine, is considered a midget in the ranks. Even enemy fans granted extra plaudits to this "little fellow" when he scored the first touchdown in his pro career by running fifty-three yards from scrimmage against the New York Giants in October 1961. (It was said afterward that he got the ball by mistake, having lined up on the wrong side of Jon Arnett, the usual carrier on the play.) But people who meet Dick on the street think of him as big, solid, and strong, and at the College of the Pacific (the school that produced *really* little Eddie LeBaron) his substitute was three inches shorter and forty pounds lighter.

Still Dick, who is master of the fake and the change of pace (he even grunts and pants to delude a defender into believing he is using the final ounce of speed he owns), is dwarfed by the monsters around him. But his size makes him quicker and he finds blocking the big men somewhat easier because he can belt them below the waist before they can put a hand on him.

Other power runners, like Nick Pietrosante, who weighs 235 pounds, and John Henry Johnson, who seemed to acquire an infusion of youth in 1962, are potential leaders among the fullbacks, each with that necessary willingness to keep pounding away for an extra inch or two. But like all ball carriers, they look better when their teammates are blocking sharply and when they have someone lined up on their side who offers a substantial threat.

Indeed, any examination of the doings of the glamorous figures in football serves but to remind us that no ball carrier is much better than the men who are in there to help him. The Jimmy Browns, and the Nick Pietrosantes and the Dick Basses and the Jim Taylors may occasionally blast their way through a scrimmage line without apparent help. But five or six such attempts will slow the best of them; and without the anonymous giants who bang into the enemy with the full weight of their bodies and shove them to one side or the other, even the fleetest of speedsters never gets a chance to set his feet to flying.

Chapter XIV

Tight Ends and Loose Play

The most difficult position in professional football, some men will insist, is tight end. There was no such job in the old days, when both ends played "tight" or when both ends split together, as in the punt or short punt formations. In modern football, however, played often with three "ends" (the two proper ends, plus the flanker back) one end almost always is split wide and the other plays shoulder-to-shoulder with the tackle.

The tight end's job is unusually difficult because he is both a lineman and a ball carrier. He must often deal with the opposing end, or even with that uncaged beast known as the middle line-backer. And frequently, after a brief brush with one of these, he must speed down or across the field to take a pass and carry the ball as far as the other side will let him.

A pass to the tight end is often one of the most exciting in the game, for he usually breaks out of the melee at top speed, having gained a step or two on the man who is guarding him, and slants across the field diagonally toward the far sideline. The pass must meet him in full career, so that he need not break stride, or turn back. And when he has the ball safely in his arms, he is usually naked as a plucked chicken, as far as blockers are concerned, and must then change his direction and fight his way past the safety-men toward the goal. He can console himself usually that he is not going to be downed by five or six men in a gang, as the full-back or halfback often is, and that the men who do hit him are relatively light in weight—say a mere hundred and ninety pounds, as against the near-three-hundred pounds of many a professional tackle or guard.

But because the tight end is a potential pass receiver and plays right in close where many hands can reach him, he is subject to all sorts of tricks and devices planned to keep him from breaking into the open too quickly. The defenders who face him will sometimes "read" the play quickly enough to forestall his breaking away, or may even, in the privacy of the scrimmage, lay hold of his flying ankle and send him sprawling, where one of the opposition can drop upon him and hold him in place. Rough and technically illegal tactics of every type are the tight end's daily fare and he accepts them as part of the price of being a pro. He cannot afford to cringe from the charge of a hungry lineman, for often the success of a play will depend on the tight end's moving his opponent or at least slowing him enough to enable a helper to get an angle on him and drive him in or out, as the play may require. Yet he must contrive on pass plays to deceive the opposition for at least a half second, pretending a block before breaking for open pasture. He must therefore be fast off the mark, speedy in the open, with an ability to shift gears and directions swiftly, and still rugged and undismayed in the crunching play of the line.

Of those who made their records in the fifties and early sixties, Ron Kramer of Green Bay and Gene Brito of the Redskins were usually named as the ablest tight ends in the business. Kramer's name was seldom headlined, even when the Packers wiped up the frozen earth with the New York Giants in 1961. But the consistent brilliance of his play was acknowledged by the men who played both for and against him. It is the lot of the tight end, however, to be appreciated mainly by the men he works for and with. The passes he catches lead often to the sidelines and seldom to the goal, yet they may provide the very guts of the advance. The blocks he performs are recorded only by the observers on his bench, and by his immediate playmates, yet they may spring the halfback loose for runs that set the stands to howling.

It is like this for the offensive guards too, who still labor in the anonymity from which television has helped free the defensive men. These big men must be fast as well as solid, for it is their job in modern football to pull out of the line again and again to lead the ball carrier through the scrimmage line, to make the blocks that decide if he is going to gain or lose. They must also stand head-to-head with the giant defensive linemen and keep them from bulling through to interrupt a forward passer in the middle of his deal. To keep contact with a big, strong, and ugly man who will not boggle at using his hands and even his elbows on you to move you aside, is no work for a fellow with tender flesh or a deep concern for his features.

Modern professional football therefore seems to seek out supermen. The size of linemen, like the height of basketball players, seems to know no limit. Yet the fellows who once could hold a job in football through their ability merely to lean their weight against the foe cannot earn a living that way today. Even men of the size of Big Daddy Lipscomb, once noted as the roughest player in the league (they called him "Fifteen-Yard Daddy" because of the consistency with which he earned roughness penalties) must move like panthers or find themselves looking at the ball carrier from behind (and no one ever catches men like Jimmy Brown or Tommy McDonald from the rear).

The backs, who could occasionally list a real lightweight among them, have grown heavier as the linemen have grown faster. "Little" quarterbacks, when you meet them on the street, are likely to view you from above. A man like Eddie LeBaron, (five feet seven, and 165 pounds) who disappears from view when the team surrounds him, and who has trouble looking over the heads of his own protectors when he is passing, must depend on raw courage to keep him in the game that has outgrown him. (They had to offer him a law partnership to persuade him to come back and take his lumps another season for Dallas.)

The left halfback, or "tight" halfback, is the golden boy still in pro football and the present prototype, who actually wears the name "Golden Boy" in the press, is Paul Hornung, the reformed quarterback from Notre Dame who does most of the scoring for

Green Bay. With the gradually increasing emphasis on the ground game in professional football, Paul and his ilk have earned more and more notice in the public prints for their smashing runs and for their occasional "option" passes. Paul, however, has earned an edge on his rivals through his skill as a place-kicker. He is indeed a triple threat of the old school, runner, kicker, passer, as well as an earnest blocker when a mate is carrying the ball.

The right halfback, or flanker back in the modern game, is really an extra end, a man whose chief jobs are to receive passes, to decoy a defender in a pass pattern, or to help remove a line-backer from the play. The tight halfback is the man who will take the ball out into the alley between tackle and end, who will try sometimes to turn the end (threatening meanwhile to toss a pass over the heads of any inrushing defenders), or will pop through the line almost like the fullback. He needs to be more rugged than the other halfback, because when he is tackled he will be ganged by a half dozen overgrown linemen and linebackers, and he must be ready to hang tight to the ball and keep pumping for those extra few inches.

He is the man who earns the cheers, however, who gets his picture in the papter (and in the movies), and who gets the girls —if he wants them, as Paul Hornung is happy to confess he does. Paul, as a quarterback with Green Bay, was a man who could not quite make a star of himself. He was not fast enough on his feet nor accurate enough with his passes and the desire seemed to have left him. But when coach Vince Lombardi turned him into a halfback (and bore down on his conditioning) he became one of the finest in the game. He was fast enough to pop through the line with the force of an explosion, shifty enough to make good use of his blockers and to fake tacklers out of position, and big and strong enough to bull along despite clinging defenders, and even to break away. He could also, on the option play, where he can either run or pass, depending on whether the linebacker charges in on him or hangs back, throw a fine forward pass. On this account he seemed, on the Green Bay team, to do more work than the quarterback.

There are other tight halfbacks in the game who are far faster than Paul, and even a few linebackers who could probably catch him from behind if he ever gave them the chance. Abner Haynes of the Dallas Texans, in the new American Football League, who scored five touchdowns in a game with Oakland; Tom Watkins of Detroit, who helped bring the Green Bay Packers' 1962 winning streak to a sudden and smashing end; Bobby Mitchell of the Redskins, who had a poor day when he caught "only" five passes; Dick Christy of the New York Titans; Johnny Counts of the Giants; Don Perkins of the Dallas Cowboys; Ray Renfro of the Browns; these could probably all outrun Paul Hornung in a foot race. But Paul still outscored the lot (with the help, it must be granted, of his ability to boot field goals and extra points). And Paul's skill with passes (as either thrower or catcher), his experience at protecting the passer, his instinctive change of pace and classy faking, made him Green Bay's most valuable player— even when he was playing on weekend passes from the Army and sometimes had to go over the new plays on the morning of the game.

Paul had been a headline hero at Notre Dame, so fame was not new to him. But his long dreary term in the ranks of the second-raters may have made fame doubly sweet when it returned. By this time he was inured to the phoney stories press agents and columnists seem to feel make exciting reading and it hardly caused him to wince when he read that he was engaged to a girl he had never heard of or had presented some idiotic gift to a girl whose name he barely recognized. He was secure in his success and owned the precious ability to play his best when pressure was greatest. His new coach bore down on him to keep him in trim and Paul responded with increasing willingness. Nothing inspires a football player, nor increases his love of his coach, so much as winning ball games. And Vince Lombardi was showing Green Bay—the league's punching bag—how to win.

Paul became almost the symbol of the new professional football player; no longer a hard-handed roughneck who spent his off hours in a steel mill or in taking nightsticks away from policemen, but a handsome, sleekly dressed, obviously well-heeled young man, with two or three expensive automobiles and a private box at the Kentucky Derby, in love with girls and race horses, admired by men, worshiped by small boys, and openly adored by ladies of every age and condition.

In modern professional football, a man can afford to give all his time to the game, if he has earned any fame at all. Frank Gifford of the Giants found an opportunity to act in the movies and, during his "Bednarik" sabbatical, to broadcast football games. There are always "endorsements" to sell, books to "write," or articles to by-line and speeches to make. A man like Johnny Unitas can earn up to forty thousand dollars a year from all his enterprises. Hornung probably makes just as much. And even lesser lights have sales jobs in industry awaiting them, with understanding employers who are happy to grant them time off from July to January.

These attributes are what make the game so attractive now to college players and they help too in luring back to the game men who, at the end of a season, sometimes find themselves almost too black and blue to carry the groceries home. It is still true, however, that there has to be more than money in the game for the player or he will not really put out as he should. The "inspiration" provided in secondary school and in college by purple exhortations to defend the sacred honor of the academy or college means about as much to the professional ballplayer as the fine print on a cigar band. Still, he does receive some uplift from the game that will keep him straining his heart and muscles sometimes all season. The urge to win, to earn the extra stipend that accrues to the champion, has a strong effect, of course. But even losers will scramble in this game as if they really had a chance. Some men react naturally this way to physical violence and most strong men find a secret delight in overpowering an enemy. Others will almost by instinct dig, claw, and wrestle for an advantage when the opposition is especially strong. Then there is the atavistic exhilaration that comes to every member of the race when he is fighting in concert against a common enemy. This *esprit de corps,* which may last no more than the length of a ball game, is what lifts men out of themselves and what inspires in all such games—stirring it in participants and spectators as well—that indescribable frenzy that will drive men to deeds they would never contemplate in hours of weekday sanity.

It is true also that from time to time personal feuds have flourished in professional football to provide a villainous incentive to individual players and even whole teams. The Chicago Bears had been known ever since the days of George Trafton as an "aggressive," not to say, roughneck team that sometimes concentrated so on punishing the opposition that they forgot to win ball games. (Their habit of using extreme forms of the blitz—even occasionally shooting the safetyman through the scrimmage line to batter the passer—often so weakened their pass defense as to render it useless. It was not until late 1962 that they grew out of these tactics.) Some teams go into games with the Bears intent on nailing one particular competitor in response to an earlier act of near-mayhem, or alert to keep their eyes on some favorite rowdy, who reputedly is ready to damage any man who turns his back on him during the play.

A quarterback especially, who must turn his back on the play and make a sort of fake "fade" to the passing spot on almost every run, can develop special hates that will keep his blood simmering even when common sense tells him he had better contemplate retirement. Bobby Layne, for instance, long nursed a special hate for Ed Meadows, an end on the Pittsburgh Steelers and the Chicago Bears, who clouted Bobby from behind several seconds after Bobby had gotten rid of the ball on a pitch-out and the carrier was yards away. (Layne was notoriously reluctant to do more than go through the motions of a fake and was often found watching the ball carrier hasten downfield.) Because the referee habitually watches the ball rather than the quarterback, Meadows was able to separate Bobby from his senses without anyone's seeing it except all the players on the bench and most of the spectators.

The Philadelphia Eagles owned a rough customer named Kilroy who was not averse to leaving his signature on the countenance of any man who opposed him too strongly, and who was supposed to be especially adept at "getting" a key man whose absence was required for victory. Kilroy had his picture taken in 1953 in the act (according to the captions) of finishing off New York and former Army star quarterback Arnold Galiffa, and the New York Giants nursed a hatred for Kilroy for the rest of his career, which ended in 1956 (Galiffa left the game in 1954). Kilroy, however, seemed to welcome such grudges and was never known even to whimper a complaint at the retaliation he was handed, except that he took care not to walk too close to the stands in alien cities, lest some fan set a bruising object adrift in his direction.

Professional football players, however, eventually become resigned to a certain amount of illegal play and to conduct that is described in the rule book as "unsportsmanlike." It is hard to maintain grudges against players who may be lined up on your side next season, and it is sometimes more satisfying merely to take your bumps without complaint and to dish out whatever you can spare on your own account. The officials in a professional football game will sometimes admit privately that they could probably call a foul of some sort on nearly every play and all seasoned spectators can observe unpenalized holding half a dozen times in every game. Men who raise their forearms in the line to block off the defending linemen would be less than human if they did not spar with their hands against the clawing hands of the opposition and it is always a temptation, while performing a stand-up block, to close one's fingers over the other man's jersey and keep him from getting where he wants to go—or slow his progress a little.

The officials concentrate on the most dangerous violations and those that might mean a score—piling up on a limp ball carrier after the whistle, running into a kicker who is still off balance from his efforts, blocking a potential tackler from behind (called "clipping"), interference with a potential pass receiver, and the really flagrant holding of defensive men who have a chance of downing the ball carrier.

Some penalties are incurred deliberately, in exchange for a certain score. Occasionally a defender will knock a pass receiver right off his feet rather than see him catch a pass for a sure touchdown. And, of course, a penalty for delaying the game is often worth the time it provides, either to bring in a new play or take the steam out of the opposition.

In all, professional football is probably a cleaner game even than college ball—or at least one that produces fewer injuries. The modern professional football player is almost always in better physical condition than his college counterpart. In addition, he seldom plays the full sixty minutes of a game, as many college men still do. In the many universities which go in for wholesale subsidization of athletes, "sportsmanship" is at a minimum anyway, and most of the stars are thoroughly cynical in their approach to the game, far more so than the men who openly take pay for playing.

Despite the game's rowdy and cynical undertones (which are not much different from baseball's), the heroes of professional football still retain their bloom in public and the game itself has devotees so wholeheartedly committed that they will subject themselves to severe discomfort to do their champions honor. Paul Hornung, although he seems to wear his mantle sometimes with the swagger of a Caesar, is as beloved in Wisconsin as he ever was at Notre Dame (or at Louisville, Kentucky, where, like John Unitas, he was a high school hero). And Vince Lombardi, the former Englewood, New Jersey, high school coach who learned his trade from Earl Blaik at West Point and Jim Lee Howell of the New York Giants, and who turned Paul Hornung from a discouraged and defeated quarterback to the best halfback in the game, could probably take the city of Green Bay out and sell it to buy him food and raiment—with never a peep of protest from his devoted followers there.

The game that proved both men to be the best in their trade at the moment was the championship game at Green Bay, Wisconsin in December 1961, when the fierce wind whistled off the ice-bound lake and the mercury, in bright sunshine, could not crawl above twenty-three degrees. Yet thousands gathered in the small arena at Green Bay, to dare the grinning pneumococci and happily gather chilblains for the greater glory of their hometown.

Most people who had really considered the capabilities of both teams before the game gave a wide edge to the Green Bay Packers, who had been handicapped earlier by Hornung's inability to practice with the club. But this time he had frequent opportunities to work out, to sharpen his timing, and to drill himself in the moves. The New York partisans, none the less, gathered in the impossible weather to chuckle at the signs that named Green Bay "Titletown, U.S.A." and suggest that it would soon be "Tittletown, U.S.A.," after the Giants' invincible bald-headed passer. And the New York team kept telling everyone, including themselves, that they were "staying loose" and treating this title game as "just another ball game." If that was truly their attitude, it forecast their doom. For the Packers were "up" for this game as no Army team had ever been "up" for Navy. The town, as it had been several times in more than forty years, was in a state of happy hysteria. And coach Vince Lombardi exuded grim confidence.

When the game began it soon became clear that Paul Hornung and Jim Taylor were red hot and the Giants were deathly cold—literally as well as figuratively. The Giants took the ball away from Green Bay on downs, to start their first offense. Then, after moving from their own thirty to the Green Bay forty-seven on two runs and a pass, they had a touchdown play in the making. Kyle Rote, their veteran receiver, playing his last ball game, had just caught a pass for a sixteen-yard gain, and had another pass from Tittle right in his hands on the enemy ten-yard line. But his hands were cold and he could not clutch the ball. That just about finished the Giants, although they did not realize it yet.

The Packers, after New York's Chandler had punted the ball

into the end zone, started a new offense on their own twenty-yard line and moved the whole eighty yards to the Giants' goal in just eleven plays, ending the first quarter on the New York seven-yard line and opening the second quarter with the game's first score on a run by Hornung that operated exactly as it had in practice, with every lineman moving his private enemy and Paul cutting at precisely the right moment to charge into the end zone uninterrupted. What dismayed the Giants most at this point—and what continued to dismay them—was that the Green Bay linemen were moving the immovable Roosevelt Grier as if he were a halfback. If the mighty Grier, staunchest defensive tackle in the game, could be shoved aside by the quick-starting Green Bay line, what next?

Next was one petty disaster after another. The Packers intercepted a Tittle pass on the New York thirty-three-yard line and made themselves a second touchdown, this time chiefly on passes to Kramer and to six-foot five-inch Boyd Dowler, who caught the touchdown pass in the end zone after deftly out-maneuvering New York's Erich Barnes—a sprinter who had celebrated his joining the Giants by intercepting an end-zone pass early in the season and outracing everyone to the other goal line. (On the previous score, Barnes, in desperation, had clutched at the faking and twisting Dowler and earned himself an interference penalty that gave Green Bay first down on the seven.)

In the previous game between the Packers and the Giants, played in Milwaukee on December 3, the Giants had actually led the Packers at the half and went home feeling that they had been done out of victory through a breathtaking and once-in-a-lifetime stunt by defensive halfback Jess Whittenton who, with a chance to tackle Alex Webster in the open, decided instead to make a grab at the ball—and got the ball and took away the ball game. At the half in the championship game, however, the Giants were already out of the running. The Packer defense had so stifled the indomitable Tittle that Charles Conerly, wearing sneakers to give him some footing on the frozen turf, had to come in to attempt to make connections on a forward pass or two. By this time, the spectators, what few had not numbed themselves by frequent applications of spirituous liquors, were near frozen in their spots, clad in eskimo parkas, in mother's best blankets, in daddy's hunting jacket, in thermoboots, even in sleeping bags. But the Giants, who had been moving across the gelid ground like men in a frozen trance, finally stirred to life. Conerly whipped a pass to Rote that that young man was able to hold on to until he was at the Green Bay fifteen-yard line. A score seemed certain now and while few sensible people believed that the Giants had a hope of winning the game, there was always that chance of a few wild breaks, a long run, an interception, a fumble, a blocked kick, or a combination of all that could turn dream into reality. Two short runs moved the ball within a yard of first down, where Webster failed to make the distance. The obvious move was a field goal attempt, but Coach Allie Sherman of the Giants sent in a razzle-dazzle play he had been saving for just such a moment—an option reverse, with Gaiters carrying and passing to Rote. Gaiters, quick as a spider, scooted wide with the ball. Kyle Rote ducked into the end zone and stood there isolated as a statue. Gaiters spotted him and let fly. And the ball went far over Rote's head into no man's land. The Giant fans in the stands were too frozen to moan but the howls of anguish that rose from television sets all over the Northeast could have broken windows in Chicago.

The smoothly operating Packers, moving as if it were a mild midautumn day, took over the ball and had it at the other end of the field, on the Giants' fifteen-yard line, in a matter of seconds, Paul Hornung first sweeping down the alley for seventeen yards and Bart Starr drilling a long straight pass to Ron Kramer that added forty yards more. The halftime clock was breathing its last so Starr called a play without a huddle, so startling the Giants—some of whom had their backs turned to the play—that one or two of them wildly plunged offside. The play was an incomplete pass, with a five-yard penalty (against the Giants) on top of it. That put the ball on the ten and provided just time enough for Paul Hornung to kick a field goal and make the score 24–0 at the half.

The Packers started the third quarter by recovering a punt that frozen-fingered Giant safetyman Morrison let slip away. Unable to turn this into a touchdown, the Packers let Paul Hornung try a field goal and he made it good from the twenty-two-yard line. The next and final touchdown by the Packers came on a swift pass to Ron Kramer in the end zone, where the hapless Morrison, who had kept Ron well covered, slipped on the hard ground and let Kramer go free.

Y. A. Tittle came back to salvage a scrap or two of honor for the Giants but, after getting the ball past midfield, he stalled the machine. Usually cool and in utter command, and supposedly gifted at calling the automatics, Tittle could not seem to get himself off a single track. With the Packer linebackers apparently reading his mind, and stacking their defense to meet him, he kept vainly whanging away at the right side as if he were determined to prove it *could* be done. Ultimately Jess Whittenton, the ball-stealing hero of the earlier meeting, intercepted a Tittle pass and downed the ball on the Green Bay thirty-eight-yard line. Green Bay, who seemed to prefer to play in the other fellow's yard, quickly moved the ball over there. The longest gain in this series came on a breathtaking draw play by plunging Jim Taylor, the man who does acrobatic flip-flops to develop his sense of balance. Jim kept his balance for thirty-three yards, after sucking in the entire Giant forward defense on one of the prettiest plays in the game, in which Bart Starr so convincingly acted out the part of a man fading back to pass that he took all the Giant defenders with him. They did not see him slip the ball to the crouching Taylor on the way and when they found that Bart did not have the ball, Jim was already down among the halfbacks.

Chapter XV

Is There Really such a Thing as a Coach?

With increasing frequency, in the 1960's men have been saying out loud (or ghost writers have been saying for them) that the easiest job in professional football is the coach's job. One coach, in a moment of exuberance, even made that statement himself. And the owner of the champion Houston Oilers in the new American Football League gleefully pointed out that they won the flag with a different coach each time.

It makes a sort of hard-rock sense, of course, to say that the man with the horses is going to win the race regardless. But what then are you going to say about Vince Lombardi, who took over a collection of chronic losers and made champions out of them within three seasons? Or about Paul Brown who, despite the fact that he never had first-draft choice of rookies, kept winning conference championships so steadily that certain handicappers would make him the favorite before they even read his roster?

Pro football players themselves, when their team is winning, will generally acknowledge that their coach is the nation's shrewdest, handsomest, most inspiring and beloved. And there are losers who will, in private, and despite their earnest avowals of personal devotion to the man, suggest that the coach's gears are not meshing the way they did. So the coach must at least own a share in the fortunes of the team; and his regimen certainly must work some consequence upon the players.

Coaches, like teachers and politicians, often have to choose between winning love and winning a goal. Weeb Ewbank, at Baltimore, could not provide that city with a championship team until he had invited the growling disfavor of his men by drilling them just as his former employer, Paul Brown, had always done, until they could make their moves in their sleep.

Most players and private observers will grant that Vince Lombardi is one of the ablest coaches in professional football; and he is not one who makes his job a four-hour armchair role. He is a tough teamster, just as most successful baseball managers have been, and he gives even more time to his work than he asks his players to give. When he was coaching football at a Catholic secondary school in New Jersey, he taught the game as some men teach mathematics, providing his linemen particularly with a set of rules that would serve to guide them to their assignments no matter what type of defense they might face. This "rule blocking" (one of Vince's associates at West Point described it as a combination of Sanskrit, Algebra, and Infantry Tactics) provided head-cracking homework for football players and demanded rather more than a minimum of intellectual capacity. It was *taught* to the men and not merely thrown out as a useful tidbit of wisdom that they might pick up or discard as the mood prompted them. Lumbering lads who were too slow-witted to remember the "if nots" and the angles just did not make the team; and no player was left to perform his tasks by instinct.

The offensive linemen under Vince Lombardi are drilled like a ballet. It is not enough for each man to know how and when to charge and whether to move his man in or out, or when to pull and lead the play, and when to trap a defender. He must charge in complete accord with all the men alongside him. Not, as Vince says, like typewriter keys, but together! together! together! This sharp, utterly unified, and mighty forward surge on the offense is what makes great ball carriers out of adequate ones and what practically guarantees a yard or a few inches when the need is acute. It smashed the "immovable" New York defense of 1961 and it turned Paul Hornung and Jim Taylor loose on runs that made heroes out of them.

Vince, besides earning the adoration of the citizens of Green Bay and Milwaukee, won the devotion of all his players, who will not hesitate to avow that he deserves a full share of the credit for their return to form as a team. But let him miss a few titles and the grousing against his tough regime may become audible. He is not the beloved, offhand, sleepy-eyed elder of the game who merely corrects his lads when they do something wrong, nor the chalk-talk genius who comes up with intricate devices for hoodwinking opponents at the moment of crisis. He is a hard-boiled, whip-cracking drill sergeant who asks even the famous players to run through their moves until they have perfected them. And he is a hell-fire fundamentalist who believes that football is made up mainly of blocking and tackling and who makes his men practice these simple deeds rather than run through triple passes or hipper-dipper sleeper plays.

He also, be it known, subjects his grown-up charges to intelligence tests of a sort. How he appraises these tests and exactly what use he makes of them Vince may be the only one who really knows. But he does look into the brains of his football players to discover just how much their skulls will hold and no doubt he requires of them whatever he knows they can deliver.

Vince is a good-natured man, always well conditioned, so heavily muscled indeed that once on a canoe trip he proved too muscle-bound to perform his full share of the paddling with the smoothness and stamina required. (He did, however, one of his companions attested with a grin, paddle pretty fast down to the village after groceries and meat.) But he is not a jolly-good-fellow type on the job, or after hours. He allows no dissipation (even though he is wise enough to know when the horse will respond to a slightly slackened rein) and he sweats his men into condition until they begin to pray for the season to begin so the work will grow easier.

Nowadays some people like to contrast him to Paul Brown, as being an inspirational leader rather than a slave driver. And it is true that Vince is not ashamed to grow sentimental at times, and to lead his whole herd of sweaty, half-dressed monsters in prayer. But he is far more like Paul Brown than unlike him. He does not use the famed Paul Brown system of sending a play in on every down. But he works out his attack in detail and insists on perfection. He can roar at a dumb mistake and lash at a loafer with all the vehemence of a muleteer. And he does not believe in letting up, either in the game or in practice. In professional football, with its swift and unforeseen reversals, no one can ever tell for sure when a score is big enough, not at least until the last few minutes, so Lombardi does not countenance habits of dogging it, whatever the excuse. His teams habitually scratch for every advantage, as they did in the first half of the 1961 championship game when, with a twenty-one-point lead in the first half and only seconds to play, they dispensed with a huddle so that they might save a few split seconds in which to make a score.

Lombardi, as Paul Brown did, makes extreme demands of his performers. They are all supposed to be in top shape and ready at any time in the game to put out their utmost. There are no free riders on the squad nor any semispectators who coast along until the enemy is close to the goal.

Paul Brown is a different sort of man from Lombardi, one who gives the impression of mental rather than muscular power. Where Brown is slender, nervous, and even withdrawn, Lombardi is solid and tough and outgoing. No one can imagine Vince Lombardi leaving his lights on at night while he slept, as Paul Brown has been accused of doing. And it would be hard to picture Paul Brown leading his squad in a tearful prayer of thanksgiving. Yet a man who was swapped from Cleveland to Green Bay might have a hard time telling the difference when it came to toeing the line in off-hours and during on-hours, redoing a hundred times the things he thought he knew. Paul Brown undoubtedly ruled his men's lives more closely. But if Vince Lombardi thought proper conditioning required it and if he needed better condition on his squad to bring him another title, you can be sure no consideration of shyness or possible player resentment would restrain him from declaring every gin mill, soda shop, or even late-hour movie off limits for his boys.

There may still be a coach or two who operates on luck and loving kindness, who lets his players condition themselves and who never requires that they strain their muscles to the aching point in practice. But no such man will win championships in a professional football league where the teams are evenly matched. And "inspiration" of the old high school or college locker room type, the "win this one for poor dying Charlie" or "Yale expects every man to do his duty" sort of thing, would simply convince a professional squad that the old man had been beating the bar rail too long.

Weeb Ewbank, former Baltimore coach, once managed to provide inspiration of a sort to his championship collection of carnivores by merely reciting to each one, in the full hearing of his fellows, how many other coaches had deemed the guy not worth the waiver price and how many teams had declared him over the hill. And once he asked his men to charge out on the field at the half and imagine that, instead of being a score or two ahead, they were still two touchdowns behind.

George Halas needled his rowdy Bears into whomping the Redskins far past the fun of it by reminding them constantly of what George Preston Marshall had said about them—that they were front-runners who quickly used up their supply of gas.

Far back in professional football's long-underwear days there were coaches no doubt who asked their hired hands to undergo sprains and strains and broken noses for the honor of this small town or that or in order to settle a score with some big city boys who thought they were "It." And other coaches from time to time have gotten by on the strength of their inventive genius and their ability to find the strongest and shiftiest ballplayers and sign them to contracts.

In the modern era, however, a coach must needs organize his squad as a military commander does and drill them, despite protests and rebellion, until they perform his will almost automatically and in complete harmony with their comrades. The professional game is getting back at last to fundamentals, and the running game will require more emphasis, as pass defenses become more wily and more practiced in the ways of their opponents. This means that wind sprints and blocking and tackling and calisthenics and every manner of exercise that will make a man grunt and groan—and will increase his stamina—along with severe drill in unified performance must fill even more of a professional football players' days. The coach cannot, of course, provide a lineman with his strength, his speed, his alertness, and his desire, give a ball carrier his swiftness, his willingness to accept a pounding without slowing down, his quickness at cutting or at changing his pace, his ability to time a pass receiver or throw a ball a long long way. But he can insure his being in condition to perform his required tasks for many minutes on end in all sorts of weather, his knowledge of where all his mates may stand or be moving at any moment, his getting off the mark at the precise instant that the play will start, and his using his strength on the proper opponent and in the right direction.

The Paul Brown system of leaving all play choice to the coach —just as it is done in baseball—may win more adherents, even though Paul Brown is supposed to have lost his job partly because of this system. (There was also an unpublicized player "rebellion" before the final game in Los Angeles in 1962 in which the players were growling that they wanted to be treated "more like human beings," but that may merely have anticipated the move instead of prompting it.) No matter what happens to Paul Brown, however, it does not seem likely he will ever agree that his system was not the correct one. The coach, he always held, was less likely to be fooled by defensive feints. Besides, he would argue, when the coaches know what play has been called they can size up its execution more readily, because they know just what each man is to do. (When Detroit put an end to Green Bay's amazing ten-game win streak in 1962, Bart Starr, the Packers' quarterback, called many an "audible," as he tried to outguess big Joe Schmidt of Detroit, who was stunting back and forth, into the line and out of it. Starr guessed wrong more often than he guessed right, despite his owning the supposed advantage of being right on hand to read the intent of the enemy.)

The Cleveland team, one observes, will still be called the Browns, to honor the man who made them. But it would be well too if Paul Brown could be honored in every football city for what he has done to make the game the glorious spectacle it is today. No single man has to his credit so many and such multifarious improvements in planning, coaching, playing, and even equipping the game. The souls of pro football players everywhere, and of magnates as well, would suffer nothing but improvement were they required to give thanks to Paul Brown every time they profited by what he contributed to the game. The handsome young ball carriers who do not grow to look like toothless plug-uglies can mutter daily thanks to Paul Brown as they put their face masks on, for it was he who invented the standard face-bar. The coaches who pore over films of earlier games, to mark and number every move on offense and defense, can bow their heads briefly in memory of the man who taught them the value of this practice. The players who suddenly discover that when they begin to play as a team, with each man doing his one job to perfection and in unison with the others—that only then does each man become great at his position—they too can remember in their prayers each night the slender, hard-fibered fellow from Ohio who taught this lesson to the whole football profession. When the current Golden Boy of the game, whether he be Brown, Hornung, Johnson, Robinson, Jones, or Smith, counts all the round zeroes that make his paycheck fat, he can utter a special thanksgiving to the man who planted in the profession the theory that the laborer was worthy of his hire. And when the spectator jumps to his feet, gasping with wonder and joy, to see a complex pass pattern unfold and bear fruit on the field, like some war dance from another world, he too can remind himself to tell his children that the man who first dreamed all this was one whom fate concealed by naming him Brown.

Some quarterbacks, even now, will whisper to their friends that they would actually prefer the Paul Brown system, which has been reviled in purple prose as robbing humans of their dignity and purpose in life. The coach after all has definite plays in mind that he wants called and some quarterbacks find themselves occasionally trying to read the old sorehead's mind and wishing that he would tell them. There are coaches who will promulgate a sort of unspoken rule that automatics must be called a certain percentage of the time, so that a quarterback, especially when the pressure is heavy, may find himself swayed by his desire to fulfill the coach's requirements as much as by trying to adjust to the strengths and weaknesses of the opponent.

It is particularly true of an untried quarterback, that he will endeavor in spite of himself to do what the coach thinks he ought to do, or what *he* thinks the coach thinks ought to be done. Untried quarterbacks are not often left in the lineup to worry their own way through a series of mistakes, unless, as sometimes does happen, the other quarterbacks are lamed or off the beam. Yet a study of the records of every top quarterback will reveal that he often misses three passes in a row and frequently calls a third-down play that leaves him dumped on his helpless haunches ten yards behind the line—mishaps that will occasionally cause a coach to yank a rookie and ask himself whatever made him think *that* guy was ready.

The confidence a coach has in his quarterback will be reflected by the confidence the quarterback has in himself—and that self-confidence will breed confidence on the part of the team.

No doubt there are still coaches in the professional game who, recalling their own active days, will spoil their players, as parents who have known adversity will spoil their children, by allowing them to go their own way too much. Voluntary conditioning is like voluntary wartime rationing—it works with only a few of the truly dedicated, and even they will begin to backslide when they see everyone else is getting by with it. So eventually the coach must really take charge and really crack the whip, or else resign himself, after his monopoly of big-time stars has been broken, to continually playing off the pace. Fear of unpopularity has weakened the resolve of some coaches; fear of organized grumbling and the opposition of the team's top stars has kept some coaches from asserting themselves. But there is always resentment under any tough regime, as in the Army or the Marines. It is quickly cured by victories and can transform itself then into personal loyalty that is almost like worship.

The old tough college coach who would, as they said, play his mother in the line if it would win him a game, sometimes had to reveal his "heart-of-gold" side to his charges in semi-tearful pep talks or fierce exhortations before the major games, on which his contract often depended. But football players who are in the business for a living—as many college stars have been for three or four years before they turn professional—are not to be cozened by fairy tales. Yet they are all of them still close enough to their own boyhood to require some degree of discipline, even in their off-hours.

Vince Lombardi, it is said, knows when to keep his eyes closed to transgressions of a minor sort, while Paul Brown was accused of making such a fetish of regulation that a man almost had to raise his hand to leave the room. Yet each man in his own way has demonstrated to the league, and to the public, the value of rigid conditioning and constant drill. And while Lombardi may be blunt where Paul Brown was sarcastic (he once asked of a quarterback who had been dumped on the seat of his pants: "Did you get a concussion?") they both use essentially the same system—even to the point of assaying the intellectual capacities of their prospects.

And both are long separated, in time, in attitudes, and in skills, from the coach of two decades ago who, preparing his legions for combat with Chicago, addressed them in these words:

"Now we meet the Bears. The big bad Bears. We're going on the field and get the spit kicked out of us. Then we'll go out and get drunk and go home and get fired."

(He was wrong on only one score. He did not get fired until the season was over. But the speech did "inspire" his soldiers so that they actually led Chicago in the first period.)

Chapter XVI

Who Will Die for Dear Old Rutgers?

It is almost a hundred years now since big Mike Michael of Nassau Hall, in plain wool trousers and jersey sweater, knocked young George Large of Rutgers right through the rail fence in New Brunswick as they raced to recover the round rubber ball in what has been called the first intercollegiate football match ever played. Since that day Americans have all grown up thinking of football as a college game, and even sometimes thinking of college as a football game.

The day cannot be too far off, however, when professional football will replace the college game completely, or reduce it to the status of college baseball, many many levels below the big-time game. Football does have the advantage, of course, of belonging to the months when college is in session, while baseball is played mostly during vacation days. But how can grown men much longer pretend that big-time college football is really amateur, or has anything at all to do with scholastic attainment? The finest college football now is played in those institutions that proselytize crudely or maintain courses for athletes that make a mockery of learning—classes in how to play games, or how to make friends, or how to stay married—and that even recruit baton twirlers and offer scholarships for beaters of the bass drum.

The public patience with such grown-up kindergartens cannot be limitless and the day must come when schools are given back to the scholars. It is true that many a young man who would have missed a college degree has been able to earn one because of an athletic scholarship. But they must be few indeed compared to the many who missed a degree because they could not play a team game with skill enough, or because they just did not have the money—not to mention the young men who have had their secondary education stolen from them because they could play basketball or football so well they were not required to do their homework, or even pay attention to their classes.

Big-time college football nowadays engages in recruiting contests that in some parts of the country can only be described as degraded and vicious. Teen-age boys are set upon by ardent alumni or "unofficial" recruiters with all the fervor of a horde of bucket shop salesmen zeroing in on a wealthy widow. Their parents are promised jobs, their sweethearts are offered scholarships, their fathers may be given eight-cylinder cars, and the boys themselves can sometimes win "guarantees" that include girls, degrees, and even post-graduation contracts. Occasionally a boy will succumb to all the lures and "sign" with two or three colleges, only to have his mind changed at the last minute by a final visit to a country club where the closing arguments will be offered by some "booster" organization or other, and underlined by a selection of fine liquors and compliant girls. Stag parties offered on the Pacific Coast to groups of football prospects have sometimes attained the rating of an open scandal.

In this sort of recruiting, teen-age boys are taught to develop a loyalty to the high dollar that can sometimes develop into a cynical willingness to make a deal with anyone for nearly anything, including, of course, the shaving of points in a football game—college football being one of the major gambling vehicles in the country. On the Coast and elsewhere, leading players have been known to fatten their take on a game by scalping tickets at five and six times their face value—this privilege being part of their "contract" with the alumni organization that brought them in.

In a magazine story some years ago, Al Stump, one of California's (and the country's) best sports reporters, told tales of recruiting by California colleges that should have caused the eyes of college presidents everywhere to start from their spheres, for Stump named names and places and amounts of money, and gave details of "entertainment" of high school prospects by ancient alumni at beach clubs that read like reports of Roman orgies. Yet there has been apparently no more than an occasional lull in the ferocity with which certain colleges vie with each other in buying new players from everywhere. (Stump said that Johnny Olszewski, the famous Johnny O, of the Cardinals, Redskins, and Denver Broncos, cost the University of California twenty-five thousand dollars when they "signed" him in 1949.) Even today professional teams sometimes find that recruits from the colleges feel they are taking a pay cut when they hear what the professional team can offer.

There are earnest devotees of the college game who sincerely feel that it is an important, or even the most important part of the American educational process. They like to talk of the college gridiron as the modern counterpart of the Duke of Wellington's "playing fields of Eton." And one former coach even set forth solemnly, as if he knew half the country would agree with him, that the empty grandstand at Stagg Stadium (where the University of Chicago once played big-league football) remains as a dreadful example of "what can happen to the game when operated on by such minds." The minds in question, one need hardly remark, belonged to men like Robert Hutchins, and others, who felt that the real business of a university was intellectual development and that big-time football tended to belittle that primary purpose.

In the service academies (although even they have been accused of promising appointments and careers to prospects) and in the de-emphasized colleges it probably is true that football has served to help turn many boys into men. But it is folly to pretend that big-time college football is any longer the property of the "boys" or that it has any relation at all to the educational process. It is merely minor league professional football, with overtones of hypocrisy and deceit such as long ago spelled the doom of "amateur" baseball. Boys who make good in the big universities are "drafted" by the professional leagues and they have learned to bargain as skillfully as professionals for the biggest bonus and the best deal. Indeed, the influence of professional football upon the colleges and its dependence upon the colleges as training ground for its young has led at least one college authority to suggest that the professional game ought to subsidize the colleges.

Before that outlandish eventuality ever comes to pass, however, it will more likely develop that professional football will reduce the college game to what it pretends to be—organized recreation for young men who are seeking advanced learning. For the professional game is developing addicts so fast that in some cities it cannot find fields big enough to seat them all. As long as the leagues remain at war, and try to bankrupt each other by stealing each other's players and patronage, the true popularity of the game may not pay off its promoters. But no one can deny that it is gaining new fans each season. Nor can anyone who has watched both games seriously pretend that the college game is nearly as fine a spectacle as is professional football at its best.

I know men who could hardly tell a touchback from a safety in school, and others who never even learned to spell such words, who can lose themselves so utterly in professional football that they would sit for twenty-four hours, unwatered and unfed, to watch its performance if it were offered in uninterrupted stretches. In New York the possession of tickets for any one of the games the football Giants have scheduled is a status symbol almost equal to a first-name acquaintance with the mayor. People who own season boxes for the games are courted during the season like suburbanites with a swimming pool. So frantic is the urge to get in to see the games, which are not offered on TV within a fifty-mile radius, that heirs have been known to quarrel over inheritance of the right to purchase the box each season. And one mourner at the funeral of a leading civic figure choked back his tears long enough to remind one of the football

Giants' brass that "Joe always said he wanted me to have the football seats."

For a while the common herd was getting into the stadium to see the Giants' games through an intricate system of bribery and chicanery that sometimes put more than a thousand non-paying spectators into the park. Admission cost the fan but two dollars through this system, but it returned nothing to the management. The fan was asked if he wanted to see the game, then, for one dollar, given a gate number where a ticket-taker, in on the deal, would be stationed. The other dollar went to the ticket-taker. The fan got in without a ticket, and both outside man and inside man kept the dollars they received. When this scheme was uncovered at last (through accidental eavesdropping), the management estimated that there might have been as many as two thousand such gate-crashers inside the park for a single game.

Most of the pro football fancy, however, are content when the home team is out of town to watch the games on television. Football is a far better game to watch this way than baseball is. On television much of baseball's allure is missing—the signs, the shifting, the calls from the stands, the sudden streaking flight of the ball from the bat, the unexpected pickoff, and both parts of the hit-and-run. But in football, with a good camera crew at work, the game is often more enjoyable than when seen from a seat in the park. It is possible on television to remain close to the teams on every play, to see the backfield moves in detail, and to follow the ball better than half the men on the field.

While professional commentators may carp that professional football is still just basketball with bruises and that the spirit of the college game is lost, the fact is that a real football addict soon loses his taste for the college game after watching professional football for a time. The college game—except when played by the great professional university teams—is ragged and stumbling. In the college game, a back may just whang away at the weak spot in the line from nearly any angle, or may dance around awhile waiting for an opening. In pro football, there must be a definite fake by the runner and a quick hard drive from a specific spot into a sudden opening, or the play is going to be spilled.

When a college quarterback "rolls out" on the play which provides him the option of passing or running, he sometimes jogs along like a man trotting home in a shower. In the professional game, the quarterback must sprint out of his position to perform this play and not slow down for a moment lest he be eaten alive by a pursuing end.

Kicking in the college game generally is but a minor factor. In pro football all the scoring sometimes may be accomplished by place kicks, booted from incredible distances by specialists who may do nothing else. (Men like Ken Strong, Lou Groza, and Ben Agajanian lasted many years past their normal expectancy in the game through their skill at putting place kicks through and over the goal.)

Pro teams are better matched, too, all up and down the line. Big men oppose big men and there are seldom any weaklings whose presence may be exploited. All the big men must move fast too, particularly in lateral directions, to concentrate strength at the point of attack and do it quickly. Many of the leading linebackers are as fast as halfbacks and can even catch some of the lesser speedsters from behind. (Sam Huff, who makes a specialty of high tackles that occasionally wind up in a stranglehold, is a real sprinter and a hard man to run away from.)

The professionals play a tougher game, although there may actually be more dirty play in some college contests, where an outclassed lineman may even things up with a knee or a fist. (In one college game where a Negro back appeared against a southwestern college, a photographer immortalized one gallant rebel in the act of smashing his fist to the Negro's jaw while "tackling" him.) In a professional game, as has been noted earlier, a man who stands to watch the play, thinking the runner as good as down, is deemed fair game for a blindside block and not even his coach will sympathize with him when he is carted off for readjustment. Nothing, in a pro game, is conceded or given away. No margin is too wide and no one expects a coach to ease up on an opponent when the lead is "too big." Nearly every professional team owns a sprinter among the pass defenders who is likely, under the proper circumstances, to intercept a pass and take it all the way from one goal line to another in less time than it takes a college team to get a play off.

Nor are there any men in the professional game whose speed alone will keep them safe, as there are in colleges. Some college speedsters find themselves unfit for professional ball because of their incurable habit of "hearing footsteps"—that is, failing to concentrate on catching the ball because always at their backs they hear some tough tackler hurrying near.

Few indeed are the football players who can step from stardom in college right into the front ranks of the pros. Invariably they discover that what they could do with half their hearts in college, they must use their last ounce of courage and skill to perform in professional football. Sure-handed safetymen will fumble again and again in the approaching thunder of the herd of three-hundred-pound tacklers. Slippery halfbacks will find themselves closeted in their own backfield, until they learn to perform in professional football. Sure-handed safetymen will them. Quarterbacks who have grown used to "fading back" ten to twenty yards before finally unleashing the touchdown pass find themselves learning the game all over again, once they are limited to the seven to nine yards the professional coach allows them. And light-footed fellows who have been able to dodge and dance away from defenders while looking for pass receivers soon discover that the price of jumping out of the "pocket" in professional football is a sudden murderous collision with a fleet of armored trucks.

Injuries in professional football, while often severe (because of the great size and strength of the players) are not nearly as common as in the secondary schools and colleges, and they have been diminishing over the past decade, with improved equipment and better conditioning. Too often, in college as well as in high school, part of the "character building" aspect of the game has been to belittle injuries, and to leave their care in the hands of "trainers" who sometimes lack even a degree in physical therapy. (Once in a game at West Point, when an obviously badly injured foe was offered the use of the Academy's hospital facilities during a football game, the "trainer" who was half carrying the boy off the field could not conceal his scorn at the suggestion. "Hospital?" he snarled. "Nah!") Fatalities in football are most common in the secondary schools, where half-grown boys sometimes find themselves outweighed by as much as a hundred pounds and where head injuries are sometimes treated casually if there is no immediate serious symptom.

In the professional game, which undertakes not to build character but to build gate receipts, the players nowadays are under the immediate care of a physician and almost always will be hospitalized after a head injury, no matter how trifling it may seem. Their physical condition is closely checked too, and no man is sent on the field just because he "feels all right." (It was not always this way, as old-timers will testify.)

Of course, when football is a game, and not a spectacle (as it has become in the big-time universities), it does have exhilarating effects and perhaps even builds character—although that always seemed an odd motive for playing any game. But it must be played to win, and played with both mind and body if it is to provide the participant any real joy. And joy, after all, is its prime purpose when young men play it in school.

Much of the pleasure that is derived from college football develops from the settling of old scores and the exacerbation of synthetic rivalries. Most universities play only one or two "big" games in a season and the older colleges have only one, the final game with the favorite rival. In these contests—Army vs. Navy; Yale vs. Harvard; Wisconsin vs. Minnesota; Holy Cross vs. Boston College—the quality of the play is of no great moment, as long as our side comes out ahead. Alumni will thrill as much to a lucky touchdown that results from a bad pass by a nervous center as to a perfectly executed scoring play from scrimmage. But professional football has built its own "alumni," wherever a team has been developed that has at least a chance of winning the divisional or national championship. Strangers caught in the rush after a league football game in Baltimore, Philadelphia, Chicago, New York, Green Bay, Cleveland, or San Francisco might not be able to detect (except for the uncollegiate bearing of some of the fans) any difference between the unbalanced behavior of the pro football fancy and that of the most rabid of college rooters. Grown men in subway cars still shout into a horde of strangers "Bring on the Giants!" or "What will we do to the Browns?" and get a roaring reply from half a hundred happy throats.

Inasmuch as it is the spectators who take the greatest pleasure in a football game, one must assume that whatever beneficent effect upon character such wholesale participation may provide is visited upon the fans of professional football and of college football with equal strength.

As for the educational value of big-time university football or its importance in providing culture to men who might otherwise find it out of reach, I think this side of the problem needs no commentary more final than that provided in a recent interview with one of the best football players in university ranks. Asked, just before graduation, why he had chosen this particular school above all others, he replied:

"I could of went to another college, but they wouldn't take me brudder."

Chapter XVII

Point after Touchdown

As sports columnist Red Smith (no kin) remarked one day, the word "professional" carries a hint of opprobrium in Great Britain, while in our country the term is offered, at least to males, as a compliment. And when a professional football player wants to indicate high approval of your effort in literature, business, sports, cocktail-mixing, or the cooking of eggs, he will name it "all-pro." For to be "all-pro" is to be a professional of professionals, a man selected as the most highly skilled among the most skilled in the world.

Nowadays "All-American" is still used to describe a football player who is the best at his job, for, despite the proliferation of "All-American" selections, the designation first applied by Walter Camp over a half century ago carries yet its implication of excellence. It should not be long, however, before "All-Pro" supplants "All-American" as the adjective indicating supremacy in football. For professional football today is superior to the college game in every degree. The effort of a professional football player nearly always surpasses that of his younger counterpart. He is usually bigger too and invariably more knowledgeable and more skilled in the art of transporting a football or of preventing the enemy from doing so. (In the 1963 Rose Bowl game at Pasadena, between Wisconsin and the University of Southern California, the USC rooters, after their heroes had made their sixth touchdown, began to chant "We want the Packers"—as if their club were the equal of the professional champions. But if they had gotten the Packers they would have wished they hadn't—just as for a while toward the end of the game they began to wish time would run out before Wisconsin scored again. The 1962 Packers were a college championship team multiplied by three—fast, tough, thoroughly conditioned, and expertly coached.)

The professional game, too, takes a far tighter grip on its adherents, who will stand in freezing cold all night lest they be denied admittance to a championship game, or who will sit through a blizzard or a howling gale to watch two teams decide which one shall own the year's national title. To the benighted who had never seen professional football, or to a stranger from beyond the stratosphere, or to any innocents who might have come upon the spectacle unawares, the championship game of 1962, between the Green Bay Packers and the New York Giants, would have brought astonishment, bewilderment, even dismay. For here, in a park designed for playing baseball and now a veritable steppe of browned sod and frozen dust, with bunting all torn by gale winds and hats sent skittering like small hoops across the playing field, with some spectators bundled like mummies and others everlastingly bouncing up and down like wound-up Christmas toys, as they sought to set their congealed blood to stirring—here where no sane man would have undertaken to do much more than get a fire going and put up some shelter against the wind, two uniformed and helmeted teams lined up head-to-head upon the concrete sod and a cityful of people gathered to howl their delight. And before ever the game began more than half the sixty-five thousand people present joined in a unified chant, like the thumping of some monstrous drum: "Beat Green Bay! Beat Green Bay!"

More men and women than this, be it known, had gathered to watch two of the service academies play with a football, but not even those eternal adolescents who still could shed real tears over an Army (or Navy) defeat had ever joined in a spontaneous chorus like this, without any prompting but their own wild desire to see their city triumphant. College cheering sections, in response to the exhortations of cavorting leaders, had often engaged in such displays. But never before had so many men and women, in so heterogeneous a mass, at any sort of sports spectacle, all sounded off with the same throat. It was both pathetic and exhilarating. But it surely marked the final emergence of professional football as the sport that takes tightest hold of the hearts of Americans.

Baseball will perhaps forever remain the summer sport that Americans are addicted to most devoutly. But professional football has now turned into a cause that affords to all manner of men, to the well-placed and the woebegone, to the college-bred and the half educated, to the "in" group and the "out" group, as well as to the dispossessed, an opportunity to savor in common both the joy of bloody victory and the dismal emptiness of defeat.

The game itself disproved most of the major libels laid against the professional game by those who persisted in believing that the college game was still superior. The enemies of professional football had said that the college attack was always more imaginative, the college effort more wholehearted, and the spirit more intense.

As to the spirit, one had only to be there to marvel at that. And the game offered a display of reckless effort that caused some men to cringe. Even though the ground was less yielding than a steel deck, these players hurled themselves head-first at loose footballs, or threw themselves at a ball carrier without regard. The Giants, obviously the less talented team, fought the mighty Green Bays to a standstill at one point, pushing them back a yard or more at every down. And later on the Packers, determined to control the football in the final quarter, called running plays time after time that gained acreage over the middle, around the end, off tackle, or down the wide alley between tackle and split end. There was passing aplenty too but no man could have complained that the ball was too often in the air. Erich Barnes of New York flung himself in front of a Green Bay kick and blocked it, to create a New York touchdown, without concern for the manner in which his body would bounce off the icy turf. Paul Hornung, with a newly healed knee, ran the ends as recklessly as if he had foam rubber under his feet. And Willie Wood of Green Bay, in hysterical dismay over an interference call, pounded the air with a protesting fist and caught an approaching official amidships, foundering him on the instant— and earning his own immediate dismissal from the game.

Each run and each screen pass by either team brought vicious pursuit by the "opposite" end of the line that sometimes spilled the play before it could get well started. Runners, especially Jim Taylor of Green Bay, who required stitches to mend a gash in his flesh, fought free of mighty tacklers and struggled on for yards until hordes of the enemy met them and beat them down. Even in the final moments of the game, with hope but a glimmer, the New York team stopped the clock to eke out the seconds and tried complicated pass plays that might bring a desperation score. As for imagination, there was at least one wildly improbable play, in which a double reverse wound up with a backward toss to the deeply retreated quarterback (Y. A. Tittle) and then a long, long forward pass that availed nothing.

Bart Starr, the Green Bay quarterback, faked effectively to make his draw plays work, and Tittle stepped coolly forward into the pocket to hit his frozen-fingered receivers on patterns that often left the Green Bay secondary flat-footed. (The passes, unhappily, were too often dropped.) And when his final effort went for naught, Tittle pounded the frozen turf with his fists— as heartbroken as any college champion could have been. Anyone who had watched the Army-Navy game should have had no complaint at the effort of the pros, for there were no halfhearted blockers, nor any of the reluctant tacklers such as had permitted the Navy quarterback to zigzag about on the field as if he had poison ivy on his pants. The tackles were hard, persistent, and blazingly determined. The defensive linemen fought with wild abandon to lay their mittened hands on the enemy quarterback. And no man ever seemed to count himself out of a play, nor was any runner stopped until there were men enough clutching him to push him backwards or turn him upside down.

But men and women who had watched professional football all season, in Dallas, San Diego, Los Angeles, Milwaukee, Chicago, Philadelphia, or any of the other towns where the leagues held franchises, could not have been surprised at the manner in which these champions fought each other. There was hardly a team in either league—even though the play in the American Football League still looked inferior—that had not staged an effort as earnest and sustained as this, not just in one game but in many. The Washington Redskins, having joined the republic at last by admitting Negroes to their backfield, started off their season as if they would take the championship and revealed a stylish quarterback in Norman Snead, who was big and strong, and accomplished at ball handling, one of the neatest in the business at faking handoffs. Pittsburgh, a team that had never won a championship, offered a rejuvenated John Henry Johnson, who is surely one of the strongest and most elusive ball carriers in the game. And even though the hometown fans booed the veteran quarterback Bobby Layne right off the field, the club still earned a chance to play in the runner-up playoff, staged in civilized weather, far from home, in Florida. The effort in this game was just as spectacular as that in the game for the league championship. There was less blood, for the ground was not frozen. But the tackles were smashing, the blocking brutal, and hard feelings flared at one point when big John Henry Johnson felt he had been rudely handled and set out to wallop any one or all of his opponents. Detroit won this game, which may have rung down the curtain on Bobby Layne's career. But Pittsburgh came close. And when Bobby realized hope was lost, even the distant television fans could see that he was angrily reviling the fates on his way off the field.

Cleveland, the team chosen as most likely to earn the eastern championship, and the one that probably disappointed its fans the most, still scrambled for every inch of ground and ended its season with a desperate victory in a sea of mud, in which the mighty Jim Brown, who had been handicapped by a broken wrist that robbed him of his potent forearm wallop, showed the world once more that he was the greatest ball carrier alive.

The Philadelphia Eagles, who had been champions not long before and who looked as if they could be again, lost games they should have won and had their great stars slighted by the distant geniuses who picked the "All-Star" team. Sonny Jurgenson, the owner of the strongest and most accurate arm of any professional quarterback, won hardly a mention for his play. Yet, with more experienced protectors to keep the enemy off him, he might have been the greatest of them all. Nor were there many pass receivers drawing pay whom a professional coach would have sought more earnestly from Santa Claus than Tommy McDonald and Pete Retzlaff.

The Baltimore Colts, in a "bad" season, still came within a nose of beating the Green Bay Packers, whom they outran and outpassed like the Colts of 1958. And the Detroit Lions, the fiercest defensive team in the league, did beat the Packers finally, and did them up so brown that some of the wallops must have been felt home in Wisconsin. Joe Schmidt, mightiest of the middle linebackers, had his greatest day. And a well-filled-out fellow named Roger Brown, who would weigh in at three hundred pounds before lunch, visited such startling punishment on Bart Starr, the Green Bay quarterback, that Starr hardly got a forward pass out of his fist the whole first half.

The Chicago Bears maintained their pose as the roughest gang in pro football, especially on their home grounds. But in their last few games they foxed their opponents by giving over, from time to time, their all-out aggressive defense in which the whole team would seem to unload on the quarterback. Instead, they occasionally played the linebackers "soft," flooding the secondary with so many defenders that they could occasionally spare two defenders for each receiver. This maneuver, of course, delayed the quarterback's release of the ball long enough for the "front four" to get in there and start to grind him to powder. And once, against the Los Angeles Rams, it brought about an interception by Rich Petitbon, the six-foot-three safety man of the Bears. Rich helped himself to a Los Angeles pass in his own end zone and carried the ball all the way to the other end of the field, where they gave him six points for it.

Even the San Francisco 49ers, who were occasionally considered the sorriest team in the league, still earned the limited devotion of hometown fans by exhibitions of heart-lifting football, particularly when a young man named Abe Woodson received the kickoff and undertook to return it to the other team's goal line. (Against the Bears he nearly did, returning the ball fifty-one yards on one play, only to have the run rubbed out by a clipping penalty.) And on defense, Leo Nomellini, the ageless linebacker, who had grown up in Italy without ever seeing anyone engage in the hand-to-hand bloodletting called football in America, continued to harry enemy quarterbacks and to manhandle even the mightiest linemen who dared interrupt him.

The Los Angeles Rams were named here and there as the team that promised most and delivered the least. But their smog-sozzled fans almost forgave them all their derelictions when "little" Dick Bass would take the ball on one of his long, long runs, in which he often sent big men sprawling who tried to halt this human Volkswagen. And some professed to see in Roman Gabriel, the new quarterback, the delivering angel long promised them in song and story.

In Bloomington, Minnesota, the Vikings, having escaped alive from threatened inclusion in the American Football League, boasted in Norm Van Brocklin—an antidisciplinarian in his playing days—a metal-fisted mentor who made Paul Brown and Vince Lombardi look like playground supervisors. It was full-pad practice for the Vikings, day in and day out, even during the playing season, when other teams were working out in sweat suits. And some observers whispered that it was sheer exhaustion that made the Minnesota team so often a first-half winner and a full-game loser, for they led the enemy time after time when they went to the locker room at the end of the second period.

And often, when the full game was over, they were so far behind they might as well have been in the other league. Still, they had men on their side who could fight back against the league's best. Their best runner was no longer aging Hugh McElhenny but young Tommy Mason, who is almost exactly of a size with Hugh. Mason even ran loose against the Detroit Lions, who have been known to chew rookie runners into hamburg steak. In a late-season loss to the Lions, Mason made one run from scrimmage of seventy-one yards and earned an average of better than eight yards a carry.

An injury to John David Crow, the man whose mild facial paralysis gives him an almost permanently fearsome look, broke the stride of the St. Louis Cardinals just when it seemed that the mighty John David was fashioning his finest year. Crow has long been one of the hardest men in the world to tackle and in the first few games of the season it looked as if no two men together were ever going to manage to get him down. And as if there weren't enough Johnsons in the world already, the Cardinals hired one named Charley to act as quarterback for their side and he set out to make new records for them. In one game (against the Dallas Cowboys) he not only threw the ball to somebody else five times to make five touchdowns, but he carried the ball across the goal line in his own hands once, to make it six touchdowns altogether that he had a claim to.

The 1962 Dallas Cowboys owned the smallest man in the league, Eddie LeBaron, whom they almost had to blackmail into playing another year, and at the beginning of the season they seemed also to own the smallest chance of winning any ball games. They did lose one or two by mighty margins. But they won some they seemed to have no right to win and at the end of the year came to New York, after having been hopelessly trounced by the Giants, and in losing another ball game still staged one of the most exciting games New York had seen all season, with scores rocking back and forth as in a basketball game. This game had real bruises, however, and much hard running. The alternating quarterbacks, LeBaron and Don Meredith, kept firing into the maw of the cannonading Giants, despite being slammed regularly to the granite-hard ground. Indeed Meredith, entering the game with the coach's new play on his lips, limped markedly almost all through the game and still managed to frighten the Giants with cool completions of his passes.

The American Football League, despite the loss of its expensive lawsuit to force the National League to acknowledge its prior claim to certain territories, began to breathe more steadily, as if it might live and grow strong. Some franchises actually started to draw patronage and prosper and certain American League teams were able to outbid the rival league for football players. Men who had been put out to pasture by the older league found they could perform well enough to star in the new league and envisioned several more years of comfortable income. Certain players who had just not been big enough or tough enough for the National League received a chance in the American League to toughen themselves up on the field of play, to break themselves of their habit of "hearing footsteps" or of slowing down when tacklers approached. Lee Grosscup, once named the greatest college passer of the era, let go by the New York Giants because, among other derelictions, he had failed to cut his hair like a football player, and dropped by the Minnesota Vikings because his pay was too high, created a sensation in his first game with the New York Titans when he went to bat twice and threw two touchdowns. A serious leg injury broke his season off short but he seemed likely to shine again if only the franchise could be kept alive until they no longer had to lie about their attendance. (The New York Titan team all walked out on strike during the 1962 season and stayed away from practice for a week, because they had not received their paychecks. Then, with their pay finally in their pockets, they went out and beat the Buffalo Bills, who had been practicing steadily. Soon after this, the American League authorities took over the club's finances and met the payroll on time.)

The Buffalo team in the new league exhibited one of the

most terrifying fullbacks ever seen on any field in the person of Cookie Gilchrist, lured across the river from Toronto (where he played with the Argonauts of the Canadian League) and paid twenty thousand dollars a year to make touchdowns for Buffalo.

The "championship" contest in the new league, matching the two Texas teams (Houston from the "East" and Dallas from the "West") seemed destined to be mere entropy, or wasted motion. But it turned out to be a slam-bang football game, played with a recklessness that apparently has become a trademark of the younger league, and lasting longer than any football game previously recorded—seventy-seven minutes and fifty-four seconds. The Dallas team, with swift Abner Haynes playing flanker back and two fullbacks, Jack Spikes and Curt McClinton, plus quarterback Len Dawson, making up the backfield, easily won the first half, 17–0. Then the favored Houston team took the second half by the same score and forced the game into sudden-death overtime—a fifth "quarter" and then even a sixth. The game might have ended sooner but Dallas' Haynes, having won the toss at the start of the sudden-death period and having been instructed by his coach to choose the goal that would give him the advantage of the fifteen-mile-an-hour breeze, became confused and told the referee, "We'll kick." That meant that Houston not only received the ball but chose the goal as well. Happily for Haynes, Houston could not cash in on either advantage and when the second sudden-death period began Dallas finally had the wind at its back. Whether the wind was any aid to Tommy Brooker of Dallas in kicking his winning field goal from the twenty-five-yard line, no one knows. Brooker counted the points in the bank before he even backed off for the kick and afterwards insisted there was just no way he could have missed when the ball was so close.

The American Football League was not the only effort to divert a runlet or two of the National League's golden river of profit into different pockets. In 1961 a truly minor league, the United Football League, that put pro teams back into Columbus,

Ohio, and Akron (which shifted to Toledo in 1962), under-took to find room for itself somewhere beneath the American League, and far below the National. With almost pathetic opti-mism, it even placed teams in Cleveland and Chicago, where semipro football had long thrived but where league "opposition" had been reduced to beggary in earlier years.

Almost inevitably, considering the whacking sums of money wagered each week on football games, professional football in 1962 caught a few dismaying whiffs of scandal that frightened some men into imagining that the golden stream might dry up altogether. Starting with faint whispers in Los Angeles, where the police department had begun a quiet investigation, talk of "fix" spread to Chicago, to Detroit, and to New York, wherever big money was handled. Young men made suddenly rich have frequently found themselves courted by the type of citizens our grandmothers always called bad company, and professional foot-ball players, it developed, were no exceptions. Investigators be-gan to question some players about their associates. Rumors that certain players often bet heavily on themselves caused wary bookmakers here and there to refuse bets on certain teams. And Washington politicians, scenting national headlines, wheeled their investigative artillery into position.

Because of the extreme difficulty of fixing a football game without the cooperation of several players, most people close to the sport felt certain that the worst that might develop would be a failure to report some clumsy bribe attempt. But back in the hand-to-mouth days there had been a real bribe effort in New York which the league mishandled by suspending one player while keeping the other suspect—a backfield star—eligible for a "crucial game." And there was fear that some such clumsy cover-up as this would, now that pro football rated so much more public attention, cause this noisome molehill to swell into a nasty mountain.

Whatever may develop from the investigations—and they seem certain to uncover a fair amount of unpleasant matter—the football leagues must eventually purify themselves in the strongest way possible, by smiting the unrighteous without regard for their fame, and by putting regulation in the hands of some quasi-public official, who is not beholden to the club owners in any way, and who is granted power to take whatever action may be needed for the good of the game. If they try to dodge out short of some radical commitment of this kind, they may find the golden flow suddenly turned to mud in their fingers.

The strategy of the professional game by the end of 1962 appeared to have reached a plateau again. Ever since Greasy Neale, many years before, had stumped the "new" T-formation offense by setting his linebackers to playing nose-to-nose with the attacking ends, there had been spasmodic efforts to devise some unheard-of ways to spread the defense and set pass receivers free. The split end and the "slot" back had provided an early answer but other refinements, such as the "shotgun," lasted hardly long enough for the rival coaches to dream up a defense. Now it began to appear that football games once more were going to be won on fundamentals, on fast charging, on solid blocking, on hard tackling, and above all on conditioning.

The champion Packers boasted no secret handbook of hipperdipper plays nor did they think only of getting a man loose to catch a killer pass. They ran the ends, and sent the fullback up the middle, and wedged out holes for the halfback so he could carry through the line. They endeavored to outcharge and outfight and outlast their opponents, as football players had in bygone days; and other coaches took heed and did likewise. (A few had long been doing so but none with quite the drive and dedication Lombardi employed.)

The professional football fan, meanwhile, waxed fruitful and multiplied, and he continued to trace out his own peculiar behavior patterns. In some cities, where the teams had had a taste of glory—as in Philadelphia, Baltimore, New York, and Green Bay—the fan was wed as tightly to his home club as ever the Brooklyn faithful were to the baseball Dodgers. He offered up his heart's blood when his darlings lost and when they won he fought with the local police for the right to unseat the cemented goalposts. He hated the enemy out loud and yelled with joy when one of the opposing champions was injured badly enough to require his removal from the game—not glorying in the man's pain at all but simply glad that the home team's hope of victory was by that much enhanced. He booed his own team angrily if they fumbled the ball or foozled a series of passes. He criticized play choices and called for pet substitutes by name. And he thirsted constantly for action. For he came to the park to see the team in motion and the ground being contested and had no stomach for long delays or those irritating "time outs" that were called to give the television advertiser time to brag about his cigarette, his beer, or his patent sweat-inhibitor. Typical of his apparent hardness of heart, his true worldly wisdom, and his impatience with the complex hypocrisies of "sportsmanship" was a raucous cry that went up one day at Yankee Stadium, when the game was stopped to deal with a man who lay injured on the turf.

There was no telling what ailed the man, except that he was obviously some half a century from death's door, nor was there any knowing just why the men in windbreaker jackets, and the officials, and the man in the felt hat all had to meet by his body and stare down at him, while the two teams dawdled in the background. Then one man arose in the grandstand and gave sudden voice to a wicked desire that slumbered in every heart:

"Oh, play around him!" he yelled.

Index